OLIVER WENDELL HOLMES, JR.

Oliver Wendell Holmes, Jr., was one of the most influential jurists of his time. From the antebellum era and the Civil War through the First World War and into the New Deal years, Holmes' long life and career as a Supreme Court Justice spanned an eventful period of American history, as the country went from an agrarian republic to an industrialized world power.

In this concise, engaging book, Susan-Mary Grant puts Holmes' life in national context, exploring how he both shaped and reflected his changing country. She examines the impact of the Civil War on his life and his thinking, his role in key cases ranging from the issue of free speech in *Schenck v. United States* to the infamous ruling in favor of eugenics in *Buck v. Bell*, showing how behind Holmes' reputation as a liberal justice lay a more complex approach to law that did not neatly align with political divisions. Including a selection of key primary documents, *Oliver Wendell Holmes, Jr.* introduces students of the United States, Civil War, and legal history to a game-changing figure and his times.

Susan–Mary Grant is Professor of American History at Newcastle University. Her previous books include *A Concise History of the United States of America, The War for a Nation: The American Civil War, North Over South: Northern Nationalism and American Identity in the Antebellum Era*, and *Themes of the American Civil War: The War Between the States* (co-edited with Brian Holden-Reid).

ROUTLEDGE HISTORICAL AMERICANS

SERIES EDITOR: PAUL FINKELMAN

Routledge Historical Americans is a series of short, vibrant biographies that illuminate the lives of Americans who have had an impact on the world. Each book includes a short overview of the person's life and puts that person into historical context through essential primary documents, written both by the subjects and about them. A series website supports the books, containing extra images and documents, links to further research, and, where possible, multi-media sources on the subjects. Perfect for including in any course on American History, the books in the Routledge Historical Americans series show the impact everyday people can have on the course of history.

Woody Guthrie: Writing America's Songs
Ronald D. Cohen

Frederick Douglass: Reformer and Statesman
L. Diane Barnes

Thurgood Marshall: Race, Rights, and the Struggle for a More Perfect Union
Charles L. Zelden

Harry S. Truman: The Coming of the Cold War
Nicole L. Anslover

John Winthrop: Founding the City upon a Hill
Michael Parker

John F. Kennedy: The Spirit of Cold War Liberalism
Jason K. Duncan

Bill Clinton: Building a Bridge to the New Millennium
David H. Bennett

Ronald Reagan: Champion of Conservative America
James H. Broussard

Laura Ingalls Wilder: American Writer on the Prairie
Sallie Ketcham

Benjamin Franklin: American Founder, Atlantic Citizen
Nathan R. Kozuskanich

Brigham Young: Sovereign in America
David Vaughn Mason

Mary Lincoln: Southern Girl, Northern Woman
Stacy Pratt McDermott

Oliver Wendell Holmes, Jr.: Civil War Soldier, Supreme Court Justice
Susan-Mary Grant

Oliver Wendell Holmes, Jr.
Civil War Soldier, Supreme Court Justice

SUSAN-MARY GRANT

Routledge
Taylor & Francis Group

NEW YORK AND LONDON

http://www.routledge.com/cw/historicalamericans

First published 2016
by Routledge
711 Third Avenue, New York, NY 10017

and by Routledge
2 Park Square, Milton Park, Abingdon, Oxon OX14 4RN

Routledge is an imprint of the Taylor & Francis Group, an informa business

Library of Congress Cataloging-in-Publication Data

Grant, Susan-Mary, author.
    Oliver Wendell Holmes, Jr. : Civil War soldier, Supreme Court Justice/
Susan-Mary Grant.
        pages cm. — (Routledge Historical Americans)
    Includes bibliographical references and index.
    1. Holmes, Oliver Wendell, Jr., 1841–1935.   2. Judges—United States—Biography.
I. Title.
    KF8745.H6G73   2015
    347.73'2634—dc23
    [B]
    2015002931

ISBN: 978-0-415-65653-5 (hbk)
ISBN: 978-0-415-65654-2 (pbk)
ISBN: 978-0-203-07770-2 (ebk)

Typeset in Bembo and Scala Sans
by Apex CoVantage, LLC

For MHS
A small token.

CONTENTS

INTRODUCTION

"I wonder whether it ever occurred to you to reflect upon another horror there must be in leaving a name behind you . . . condemned to walk the earth in a biography."
(Oliver Wendell Holmes, Sr., *The Poet at the Breakfast-Table*)

"The life of an individual is in many respects like a child's dissected map," observed noted nineteenth-century doctor and author Oliver Wendell Holmes, Sr., and only the passage of time enables the pieces to be brought together to form "a properly connected whole." Speaking for himself, he felt that living a hundred years might still not reveal the full picture. For his son, who almost achieved this, the pattern, if not the resultant portrait, can seem, in hindsight, almost to have been predetermined by: the "blueprint" provided by his father's fame, the cultural values of the conservative class into which he was born, the wider New England religious and reform traditions in which he was raised, and, above all, his traumatic transition into adulthood in the Civil War of 1861–1865.[1]

Lineage and longevity, in and of themselves, of course, may reveal little of the life and times of an individual, but Oliver Wendell Holmes, Jr. (1841–1935) was no ordinary individual: briefly professor of law at Harvard Law School, he became Associate Justice of the Supreme Judicial Court of Massachusetts in 1883, Chief Justice in 1899, and was appointed by Theodore Roosevelt to the Supreme Court in 1902, where he served as Associate Justice until 1932. By then, as economist and law professor Walton H. Hamilton commented just before the retired justice died, Holmes "was an Olympian who in judgment could do no wrong." Certainly, for the noted journalist Max Lerner, writing just after Holmes' death, there was a "wholeness about Holmes which could come only from the flowering of the greatest aristocracy America has so far had—the New England aristocracy."[2]

Holmes was over ninety when he finally retired, and his ninetieth birthday was marked by a coast-to-coast radio broadcast, still a technological marvel in 1931, but one unimaginable in the year of his birth when the nation's first telegraph message was still three years away. He remains, to this day, perhaps the best-known justice to have served on the Supreme Court, portrayed on stage, film, and fiction, on a stamp, in three substantial biographies, and in countless other shorter studies of his life and his legal legacy. In honor of his birthday, a valley in the Central Brooks Range in Alaska was named after him by explorer Robert Marshall. His legend began in his lifetime; the debate over his legacy has continued ever since.[3]

It would be an exaggeration to say that those who, through writing about Holmes, have come to know him best like him least. It is true, however, that many modern assessments complicate, if they do not entirely contradict, the positive image crafted by such contemporary colleagues and admirers as British political theorist and long-time Holmes correspondent, Harold Laski, Associate Justice Felix Frankfurter, and journalist and author Elizabeth Shepley Sergeant. It is, of course, the plethora of contradictory accounts of him that accords Holmes his persistent cultural influence in contemporary America, even if it was mainly positive interpretations that began the process. And among those, Sergeant's still stands out. For her, Holmes was "a Yankee, strayed from Olympus," who knew "truth in flashes of fire" and revealed "its immortal essence in cryptic phrase."[4]

Holmes' detractors have largely concurred with the "cryptic phrase" concept, but from there on in they part company with Sergeant to bring Holmes down to earth; with a bump, in some cases. "Put out of your mind the picture of the tolerant aristocrat, the great liberal, the eloquent defender of our liberties, the Yankee from Olympus," urged leading legal scholar Grant Gilmore, who after over a decade of working on a biography of Holmes concluded that he could not complete it. "The real Holmes," Gilmore asserted, "was savage, harsh, and cruel, a bitter and lifelong pessimist who saw in the course of human life nothing but a continuing struggle in which the rich and powerful impose their will on the poor and weak."[5]

So far from Olympus, Gilmore's Holmes inhabited "a bleak and terrifying universe," delineated by his own "radical and despairing pessimism." In this respect, Gilmore suggests, Holmes "cut against the grain of most nineteenth-century thought." But did he? Holmes might have been out on a legal limb, the dark prince of what Gilmore described as "law's black night," but how far was he from the social and political beliefs of his time? Moving Holmes out from the shadow cast over him by some of the specialist scholarship and locating him in the relative sunlight of a broader historical landscape not only shifts our perspective on Holmes as an individual, but on America as a nation. After all, the "story of Justice Oliver Wendell Holmes," as one of his first unofficial biographers asserted, "is the story of his country."[6]

Although in some respects Holmes was hardly typical of his time, in others his experiences and outlook do reveal a particular class, cultural, and generational perspective that informed the emergence of the United States as a global power in the twentieth century. Holmes' long life, in effect, can serve as a lens that focuses, or perhaps more accurately a kaleidoscope that reflects and refracts, through its various shifting shapes and shades, the tremendous social, legal, and economic upheavals of nearly a century of America's history, from the Antebellum Era through the First World War and into the New Deal years.

The man whom Franklin Delano Roosevelt (FDR) once called "the greatest living American," and whom legal scholars are apt to term the "Great Dissenter," was born in Boston, Massachusetts just as Martin Van Buren's presidency had ended, and that of William Henry Harrison begun. It would not last long. Dying of pneumonia barely a month into his term of office, Harrison became the shortest-serving president in the nation's history. By the year of Holmes's death, FDR, America's longest-serving president, was in the White House, steering the nation through the economic and emotional trauma of the Great Depression that had followed the global stock-market crash of 1929. When Holmes was born the population of the United States was around 17 million, an increase of over 30 percent over the previous decade; by the time of his death it had risen to over 124 million, although its rate of increase, at about 16 percent, was almost half that of the Antebellum Era. Both demographically and economically, America had become a bigger but, perhaps inevitably, slower nation, albeit one positioned, although not yet fully prepared, for the superpower status it would acquire after the Second World War.

Born into what his father would later define as the Brahmin class of antebellum Boston, Holmes was raised in the intense intellectual atmosphere of a social stratum—a "harmless, inoffensive, untitled aristocracy," as his father described it—whose conservative cultural and political tendencies were increasingly untenable in the context of the sectional squabbles over slavery that suffused not just the city, but the nation by the 1840s.[7] The very day after Holmes' birth on March 8, 1841, the Supreme Court ruled in the famous *Amistad* case that revolved around the legal status of forty-four African captives who, in 1839, had seized the ship on which they were being transported, but ended up in Connecticut instead of being able to sail back to Africa.

The eventual decision in favor of the right of the Africans to their freedom was based on international law and had no direct legal impact on slavery within the United States. Nevertheless, former president John Quincy

Adams emphasized its national implications when he asserted before the court that the "moment you come to the Declaration of Independence, . . . every man has a right to life and liberty, an inalienable right, this case is decided."[8] By the year of Holmes' death, however, although slavery had long since been abolished, future Associate Justice Thurgood Marshall, arguing for educational equality at the University of Maryland law school, similarly reminded the Maryland Supreme Court that the case in question hinged on "the moral commitment stated in our country's creed."[9]

Highlighting these arguments is not to suggest that little had changed over the course of Holmes' life; far from it. As Holmes himself asserted, "[the] law is the witness and external deposit of our moral life. Its history is the history of the moral development of the race."[10] And it is the changes between 1841 and 1935 that locate the man within a nation that faced a perennial struggle to secure and to implement the right to liberty and equality for its citizens. When Holmes was born, slavery was still legal, but when he died the civil rights movement as modern scholars understand it was already in its infancy. And certainly, over the course of his life there were other, internal and external, challenges facing the nation besides racial equality. Holmes lived through the Mexican-American War, the Civil War, the Spanish-American War, and the First World War; all changed the nation in significant ways but it was the Civil War, most scholars concur, that changed Holmes.

That the Civil War is deemed to have been the formative event in Holmes' life, the origin of what is sometimes described as his moral skepticism, is partly because, toward the end of the century, he delivered two notable addresses on the subject of war and the life struggle. In 1884, in a Memorial Day Address delivered to the Union veterans' association, the Grand Army of the Republic, Holmes famously declaimed that "the generation that carried on the war has been set apart by its experience. Through our great good fortune, in our youth our hearts were touched with fire. It was given to us to learn at the outset that life is a profound and passionate thing." Just over a decade later, speaking before the graduating class at Harvard on Memorial Day 1895, he again invoked his own Civil War past and urged the students "to keep the soldier's faith against the doubts of civil life."[11] These speeches, of course, may have been little more than the romanticized recollections of a conflict faced in his youth, but Holmes' scholars have tended to read more into them than that.

For Holmes' first official biographer and former law clerk, Mark DeWolfe Howe, the tension between "the war in fact and the war in retrospect" was "dominantly formative of his philosophy," an assessment with which one of America's foremost literary scholars and critics, Edmund Wilson, concurred. The "conclusions to which Holmes had been brought under pressure of his service in the Civil War," he asserted, "were to affect in fundamental ways the whole of his subsequent thinking," in matters metaphysical and material, political, personal, and pragmatic. He "brought out of the war a tough character, purposive, disciplined, and not a little hard, a clearly defined personality," Wilson argued, that nevertheless contained a strain of "bleakness." And it was this bleakness in Holmes that historian Louis Menand, in search of the Civil War's individual, intellectual, and ideological impact, also emphasized. "The war was the central experience" of Holmes' life, Menand proposed, but it produced in him "a grimness and, at times, a cynicism that have occasionally repelled people who have studied his life and thought." Although the man left the war, most scholars agree, the war never fully left the man.[12]

Whether Holmes' entire life and career can be regarded as informed, or at least influenced, by his Civil War experiences, however, or whether there is an element of the *post hoc ergo propter hoc* fallacy about this perspective, is one of the issues that this short study will explore. It will do so not least because the question takes us beyond Holmes the individual to a wider consideration of the development of the United States as a nation between his birth in 1841 and his death in 1935 by which point the Civil War was a distant, if politically persistent, memory and the Second World War was already on the horizon. In this respect it is worth recalling Don Fehrenbacher's astute observation that with a single event as with a solitary individual, the "principal fallacy to be avoided is a tendency to view one's subject as the matrix of forces when it is usually instead a mere channel of their passage." A broader approach, hopefully, avoids this danger, and enables us to assess Holmes' own role in and contribution to "the birth of modern America," as well as explore what the social, political, cultural, economic, and legal lineaments of this rather traumatic birth entailed.[13]

The Civil War has, of course, long been conceptualized as a dividing line between two quite distinct worlds. On one side there is the world of Thomas Jefferson and James Madison, a world comprising, for much of the nation, small-scale farms, local communities, and, for some of the Southern states, larger-scale, slave-run plantations; but essentially a human-sized world, albeit one with an inhuman labor system at its core. On the other side lies the "monied metropolis" of the Gilded Age, a world dominated by John D. Rockefeller and Standard Oil, Andrew Carnegie, and J.P. Morgan, and driven by a "new industrial discipline" the origins of which, many scholars conclude, lay in the Civil War itself. The life of Oliver Wendell Holmes, Jr. reminds us, however, that this dividing line may more usefully be viewed as a fence, upon which several ideas sat somewhat awkwardly; none more so than the understanding of individual freedom in a world defined by, in historian Robert Wiebe's words, "the regulative, hierarchical needs of urban-industrial life."[14]

For leading African American sociologist and historian W.E.B. Du Bois, a student of Holmes' one-time close friend, William James, the Civil War did little to resolve this national dilemma. Writing in *Black Reconstruction*, a work first published in the year Holmes died, Du Bois argued that "to the Negro, 'Freedom' was God; to the poor white, 'Freedom' was nothing—he had more than he had use for; to the planter 'Freedom' for the poor was laziness and for the rich control of the poor worker; for the Northern businessman 'Freedom' was the opportunity to get rich."[15] And over the course of his life and legal career, Holmes had cause to consider the ramifications of all the various iterations of freedom that Du Bois had outlined, and many more besides, as he confronted the economic, social, and security challenges that faced the expanding, modernizing nation. In many respects, indeed, the question posed by Henry Adams in his famous memoir might be addressed as much to Holmes as to his nation. What, Adams enquired, might become of "a child of the seventeenth and eighteenth centuries, when he should wake up to find himself required to play the game of the twentieth?" For Holmes, it would have been a rhetorical question, of course, since, as he observed "certainty generally is illusion, and repose is not the destiny of man."[16]

NOTES

1 John T. Morse, *Life and Letters of Oliver Wendell Holmes*, 2 Vols. (London: Sampson Low, Marston and Company, 1896) I, 28–29; G. Edward White, *Justice Oliver Wendell Holmes: Law and the Inner Self* (New York and Oxford: Oxford University Press, 1993) 9.

2 Walton H. Hamilton, "On Dating Mr. Justice Holmes," *The University of Chicago Law Review*, 9:1 (December 1941) 1–29, 1; Max Lerner, intro. to "The Scar Holmes Leaves," in *Ideas Are Weapons: The History and Uses of Ideas* (1939. Reprint. New Brunswick, NJ: Transaction Publishers, 1991) 54–55.

3 The play (1946) and the film (1950) derived from it was *The Magnificent Yankee*, by Emmet Lavery, derived from an early (1942) biography of Holmes by lawyer and judge Francis Biddle, who had known Holmes. Holmes appears in modern fiction in, e.g., Harry Turtledove's "alternative history" stories that revolve around the Civil War, notably his "Southern Victory" series. Some scholars, possibly influenced by the "Olympian" label, have stated that a mountain was named after Holmes, but this seems not to have been the case; see Robert Marshall, *Alaska Wilderness: Exploring the Central Brooks Range*, Third Edition (Berkeley: University of California Press, 2005) 71–72, where Marshall recalls: "To enable us to discuss the geography without pointing we gave names to some of the valleys. The first one on the left, northeast of Boreal, we named Holmes Creek after the great jurist . . . who was celebrating his ninetieth birthday at about that time."

4 Elizabeth Shepley Sergeant, *Fire Under the Andes: A Group of Literary Portraits* (1927. Reprint. New York: Kennikat Press, 1966) 307; The "Yankee from Olympus" phrase refers to Sergeant's description, which also informed the title of Catherine Drinker Bowen's, *Yankee From Olympus: Justice Holmes and His Family* (Boston: Little, Brown and Company, 1944). There are many accounts in the various biographies of the construction of the Holmes' legend, but a useful summary (the notes alone are sobering for any student of history) of the convoluted process as undertaken, controlled, and challenged by those closest to Holmes can be found in the introduction to Robert M. Mennel and Christine L. Compston, *Holmes and Frankfurter: Their Correspondence, 1912–1934* (Hanover: University of New Hampshire, 1996), esp. xxix–xlii.

5 Grant Gilmore, *The Ages of American Law* (New Haven, CT: Yale University Press, 1977) 48–49.

6 Gilmore, *Ages of American Law*, 41–42; Bowen, *Yankee from Olympus*, xi.

7   Oliver Wendell Holmes, Sr., "The Professor's Story," *The Atlantic Monthly*, 5:27 (January 1860) 88–100, 93. This was part of a series of articles subsequently published as the novel, *Elsie Venner: A Romance of Destiny* (New York: Grosset and Dunlap, 1861).

8   John Quincy Adams, *Argument . . . Before the Supreme Court of the United States in the Case of the United States, Appellants, vs. Cinque, and Others, Africans, Captured in the Schooner* Amistad *. . .* (New York: S.W. Benedict, 1841) 89 [40. U.S. 518 (1841)]. The literature on the Amistad case is voluminous, both online and in print, but one of the best assessments of the case can be found in Howard Jones, *Mutiny on the Amistad: The Saga of a Slave Revolt and Its Impact on American Abolition, Law, and Diplomacy* (New York: Oxford University Press, 1987). The literature on slavery and the Constitution is even more voluminous, but a recent short study by Justin Buckley Dyer, *Natural Law and the Antislavery Constitutional Tradition* (Cambridge: Cambridge University Press, 2012), offers a useful starting point.

9   Thurgood Marshall, Transcript of Oral Argument, NAACP Papers, Box I-D-94, file; *Pearson v. Murray*, 169 Md. 478 182 A.590 (1936) quoted in Mark V. Tushnet, *Making Civil Rights Law: Thurgood Marshall and the Supreme Court, 1936–1961* (New York and Oxford: Oxford University Press, 1994) 14.

10 Oliver Wendell Holmes, Jr., "The Path of the Law," *Harvard Law Review*, 10:8 (March 25, 1897) 457–478, 459.

11 Oliver Wendell Holmes, Jr., "Memorial Day Address, May 30 1884," in Richard A. Posner (ed.), *The Essential Holmes: Selections from the Letters, Speeches, Judicial Opinions, and Other Writings of Oliver Wendell Holmes, Jr.* (1992. Reprint. Chicago and London: The University of Chicago Press, 1996) 80–87; and "Memorial Day Address, May 30, 1895," ibid., 87–95.

12 Edmund Wilson, *Patriotic Gore: Studies in the Literature of the American Civil War* (1962. Reprint. London: The Hogarth Press, 1987) 743; Mark DeWolfe Howe (ed.), *Touched with Fire: Civil War Letters and Diary of Oliver Wendell Holmes, Jr., 1861–1864* (Cambridge, MA: Harvard University Press, 1946) vii; Wilson, *Patriotic Gore*, 753–754; Louis Menand, *The Metaphysical Club* (2001. Reprint. London: Harper Collins, 2002) 4; Richard Maxwell Brown, *No Duty to Retreat: Violence and Values in American History and Society* (New York and Oxford: Oxford University Press, 1991) 31. In the *Oxford Companion to the Supreme Court*, Sheldon M. Novick, author of the first full biography of Holmes, also argues that Holmes' "views of the power of government were formed in the Civil War": Kermit L. Hall, James W. Ely, Joel B. Grossman (eds.), *The Oxford Companion to the Supreme Court of the United States*, Second Edition (New York and Oxford: Oxford University Press, 2005) 472.

13 Don E. Fehrenbacher, *The Dred Scott Case: Its Significance in American Law and Politics* (New York and Oxford: Oxford University Press, 1978) 4; Menand, *Metaphysical Club*, ix.

14 Sven Beckert, *The Monied Metropolis: New York City and the Consolidation of the American Bourgeoisie, 1850–1896* (Cambridge: Cambridge University Press, 2001); Alan Trachtenberg, *Reading American Photographs: Images as History, Matthew Brady to Walker Evans* (1989. Reprint. New York: Hill and Wang, 1999) 109; Robert H. Wiebe, *The Search for Order, 1877–1920* (New York: Hill and Wang, 1967) 2. On the role of the Civil War in this process see also: Allan Nevins, *Ordeal of the Union* (1947–1971. Reprint. New York and London: Collier Books, 1992) Vol. 4, *The War for the Union*, 271–273; George M. Fredrickson, *The Inner Civil War: Northern Intellectuals and the Crisis of the Union* (New York: Harper and Row, 1965); and Leonard P. Curry, *Blueprint for Modern America: Nonmilitary Legislation of the First Civil War Congress* (Nashville, TN: Vanderbilt University Press, 1968).

15 W.E. Burghardt Du Bois, *Black Reconstruction: An Essay Toward a History of the Part which Black Folk Played in the Attempt to Reconstruct Democracy in America, 1860–1880* (New York: Harcourt, Brace and Company, 1935) 347.

16 Henry Adams, *The Education of Henry Adams*, ed. Ernest Samuels (Boston: Houghton Mifflin Company, 1973) 4; Holmes, "The Path of the Law," 167.

PART I

OLIVER WENDELL HOLMES, JR.

CHAPTER 1

An Antebellum Adolescence

"But now, look around, my history's everywhere
And I'm my own environment."
(Norman MacCaig, "Double Life," *Riding Lights*, 1955)

In the final chapter of *Patriotic Gore*, a study of the literature of the Civil War era, Edmund Wilson opened his discussion of "Justice Oliver Wendell Holmes" by merging father and son into the "Oliver Wendell Holmeses." This confluence between one generation and the next, and by extrapolation between an antebellum Union and the post-Civil War nation, offers an appropriate starting point for a study of the son whose life extended well into the twentieth century but was, arguably, influenced by "his struggle to distance himself from his famous father" and overshadowed by his nation's mid-nineteenth-century civil conflict.[1]

Oliver Wendell Holmes, Jr. was born into the "highly cultivated, homogeneous world" of antebellum Boston. Arguably he was its "consummate product: idealistic, artistic, and socially committed." But, at least as historian Louis Menand put it, his was a world that bled "to death at Fredericksburg and Antietam, in a war that learning and brilliance had been powerless to prevent."[2] It is important to emphasize, however, that the Boston of Holmes' youth was no static Christmas card caricature of a pre-war world, shaded in subtle sepia hues and inhabited primarily by the privileged progeny of its Puritan past. Antebellum Boston was neither Europe before the First World War, nor was it Eden before the Fall. It was, however, very much the world of Oliver Wendell Holmes, Sr. And in many respects, to get to the son, we must first go through the father.

★★★

Although not quite as long-lived as the son to whom he bequeathed his name, Oliver Wendell Holmes, Sr.'s life (1809–1894) nevertheless spanned the greater part of the nineteenth century. However his life was deemed by one of his earliest biographers to be "so uneventful that the utter absence of anything in it to remark became in itself remarkable." Certainly, with the exception of two years spent in Europe, largely in Paris studying medicine, and a short return visit there in later life, Dr. Holmes rarely ventured far from Boston whose State House he famously designated the "Hub of the Universe." His affection for Boston was, as noted author William Dean Howells observed, akin to "the patriotism of men in the times when a man's city was a man's country." There was "something Athenian, something Florentine" about it. This did not mean, however, that Dr. Holmes' national influence or cultural impact was insignificant; far from it. He was living proof "that identification with a locality is a surer passport to immortality than cosmopolitanism is." A notable "man of letters," as contemporary parlance put it, the output from his pen covered many more miles than he could have managed in person had he been an inveterate globetrotter. In part this was down to the inclinations of Holmes as an individual, but in large part, too, it derived from the specific circumstances of his time and place.[3]

When Dr. Holmes was born in 1809, the same year, indeed, as Abraham Lincoln, Boston was still designated a town, although it was in fact the fourth largest city in the nation at that time. Boston legally became a city only in 1822. In 1809, it was just one part of a post-Revolutionary, post-colonial, if not yet entirely post-Puritan world, but it already possessed a strong sense of its own significance. Much of this was predicated upon the past; not merely the brief past that Boston had in national terms, but the far longer past that had preceded this, all the way back, indeed, to the earliest European migrations into what became Massachusetts. Its origins lay in the Puritan exodus, the "Great Migration" from England that began in 1629. More specifically, it derived from Puritan leader John Winthrop's now famous sermon, *A Model of Christian Charity*, preached either on the eve of departure or possibly actually en route to the then New World. For Winthrop, as for his congregation, the venture was a new beginning, albeit driven by a much older religious imperative. In establishing a settlement across the Atlantic, Winthrop reminded the colonists that "we must consider that we shall be as a city upon a hill. The eyes of all people are upon us. So that if we shall deal falsely with our God in this work we have undertaken, and so cause Him to withdraw His present help from us, we shall be made a story and a by-word through the world."[4]

Over the course of the two centuries between John Winthrop's arrival and Holmes' birth, New England was largely understood, at least by its elite residents who were descendants of the first Puritans, to have achieved

Winthrop's initial ambitions as far as matters cultural and clerical, educational and economic were concerned. By the nineteenth century, New Englanders dominated the writing and therefore public dissemination of American history. This did little to contradict what was, in effect, a distinctly sectional slant on the national story that elided most of the brutal and exclusionary realities of the colonial past. As America's most famous poet, Walt Whitman, noted in 1883, for much of the nineteenth century, Americans had been overly influenced "by New England writers and schoolmaster," too accepting of "the notion that our United States have been fashion'd from the British Islands only, and essentially from a second England only." This, Whitman argued, was "a very great mistake."[5]

New England's writers were not entirely to blame for this state of affairs. Boston, by Dr. Holmes' time, already lay at the core of the national narrative as a city whose patriotic credentials had been confirmed by the central role that the city had played in fomenting the American Revolution. To live in Boston, as the Brahmin historian Henry Adams recalled, was to live "in the atmosphere of the Stamp Act, the Tea Tax, and the Boston Massacre." By the turn of the nineteenth century, therefore, even before New England historians put pen to paper, Boston's reputation was already secure. Its reality, of course, had altered considerably. Colonial Boston had been a settlement constructed, as the New England colonies as a whole were, around the rule of the elect; not in a political sense, but in a religious one. By 1809 the dominance of those who had experienced public conversion, termed "Visible Saints," was long over, but in their place a new secular elect had emerged. As Adams later described it, until "1850, and even later, New England society was still directed by the professions. Lawyers, physicians, professors, merchants were classes, and acted not as individuals, but as though they were clergymen and each profession were a church."[6]

This nineteenth-century social and economic elite "utilized an elaborate web of kinship ties" that provided it with "cohesion, continuity and stability" in a rapidly changing world. And although Boston's elite perceived its authority as stemming "not from hereditary privilege but from personal achievement," lineage had a great deal to do both with how it saw itself and how it was seen by outsiders. Writing at the end of the nineteenth century, Dr. Holmes' first biographer, in noting that his subject was descended from solid "New England stock," bemoaned the fact that "the name of New England is now a mere geographical title rather than, as it used to be, an implied expression of racial and social characteristics."[7]

For much of the nineteenth century, however, the ideals of the city on a hill were deemed largely to inhere in that part of its population later labelled by Holmes as the Brahmin class. This "republican aristocracy" perceived itself as the contemporary social and economic exemplar for the nation.

It reinforced its position through "a highly articulated social order which not only set standards but encouraged and enforced right conduct," and thereby reassured its members that stability could be maintained. Boston Brahmins largely profited from many of the strongest forces for change in mid-nineteenth-century America encapsulated in the urbanization, industrialization, and immigration paradigm. But their connection to these changes did not automatically ensure their confidence in the result. Fearful that rapid social change in Boston and elsewhere would produce "a chaotic individualism," elite families carefully constructed cultural and commercial channels through which both individual and national character could be constrained and controlled.[8]

Their fears, naturally, have to be placed in the context of Boston's rapid growth. "Possibly no city in the world," observed an early-twentieth-century study of Boston's development, "has altered more the physical conformation of its site."[9] In 1814, when the senior Holmes was just a child, the Boston and Roxbury Mill Corporation began the gradual land reclamation of the Back Bay. In time this transformed what had been marshland into fashionable residential streets. After the Civil War, both Dr. Holmes and his son would live there, on the newly-created Beacon Street. This was only one of many such projects. Over the course of the nineteenth century Boston's physical footprint increased some tenfold. This was just as well since its population, too, trebled from around 34,000 in 1810 to around 93,000 by 1840; by the eve of the Civil War it was almost 178,000. It was now the fifth largest city in the nation, and one of America's major seaports whose population comprised an increasing number of foreign-born or native-born in-migrants. By the middle of the century, indeed, only around 35 percent of the city's inhabitants had been born and raised there.

If any of those who came to Boston had done so in the hope of making their fortune, however, they would have likely been disappointed. Equally, the fears of any Boston Brahmin for the financial future proved equally unfounded. Fortunes in antebellum Boston "tended not to fall overnight but rather to persist." To those who had, the likelihood was that more would be given. Doubtless, the fact that the egalitarian ethos of the American republican experiment failed to disturb the economic equilibrium was a comfort to Boston's elite citizens. At the same time it left them increasingly isolated within a growing city that was hardly as homogeneous as they liked to believe, and in which the social, as well as the physical, distance between the parallel planes of poverty and privilege was growing ever-greater.[10]

By the early nineteenth century New England society had "lost something that was central to the cohesiveness of Puritan culture: a meaningful and functioning sense of community."[11] In this context it may be no surprise that such social stability as was to be found in nineteenth-century Boston had almost as much to do with ancestry as with assets. In 1831, Mount Auburn Cemetery in Cambridge became one of the nation's first Rural or Park cemeteries, but for contemporary Bostonians Mount Auburn was only one of the sites of memory as much as of mourning that fixed their world.[12]

The publication, just after the Civil War, of a history of the city that devoted no fewer than nine chapters to detailed descriptions of individual burial grounds and their many "interesting associations of the past" emphasized this centrality of the cemetery in nineteenth-century New England culture. For some, such as future Unitarian minister, author, and abolitionist Thomas Wentworth Higginson, the city's cemeteries were sites of curiosity as much as of historical "associations." He recalled how as a child he had "delighted to pore over the old flat tombstones in the Old Cambridge cemetery, stones . . . on which even the language was dead" but nevertheless invoked past "virtues," stones from which the "leaden coats of arms had been pried out to be melted into bullets for the Continental army . . . and so linked us to the past." And this was the crucial point. In 1838, as Massachusetts Governor Levi Lincoln observed in his dedicatory address at the Worcester Rural Cemetery, there was a danger of the past being "all but forgotten" by the generations then living. There are few left, he noted, who "can now claim affinity to the tenants of that ancient churchyard." For those few who could, however, such cemeteries represented public expressions of private success, places quite literally "rich with memories from the past" that validated the values of the present and held out hope that such values had a place in the future.[13]

★★★

This, then, was the world in which Oliver Wendell Holmes, Sr. lived. It was one in which "the ethic of individual responsibility married moral duty to the calling of trade," in which the family represented "the hub of the domestic universe." And the city of Boston, in its physical constructions as much as in its personal associations, both living and dead, expressed the outward, public ambitions and apprehensions of an inward-looking, essentially private class.[14]

Dr. Holmes' father had been a Calvinist clergyman and he himself studied law and then medicine. In this period, however, there was no expectation that medicine would represent the whole of his public life, and nor did it. Ultimately, he became better known as a novelist, poet, essayist, and public speaker, or the "Autocrat," after the series of popular essays that he began to publish in the 1850s. These were brought together as *The Autocrat at the Breakfast-Table* (1858), a bestseller and the work that established his literary reputation.[15]

Holmes was not unusual among nineteenth-century doctors in combining medical with literary pursuits. Other doctors with literary aspirations at this time included neurologist and future Surgeon General of the Army William A. Hammond and Holmes' friend and colleague the nerve specialist Silas Weir Mitchell. Both the latter, however, positioned medicine as their primary public activity; their literary endeavors were essentially extracurricular enthusiasms. For Holmes it became the reverse, to the dismay of some of his associates who felt that, in Holmes' case, literature's gain was medicine's loss. This was a view with which his son, Wendell, concurred. Had his father, he believed, "had the patience to concentrate all his energy in a single subject, which perhaps is saying if he had been a different man, he would have been less popular, but he might have produced a great work."[16]

It was perhaps inevitable, however, that Dr. Holmes would approach life in the way he did. "The values of 'Brahmin' Boston" as one of his son's biographers noted, "emphasized versatility and gentlemanly amateurishness at the expense of singleminded professionalism." And the city's reputation as the "Athens of America" certainly ensured that there was a wealth of opportunity in it for the intellectual life, more broadly conceived. This was, to use Howells' term, Boston's "Augustan" age. It was one in which literature was deemed "so respectable, and often of so high lineage, that to be a poet," Howells recalled, "was not only to be good society, but almost to be good family." And it was a fairly high-profile family, as its members sometimes liked to remind themselves, and others. Having had the many talents of "Louis Agassiz, Francis J. Child, Richard Henry Dana, Jun., John Fiske, Dr Asa Gray, the family of the Jameses, father and sons, Lowell, Longfellow, Charles Elliot Norton, Dr John G. Palfrey, James Pierce, Dr Peabody, Professor Parsons, [and] Professor Sophocles" described to him, author Bret Harte's response was pithy, and to the point. "Why, you couldn't fire a revolver from your front porch anywhere without bringing down a two-volumer!"[17]

Yet although the literati comprised a charmed circle, it was not an entirely closed one. Through a combination of informal clubs, library associations, and what were, in effect, rather rarefied nineteenth-century reading groups, Brahmin society achieved a confluence of commerce and culture—in the Unitarian sense of self-culture—that extended beyond its own class. Institutions such as the Boston Athenaeum, a private-subscription library founded in 1807, were in time joined by less elite examples, such as the Mercantile Library Association (founded 1820) and the Boston Public Library (founded 1848). And the debates conducted via Brahmin associations such as the Saturday Club, a "society of friends" founded in 1856 by a group of businessmen and intellectuals that included Holmes, Ralph Waldo Emerson, James Russell Lowell, Henry Wadsworth Longfellow, and businessman John Murray Forbes, made their way into the public arena via publications such as *The Atlantic Monthly*, launched the following year. Throughout the Antebellum Era, too, the growing popularity of public lectures, many of them delivered by future Saturday Club members, disseminated the discussions of the elite across a far wider social and economic spectrum.[18]

"Nothing is so popular just at this period as Lectures," observed Boston hardware merchant William Gray Brooks. And although Brooks was suspicious of "the great increase and diffusion of knowledge" across society, fearing that "this democratized mode of learning would contribute to cultural decline," his concerns were not universally shared. Public lectures, in particular, were social events with the added potential, as far as their organizers were concerned, for socialization. They bridged the cultural gap that Boston's elite perceived as existing between their civic ideals and the citizen masses, between the immigrant and the intellectual, the rural and the urban, and the past and the present. And as a regular feature on Boston's lecture circuit, Holmes fully grasped the many "ways in which talk or 'conversation' had become the representative verbal mode of his age—central to the era's spoken social discourse, to its written literary discourse, and even to its changing medical discourse."[19]

Holmes' decision, in the end, to make talk rather than treatment his life's work, in part derived from the fact that he did not comfortably conform to the public idea of what a doctor should be. He "who writes rhymes must not write prescriptions," he once observed, "and he who makes jests should not escort people to their graves." Yet Holmes was serious about his science, and equally serious about his prose. In the latter he worked out, or at least experimented with, many of the medical questions of his day, notably in the first and still most famous of what were termed his "medicated novels," *Elsie Venner*.[20]

It was in *Elsie Venner* that the benefits of the Brahmin class were first mooted, if also implicitly critiqued. Serialized in *The Atlantic Monthly* in 1859 and 1860 and published in book form in 1861, this was the unusual tale of a woman poisoned by snake venom whilst still *in utero*, divided in her nature between the ophidian and the human. It was, as Holmes made clear in his various prefaces to the work, a story designed "to test the doctrine of 'original sin' and human responsibility for the disordered volition coming under that technical denomination." At its heart was the issue of "moral poisoning." "[M]y poor heroine," Holmes explained, "found her origin, not in fable or romance, but in a physiological conception, fertilized by a theological dogma." The Calvinist clergy, inevitably, loathed it, but it was a novel of its time and, with rather different cultural connotations, of his son's time, too.[21]

One cannot comfortably draw a clear line between the father's fiction and the son's personal, and later legal, opinions, of course, but it would be foolish to ignore the possibility of influence entirely.[22] What can be said with certainty is that the young Wendell was born at that moment when a rather different "moral poison," America's original national sin of slavery, was beginning to dominate both social and political discourse.

As Dr. Holmes explored the lineaments of self-determination and personal freedom in his fiction, such matters were far from fictional in a nation increasingly divided over the permanence of, and political, social, and moral implications that followed from, what was, by then, the South's "peculiar institution." Even the Brahmin elite could not avoid the subject, which came increasingly to determine any and all debate from the 1840s onwards. The contentious question of whether a nation could exist, as Lincoln famously put it, "half-slave and half-free" in some senses paralleled the personal issues that Holmes struggled with in his life as in his fiction; but in his own life Holmes could afford to vacillate.[23] For his nation, however, the nation into which his son was born, on the subject of individual freedom the days of indecision were drawing to a close.

★★★

For the young Wendell, rather like Henry Adams who was only a few years older than him, life could also be described as "a double thing." Whether this can be applied to the whole of his life, and it has been, is another matter. William James famously described Holmes as being "composed of at least two and a half different people rolled into one, and the way he keeps them together in one tight skin, without quarrelling more than they do" was, in James' opinion, "remarkable." This was, of course, Holmes' character that was under consideration, rather than the world within which it was located. But if the former showed subsequent signs of division, it may be, in part at least, because the latter was, at the start of Holmes' life and for all of his adolescence, so very divided.[24]

Holmes, like Adams, grew up between two worlds, one could say quite literally. The house in which he was born in Montgomery Place (now Bosworth Street), Boston, was relatively recent, a tangible symbol of the expanding city's future, but it led out opposite the Old Granary Burying Ground, an equally tangible reminder of its past that he would pass every day on his way to school. As Holmes himself once said, of course, "our interests are in the present and the future—not the past," but that was never entirely true of him. Montgomery Place and its surroundings were both emotional and national bedrock for Holmes. In his memory they evoked "a Boston of two centuries ago" but also a more proximate time "before the war," by which he meant the Civil War, the conflict that instigated "the changes that have almost made a new art of warfare."[25] They spoke to a tradition whose historical roots, as he acknowledged, developed absent "the thicker atmosphere of the old world," ran less deep than in Europe, but deep enough for his nation, and for him.[26]

Yet if the geographical location of his birth grounded Holmes in the colonial past, his temporal placement forced him to face, as he grew up, an uncertain national future. Arguably, the coordinates of his character were established precisely at the point on the nation's moral compass when its needle wavered between past and future, North and South, slavery and freedom.

The fact is that Holmes was born on both a legal and an ideological frontier. The antebellum legal landscape might have resembled the "Garden of Eden," in which "great judges" struck "a sensitive balance between the conflicting claims of local autonomy and national uniformity in an immense, diverse, and rapidly growing country." But the snake in the garden was slavery, an inheritance from the colonial past that threatened to blight the national future. And whilst the physical violence over the issue took place on the nation's territorial edges, the legal struggle was at its center.[27]

The Boston of 1850, Henry Cabot Lodge recalled, "stood on the edge of a new time, but the old time was still visible from it, still indeed prevailed about it." If its atmosphere "was still an eighteenth-century atmosphere," nevertheless that eighteenth-century world was gradually "slipping away" under the influence of forces driving not just the United States but Europe toward modernity. This was a period that witnessed "the consolidation of the United States and of Germany . . . the unification of Italy, the liberation of the slaves, the emancipation of the Russian serfs, and the wide extension of democratic and representative government." It was, as Lodge recalled, "the day of the human-rights statesmen just rising to power, of the men who believed that in political liberty was to be found the cure for every human ill."[28] And Boston was, to a great extent, on the frontline of this new age. More socially fluid than fixed, and certainly more fluent on the contentious question of slavery than some cities, by the mid-nineteenth century Boston's apparently placid surface disguised some deep and dangerous sectional currents.

Holmes was not yet a teenager when, in the wake of the Compromise of 1850, North and South faced each other, albeit metaphorically, on the city's streets. The cause was the revised Fugitive Slave Act that was part of the Compromise. This facilitated the arrest and removal to the South of slaves who had escaped to the Northern states. In effect, it forced a city long proud of its anti-slavery credentials into complicity in chattel slavery, "bound through corruption and fraud," as the businessman John Murray Forbes put it, "to the will of the aristocratic minority."[29] The iniquity inspired Emerson to heights of Brahmin bluster that even he had not reached before:

> Boston, of whose fame for spirit and character we have all been so proud; Boston, whose citizens, intelligent people in England told me they could always distinguish by their culture among Americans; the Boston of the American Revolution, which figures so proudly in John Adams' Diary, which the whole

country has been reading; Boston, spoiled by prosperity, must bow its ancient
honor in the dust, and make us irretrievably ashamed.[30]

In response to the Fugitive Slave Act, local associations, such as the Boston
Vigilance Committee, were formed to assist fugitive slaves who had made
it as far as Boston, helping them move further North and into Canada, but
also preventing, through direct action if necessary, their seizure and return
South by their owners.

Such associations were not new to the city. Boston had a long history
of abolitionist agitation. This found public expression, and also some public censure, largely through the efforts of William Lloyd Garrison and his
famous newspaper, *The Liberator*, that began publication in 1831, and the
Massachusetts Anti-Slavery Society he founded. "Slavery," Henry Adams
argued, "drove the whole Puritan community back on its Puritanism." But
this was only partly true. What bothered Bostonians, by and large, was that
a law they had expected to see enacted solely in the South, one "merely
held *in terrorem* over the blacks, as a preventive of escape," had penetrated
the Puritan heartland. And in 1854 one particular case brought matters to a
head; that of Anthony Burns. Having escaped slavery in Richmond in 1853,
Burns was working in Boston when he was arrested. The Fugitive Slave Law
was upheld, and he was returned South, but not before Boston had been,
albeit temporarily, placed under martial law to prevent his rescue, prompting Thomas Wentworth Higginson to deliver a sermon in which he echoed
Emerson in describing Massachusetts as "a conquered province."[31]

Looking back on those days, Higginson recalled that this was, in Boston,
"a time of high moral purpose." He highlighted the extent to which "the
anti-slavery movement, reaching its climax after the passage of the Fugitive
Slave Law," was the undisputed "leader in all the reforms of the day . . . it
brought to a focus all their picturesque ingredients." Higginson was a concerned and committed abolitionist, who would go on to become an officer
of an African American regiment in the Civil War. But that did not prevent
him from poking some gentle fun at those attracted by abolitionism: the
"women who sat tranquilly knitting through a whole anti-slavery conven-
tion, however exciting, and who had that look of prolonged and self controlled patience which we associate with Sisters of Charity"; and the men
who "bore a marked resemblance to the accepted picture of Jesus Christ,"
individuals whom Emerson "tersely classified as 'men with beards.'"[32]

Yet although their worlds overlapped, and would meet most forcibly in
the years immediately prior to and during the Civil War, Higginson and
Holmes were not contemporaries; the former graduated from Harvard in
the year the latter was born. So although the young Wendell experienced the
excitement, he did not endure the absurdities of the abolitionist movement

as Higginson did; by the time Holmes came to it, it was fully formed, and rather more serious. As Holmes prepared to leave for Harvard, Higginson was in Kansas, armed and fully prepared for violence in defense of the anti-slavery settlers there.

And there was violence. In the spring of 1856, pro-slavery forces attacked the town of Lawrence and destroyed abolitionist newspaper presses, and the abolitionist forces responded in kind. "Murder and cold-blooded assassination were of almost daily occurrence," wrote English visitor Thomas H. Gladstone in his account of conditions in Kansas that appeared in the *London Times*. The most dramatic episode occurred when, in response to the raid on Lawrence, the radical abolitionist John Brown, later to lead the famous but futile attack on Harpers Ferry, Virginia in 1859, attacked and killed five pro-slavery settlers at Pottawatomie Creek. By his actions in Kansas and in Virginia, Brown was, as legal historian Paul Finkelman has argued, "the harbinger of the future." And in some respects, indeed, Brown can be seen as a harbinger of Holmes' future in his merging of "the sentimentality of the antebellum age with the very unsentimental era that followed."[33]

★★★

Assessing the extent to which the issue of slavery impacted on Holmes' world at the time, however, as well as the longer-term significance of this, is not necessarily straightforward. It may be, as Emerson wrote, that the "household is the home of the *man*, as well as of the child," and that anyone wishing to "acquaint himself with the real history of the world, with the spirit of the age . . . must not go first to the state-house or the court-room . . . It is what is done and suffered in the house," according to Emerson, "in the constitution, in the temperament, in the personal history, that has the profoundest interest for us."[34] But the initial period of Holmes' life can only ever be imperfectly reconstructed from such limited contemporary material as is available, supported, but possibly equally skewed, by later reminiscences, his own and those of others. In this respect, retrospective clarity is a real risk. Remembering always involves a degree of reorganization, of memories, of motives, and of meaning. As much may be redacted as revealed by taking this route into Holmes' past. At the same time, the closeness of his class does mean that glimpses of his environment, at least, are provided by the many literary accounts, memoirs, and recollections of those who, like Higginson, shared his world, if not his sensibilities.

Holmes was only six when his father became the Parkman Professor of Anatomy and Physiology at Harvard Medical School. It would be a decade before the "Autocrat" became a household name. So although Dr. Holmes, mainstay of the lecture circuit as he was, was often absent, for Wendell the pressures of being the son of a famous father were not an issue as he was growing up. The security of New England tradition largely dictated the structure of Holmes' early years, and especially its educational component. In his hastily composed "autobiographical sketch" for the Harvard class album, written in the period shortly after he had volunteered to fight in the Civil War, Holmes located himself in genealogical and in national terms; some "of my ancestors," he noted, "have fought in the Revolution." He then identified his grandparents, maternal and paternal, said nothing about his younger siblings, Amelia and Edward, and simply noted that he had just completed his own contribution to the family's educational tradition, "as my grandfathers, fathers and uncles . . . before me." This tradition was one shared across much of the Brahmin elite. As Adams noted, "custom, social ties, convenience, and, above all, economy, kept each generation in the track."[35]

In domestic terms, too, Holmes' world followed a pattern typical of his class and generation. Summers were spent at the family's newly-acquired, in 1849, country home in the Berkshire Hills at Pittsfield, Canoe Meadow, and winters at school. For Holmes, as for Adams, "[w]inter and summer, cold and heat, town and country, force and freedom, marked two modes of life and thought, balanced like lobes of the brain." Both also attended Epes Sargent Dixwell's school, located in Boylston Place by Boston Common. Whether Holmes shared Adams' sense that his early education was "colonial, revolutionary, almost Cromwellian" in its essence, and whether he experienced a similar "unqualified joy" when he left Dixwell's establishment, is not recorded. Since Holmes would, in 1872, marry Dixwell's daughter, Fanny, any recollections of his future father-in-law's school, had he confided them, might not have been so blunt. In later life, however, he did recollect that his general upbringing and education took place in a stifling religious atmosphere, one that he could not then, nor ever in his life after, breathe in comfortably. "I didn't get Hell talk from my parents," he recalled, "it was in the air."[36]

Apart from "the *ennui* of those Sunday morning bells, and hymn tunes," however, Holmes' life seems to have been as relatively carefree and, simultaneously, as constricted as it was for most economically and socially secure antebellum children. Probably he, like Adams and Lodge, received at least part of his education from, even if he did not "take a prominent part in," what Lodge described as the "Homeric combats with snowballs against the boys from the South Cove and the North End" waged on Boston Common. In the context of the city's growth, its expanding immigrant, especially Irish immigrant numbers, this was a game that, as Lodge noted, his class was destined to lose. Over time "the ever-increasing number of our opponents gradually by sheer weight pushed us, and still more our successors, from the Common . . . to seek coasting and skating in the country." Clearly, by this point he had more in mind than boys' games, as, indeed, did Adams. Looking back on the battles of Boston Common, Adams mused on the more serious battles that many of Boston's youth later faced on "the battle-fields of Virginia and Maryland," and "wondered whether their education on Boston Common had taught [them] how to die."[37]

This tragedy lay in the future. For Holmes, as for Adams, the dominant features of his early education derived not from quasi-class conflict conducted on Boston Common but from the intensive "literary and political" discourse that prevailed in the domestic arena. This was driven by Boston's Unitarian clergy and those trained in the ministry, and its literati as described by Howells and that included, of course, his own father. Holmes' was a very concentrated world because so many of Boston's Brahmin class, broadly defined, were located in either one, and usually both, of these twin constellations; and their intellectual orbit was necessarily determined by the other. In the Holmes' family, even more so, possibly, than in the Adams', children "joined in the dinner-table discussions," and "were accustomed to hear, almost every day, table talk as good as they were ever likely to hear again."[38]

And since this enthusiasm for debate and discussion was not restricted to the private sphere, nor to private concerns, it may be assumed—and can be traced to some extent through Holmes' later writings—that the young Wendell was at least aware of the central subject of much of this debate. Indeed, as historian Fred Somkin once argued, the Antebellum Era as whole was one that enjoyed "a certain unity of public utterance, an utterance which was perhaps representative in a way that has not been the case since." Brahmin Boston was simply an extreme example of this. For Somkin, what defined this utterance, what unified it, in effect, was a fascination with the idea of American freedom, "whether in form political, religious, or cultural." This, he argued, was pre-eminently the "*res Americana*, the *matter of America*."[39]

And yet out of this unity emerged a deadly division, and ultimately a civil conflict that would kill well over 600,000 Americans, maim as many more, and almost terminate the life of Wendell Holmes before it had really begun. The cataclysm that was the Civil War, however, can obscure the contradictions inherent in the world before war came. This was Wendell Holmes' world, one in which the Brahmin elite of which he was a member can be regarded as the beating heart of antebellum Boston, but equally can be seen as "anachronistic and socially exclusive," out of touch with its time, and susceptible to political and cultural forces beyond its control. In this context, his father's writings may have represented a "reflection of the explosive, interruptive, and multivoiced dynamics of the 'public sphere' in mid-century America," but the "conversation of the culture" was undergoing a substantial shift when Wendell was born. Words would mean something very different for the future Supreme Court Justice, equally glib with them though he was.[40]

★★★

In later life, Holmes saw this shift more clearly. Like Henry Adams, he came to believe that his father's "generation that lived from 1840 to 1870 could do very well with the old form of education," but his own generation, "which had its work to do between 1870 and 1900 needed something quite new." For Lodge, too, the generational divide was more pronounced at that time than at any other. There "was a wider difference between the men who fought at Waterloo and those who fought at Gettysburg," Lodge suggested, "than there was between the followers of Leonidas [who died at the Battle of Thermopylae in 480 BC] and the soldiers of Napoleon." For Lodge, the differences were in part ideological, but in larger part environmental. The "application of steam and electricity to transportation and communication," in his opinion, "made a greater change in human environment than had occurred since the earliest period of recorded history."[41]

For Holmes, however, the differences went even deeper, at least as he experienced them personally. He later explained to the legal scholar and philosopher Morris Cohen:

> My father was brought up scientifically—i.e. he studied medicine in France—and I was not. Yet there was with him as with the rest of his generation a certain soft-ness of attitude toward the interstitial miracle—the phenomenon without phe-nomenal antecedents—that I did not feel. The difference was in the air, although perhaps only a few of my time felt it. The Origin of Species I think came out when I was in college—H. Spencer had announced his intention to put the uni-verse into our pockets—I hadn't read either of them, to be sure, but as I say it was in the air ... Emerson and Ruskin were the men who set me on fire. Probably a skeptical temperament I got from my mother had something to do with my way of thinking. Then I was in with the abolitionists, some of whom were skeptics as well as dogmatists. But I think science was at the bottom.[42]

As Holmes' reference to the abolitionists reveals, however, it was not just generational but more fundamental divisions in the broader culture that impacted upon his world. And some of these were mirrored in his immedi-ate family.

Holmes' mother, Amelia Jackson Holmes, certainly espoused strong abo-litionist convictions. His father was more circumspect about the subject, at least prior to the Civil War. Criticized by James Russell Lowell for not discussing slavery in a lecture delivered in 1846, Dr. Holmes acknowledged that "it would have been a popular thing to do." He defended his silence, however, by noting, first, that his audience had not been "slaveholders and generally hate it pretty thoroughly already," and, second, that since "all the resources of language have been so liberally employed upon the subject" he could have added little. You "and I cannot prevent the existence of slavery," he lectured Lowell, but "the catastrophe of disunion I believe we can prevent, and thus avert a future of war and bloodshed which is equally frightful to both of us in contemplation."[43]

Holmes' mother, by contrast, has been described as fully "prepared even for war" on this issue, and offered her opinion that, whilst it was "very hard to have our sons and brothers go off" to war, "we would not keep them at home if we could. I long ago learned," she observed, "that there is no happiness to be had in this world by avoiding duty." The timing of these sentiments—in the war's third year, and following close after Lincoln's issuance of the Emancipation Proclamation—may, of course, have expressed an acceptance of trials already in train rather than anticipation of those to come. Yet in her emphasis on duty in the cause of emancipation, her willingness to see the Civil War "go on till every slave is free," and her desire that her son should "always be ready to defend and struggle for humanity," after that son had already twice been wounded, she was not alone.[44]

Maternal influence exerted a forceful pressure on Boston's Brahmin sons that was almost Spartan in its sensibilities and difficult for a modern age, less secure in its certainties about salvation, to sympathize with. It may, indeed, have been hard enough at the time for some of the sons concerned to meet such elevated expectations as their mothers imposed. One of Holmes' Harvard contemporaries and friend, Robert Gould Shaw, certainly felt frustrated, indeed defensive on the subject of slavery. He resented his own mother's assumption that because he did not "talk and think Slavery all the time," he was not in tune with her abolitionist sentiments; "you say I don't feel with you," he complained, "when I do."[45]

Amelia was not, perhaps, quite so demanding. And in some respects, although it reinforces the sense that Holmes as an adolescent was poised not just between childhood and adulthood but between his parents' perspectives on the bigger issues of the day, the question of whether the young Wendell took his mother's side rather than his father's on the specific question of slavery and its abolition has little bearing on his life before the Civil War. In others, however, the issue of influence, more broadly conceived, cuts directly to the heart of Holmes' development as an individual.

As Holmes himself once noted, "[o]ur early impressions shape our later emotional reactions." This was almost certainly true in his case. Over the span of a long career, many of the decisions he made, and opinions, both personal and legal, that he penned often carried the echoes, however faint, of antebellum arguments; not just over slavery specifically but its wider implications for the nation. As far as slavery and its abolition were concerned, however, there certainly was a degree of tension between Holmes and his father on the subject. "Holmes Sr. was at first a skeptic and later a strong enthusiast of the abolitionist cause in the Civil War," legal historian G. Edward White notes, whereas "Holmes Jr. was at first a strong enthusiast and then a skeptic of the Union War effort." This apparent reversal of roles, however, is perhaps putting it a little too tidily.[46]

Dr. Holmes was no supporter of abolition, which he regarded as unreasonably radical and, as he advised Lowell, not likely to secure its ends by the means it adopted. He would have been unlikely to have concurred with the future Secretary of State, William H. Seward, when in 1850 Seward invoked "a higher law than the Constitution" in support of his repudiation of slavery and the Fugitive Slave Law. In 1850, Dr. Holmes' position on the subject was closer to his son's argument, made many decades later, that challenging the law in this way was akin to "shaking one's fist at the sky, when the sky furnishes the energy that enables one to raise the fist." Neither judges nor the law itself, Justice Holmes emphasized, should be seen as "independent mouthpieces of the infinite," but rather as "directors of a force that comes from the source that gives them their authority." If the law was "not a brooding omnipresence in the sky," Holmes asserted, no more was the nation "subject to some mystic overlaw that it is bound to obey." Whether this was his perspective as a young man confronting the issue of abolition is certainly open to doubt. Equally, whether he was as enthused by the abolitionists' moral imperative as some have argued is also questionable.[47]

In later years, Holmes described his younger self as having been "a pretty convinced abolitionist." He recalled one occasion toward the end of January 1861 when he, along with, among others, his close friend and Harvard classmate Norwood Penrose (Pen) Hallowell and Thomas Wentworth Higginson, acted as bodyguard to abolitionist orator Wendell Phillips, who was a distant cousin of Holmes, when Phillips was due to speak at a Massachusetts Anti-Slavery Society meeting at Tremont Temple. "How coolly one looks at the question now," Holmes observed, some six decades later, but at the time, he reported, he had objected even to minstrel shows "because they seemed to belittle" blacks. From the perspective of his later years, he believed himself to be older and wiser on the subject; the question is, was he?[48]

On the one hand, Holmes would hardly have been the first person to have been more radical in youth than in old age. On the other, in juxtaposing the adolescent abolitionist prepared to take up arms in defense of a moral cause with the mature justice who never obviously went out of his way to defend, never mind advance African American rights, we may be in danger of delineating a false dichotomy, creating a contradiction that is more apparent than real. In part, this contradiction inheres in interpretations of the Civil War; but in larger part it was inherent in Holmes himself.

★★★

1857, the year that Holmes, at the age of sixteen, left for college, represented a development but also a deviation from what had gone before: personally, for him, but also politically for the nation. In some respects, the transition from school to college was, for Holmes, "no revolution . . . he was doing what his father had done."[49] Yet what his father was then doing almost certainly had an impact. Dr. Holmes' new-found wider literary success as the "Autocrat" accompanied Holmes to Harvard, ensuring that he was, from the age of sixteen at least, very much the son of a famous father. This was a potentially problematic position from which to launch any life, rendered the more challenging for Holmes because the Autocrat had a habit of discussing his son's foibles, albeit obliquely and not unkindly, in his sketches.

National politics, too, was undergoing a decisive change at that time. A new president, James Buchanan, had been elected the previous year. Crucially, the 1856 election had involved a new political party, the Republicans, whose platform was largely predicated on restricting slavery's further extension. Its slogan, "Free Soil, Free Speech, Free Labor, Free Men," extended the party's appeal across constituencies whose sympathies were not necessarily with the slave but with the economic and social effects of chattel slavery upon the white man, and especially upon the new Western territories. And only two days after Buchanan's inaugural, and two before Wendell's sixteenth birthday, in a courtroom packed with journalists and spectators the Supreme Court, under Chief Justice Roger B. Taney, handed down a controversial ruling designed to undermine the growing popularity of this new party by drawing a legal line under the sectional squabbles over slavery. Unfortunately, it had precisely the opposite effect.

Dred Scott was a slave who had lived in what became the Minnesota territory, where slavery was banned under the Missouri Compromise of 1820, and in the free state of Illinois. In 1846 he sued for his freedom in the long-running case that eventually reached the Supreme Court as *Dred Scott v. Sandford* (1857). The case was decided in favor of Scott's owner, on the legal grounds that Scott, as an African American, was not a citizen of the United States and therefore had no right to bring suit in a federal court, even if in fact he was entitled to his freedom. But this decision, described by historian Don Fehrenbacher as "the most striking instance of the Supreme Court's attempting to play the role of *deus ex machina* in a setting of national crisis," went far beyond Scott's personal case. In denying Scott's claim both to citizenship and to freedom, by establishing that slaves were property and upholding the Fifth Amendment right to property, wherever the property in question might be taken, Taney had effectively opened the free territories to slaveholding.[50]

The Fugitive Slave Law of 1850, and in Boston the rendition of the fugitive slave Anthony Burns, followed by bleeding Kansas and the Dred Scott decision stimulated anti-slavery feelings in Boston and across the North. This was especially true among Holmes' class and generation at Harvard. Over the three years that Holmes spent there, slavery was at the forefront of politics, not just in Massachusetts but nationally. In the year following Holmes' arrival at Harvard, a relatively unknown politician from Illinois, Abraham Lincoln, who was seeking election to the Senate, engaged one of the most famous orators of the day, Stephen A. Douglas, in a series of debates held across the state of Illinois. These debates effectively "transformed a statewide contest for the U.S. Senate into a watershed national disquisition on the contentious issue of slavery." And it was in the course of what became known as the Lincoln-Douglas Debates that Lincoln summed up what he viewed as "the real issue" which was "the eternal struggle between right and wrong."[51]

Abolitionism, Higginson emphasized, "drew a line of cleavage through all Boston society." Even as the church bells tolled on December 2, 1859, the day of John Brown's execution following his abortive raid on Harpers Ferry, there were many in the city who perceived anti-slavery agitation as just "one more example of the totally irresponsible Harvard-educated liberals' willingness to break the law." There was a dawning realization that the contest between slavery and its opponents was, in William H. Seward's words, an "irrepressible conflict between opposing and enduring forces." It would never be settled, Seward declared, until the United States became "either entirely a slaveholding nation, or entirely a free-labor nation."[52]

With an increasing emphasis on that crucial word "conflict," it "was observable," Higginson recalled, "that men were beginning to use firearms more . . . even in New England." Yet even as Higginson read more "military books," and "took notes on fortifications, strategy, and the principles of attack and defense," for Wendell Holmes, still safely ensconced at Harvard, his reading regime was of another nature entirely. Not all of it was related to the courses he was taking or, indeed, the abolitionist cause that, most scholars conclude, was the main motivating factor behind his decision to terminate, precipitously, his undergraduate career and join the Fourth Battalion in 1861.[53]

Harvard itself was, in Holmes' time, still largely conservative, as much of Boston Brahmin society was, on the subject of slavery, closer in its view to Dr. Holmes' concerns that agitation on the issue would achieve little, and that "emancipation would lead to instant and formidable insurrection" in the South. At the same time, the college was hardly immune to the implications of the debates over slavery. After all, its undergraduate body derived from both sides of the Mason-Dixon divide. And although Higginson's description derives from a period prior to Holmes' arrival there, Southern students were still "a distinctive element in Cambridge society" in Holmes' day, mainly because, "reared under the influence of slavery" as they were, they stood out in, and slightly apart from, New England society. As Higginson recalled it, they "usually had charming manners, social aptitudes, imperious ways, abundant leisure, and plenty of money," but were at the same time "often indolent, profligate, and quarrelsome," and included "a number who, having been brought up on remote plantations and much indulged, had remained grossly ignorant": not entirely ignorant of current events, of course. When, following the election of Lincoln, South Carolina seceded in 1860, during Holmes' final year at Harvard, the Southern students swiftly withdrew from the college.[54]

Harvard's Southern students knew where their loyalties lay, but the question is did Holmes develop a similarly strong and persistent sense of the issue whilst at college? If contemporary and some subsequent accounts are to be credited, whatever Holmes did learn at Harvard had precious little to do with an institution that Henry Adams famously dismissed as one that "taught little, and that little ill." Indeed, by far the dominant feature of Holmes' time at Harvard seems to have revolved around the reinforcement of his own already quite secure social position through his membership of various clubs and societies that his father had been a member of before him, including the Hasty Pudding and the Porcellian, and through these the forming of significant friendships, some of which would endure throughout his life. There is "little evidence," White argues, "that Holmes was any more stimulated by the academic offerings of Harvard than his contemporaries who later publicly expressed their contempt for the college as an educational institution."[55]

Certainly, for an individual such as Holmes, who had already acquired the habit of "omnivorous reading" before he arrived there, the entire college experience, with its rather dated syllabus, may have been a less than stimulating one had it not been for his extracurricular interests. Yet Holmes seemed to have enjoyed aspects of college life, which he described at one point as a "perfect delight." There is "nothing to hold you down hardly," he reported, "and you can settle for yourself what sort of a life you'll lead." The life he led was, typically for many students then and now, only tangentially related to the educational curriculum. Whether it was staying up talking into the small hours with fellow students, boating (a pastime he had taken up as a boy), or pursuing his growing appreciation of art, Holmes' life at Harvard offered him the opportunity not just to spread his social wings but to develop and deepen his intellectual interests.[56]

The evidence for what these interests were is found in several essays that Holmes wrote whilst at Harvard. And in the absence of alternative material, a great deal, possibly too much at times, has been made of these early literary endeavors. The first of these was entitled *Books*, and appeared in the *Harvard Magazine* in December 1858. It deliberately followed, and sought to emulate, an essay by Emerson, of the same title, published in *The Atlantic Monthly* in January of that year. It is often read by scholars as "evidence of high seriousness in" Holmes, proof of his sense of "intellectual urgency." The essay itself, however, seemed to revolve more around his father's concerns than those of Emerson, *per se*, with its emphasis on the value of "conversation" as either "a statement of conclusions, or of such facts as enable us to arrive at conclusions, on the great questions of right and wrong, and on the relations of man to God." In essence, it was as White has astutely described it: "a mix of passion and pomposity, some genuine critical insight and some largely deriv-ative posturing." But it did reveal Holmes' awareness of belonging to a gen-eration peculiarly adrift, in some respects, especially in regard to religion and to human rights.[57]

Holmes described himself and his contemporaries as being "in a peculiarly solemn position . . . the first of young men who have been brought up in an atmosphere of investigation, instead of having every doubt answered." Yet if this sense of discontinuity from past certainties was a generational complaint, for Holmes it may also have been a peculiarly personal one. By all accounts, including his own, he was a somewhat self-absorbed but also rather lonely individual. The self-absorption may have been his paternal inheritance. But Dr. Holmes was as socially outgoing as he was psychologically inward-looking. His son was rather different. And possibly the father knew it. Refracted through Dr. Holmes' later writings, especially in the guise of *The Poet at the Breakfast-Table*, the young Wendell appeared as "the young Astronomer," who was described as "too much given to lonely study, to self-companionship, to all sorts of questionings, to looking at life as a solemn show where he is only a spectator." And although the young Astronomer admitted that "he was lonely . . . he said it in a manly tone, and not as if he were repining at the inevi-table condition of his devoting himself to that particular branch of science."[58]

It is not difficult to see in "the young Astronomer" at least echoes of the boy who never fully engaged with the snowball fights on Boston Common. It is even easier, when one reads Holmes' *Books* essay, to imagine his similar-ity to the "pale student burning away, like his own midnight lamp, with only dead men's hands to hold, stretched out to him from the sepulchres of books, and dead men's souls imploring him from their tablets to warm them over again just for a little while in a human consciousness."[59]

Evidence for Holmes' early sense of isolation can be glimpsed not in what he said but in what he did not say in his brief autobiographical sketch. Here he described himself as the latest in a line stretching from his grand-father, Abiel, through to his father. But he did not seem to see himself as part of a family unit that included his siblings. In his *Books* essay, Holmes denied that he was "of a melancholic temperament," but in many senses that is precisely how he seemed to some as a young man, and admitted to being as an older one. On the occasion of becoming a Supreme Court Associate Justice, for example, he described the "triumph" of the occasion as having been overcast by his peculiar "perversity of temperament" which made him, so far from pleased, instead "very blue."[60]

A clearer sense of the form of this melancholic strain in Holmes' personality may be gleaned from substantial essays on Albrecht Dürer and Plato he wrote. Significantly, he sought out Emerson's advice for his essay on Plato. But Plato turned out to be rather a disappointment for Holmes, although the essay itself, one in which its author noted that "free criticism as well as praise has been used," won the prize for best article in the *University Quarterly* in 1860. Holmes had approached Plato expecting, as he later put it, "to find the secrets of life revealed," but found only a reinforcement of his own sense that life was a battle destined to be fought for no other reason than that of "preserving an ideal faith and a manly and heroic conduct." Absent any reliable ideal of faith, all that remained was the heroism, and that, for Holmes, appeared to inhere as much in the myth of the Middle Ages as in his own time. Man, he later observed some six decades later, was "a cosmic ganglion and inseparable from his time and place," but the Holmes who was at Harvard struggled to locate himself in his own time and place, for reasons that his essay on Dürer at least hints at.[61]

With Dürer, Holmes was on familiar ground, writing on a subject that he had long had an interest in, and would continue to pursue for all of his life. When well into his eighties, he described the process of "recurring to my youth by reading about engraving and etching—putting the glass to Dürers and other old prints." But his 1860 essay, rather like *Books*, owed much to *Modern Painters*, written by the artist and art critic John Ruskin. More than *Books*, however, *Notes on Albert Dürer* was potentially revealing, because the particular engraving that he focused on as evidence of Dürer's "undecaying and immortal thought" was *Melencolia* (1514).[62] In the figure of this "solitary woman," Holmes wrote:

> is the true picture of [Dürer's] soul, in its strength and in its weakness; powerful, but half overcome by the many objects of its universal study; crowned with the wreath of the elect and beautiful with ideal genius, but grave with thought and marked with the care of the world; winged, yet resting sadly on the earth.[63]

This is not to suggest that Holmes perceived any particular parallels with his own situation. He did not, in his essay, give any hint that he equated himself with the solitary figure of Genius. That link was later made for him. "The boy who could have such profound thoughts," gushed Fredrick Fiechter, "could not join his fellows in their common college life." Yet it was not, perhaps, Holmes' profundity that kept him apart, but simply his personality.[64]

★★★

Holmes' personality, of course, represents the focal point of contention in assessments of his life and legal opinions. Was it consistent, contrary, confrontational, or conservative? In some respects it appears fixed, and largely predetermined: the natural product of the Brahmin society "to whom name, family, connections are the greater part of competence." This closed class, as one of his biographers, Liva Baker, summed it up, "lived in the same neighborhoods, went to the same schools, read the same books, shared the same ignorances as well as knowledge, belonged to the same clubs, dined at the same houses, donated to the same charities, and married their cousins."[65]

Holmes was rather more intellectually intense than the class norm, perhaps, but that was inevitable given his father's influence. In its major components, as far as some scholars are concerned, his personality appears to have persisted, relatively unchanged, into his legal career. On the other hand, almost everyone who writes about Holmes identifies the Civil War as the decisive force for change in his life and in his outlook. "Philosophically, spiritually, and emotionally," historian Richard Maxwell Brown asserted, Holmes "was a product of the Civil War." The Holmes that came out of the war, however, was more closely tied to the one who entered it than this suggests. And although Baker argued that the war represented "the last great adventure" that Holmes "would share wholeheartedly with his fellow Bostonians," there are grounds for questioning the extent to which Holmes ever regarded himself as one of a Brahmin band of brothers.[66]

Part of the confusion here resides in what motivated Holmes to cut short his studies and join up. Simply to describe his motives as mixed risks cliché rather than clarity on this crucial question. Yet it is an important one, since what he, and many Northerners, took into the Civil War very much determined what, in the end, the nation got out of it. Ultimately, the secession of the Southern states in the wake of the election of 1860 invited a dual response from the Northern ones, a response that contained, and held simultaneously for much of the war itself, both conservative and revolutionary imperatives: save the Union; free the slave. For Holmes, as for many of his contemporaries in 1861, these were not necessarily seen as mutually supportive, but potentially contradictory imperatives. And, arguably, in 1861 Holmes' personal impulse toward duty was already in its nature essentially conservative rather than revolutionary.

"Perhaps no one had enlisted at the beginning of the Civil War with a more devoted ardor than Holmes," but whether this ardor derived from abolitionism or from a youthful (and, indeed, persistent) enthusiasm for the novels of Walter Scott and the "spirit of romantic chivalry" that these invoked, a spirit he readily transmuted into support for abolitionism, may be a moot point.[67] It was certainly more than coincidence that "the revival of medieval chivalry came simultaneously with a flourishing of science" in the mid-nineteenth century. As the old religious orthodoxies in New England gave way under the onslaught of science, the homogeneity of Boston's Brahmin class became overwhelmed, metaphorically, by snowballs on the

Common but in reality by the demographic expansion and growing het-erogeneity of the modern city. It would have been the more remarkable had there been no counter reaction, no emotional hankering after a lost world which still maintained some certainties of class structure and behavioral pre-cepts. To a society in flux, medieval England offered the ideal of social, reli-gious, and cultural stability, albeit via a cultural construct that was not only not American, but that had never even been real. Chivalry, as Scott himself noted, belonged to the mythical past. "We can only look back on it as a beautiful and fantastic piece of frostwork," he wrote, "which has dissolved in the beams of the sun."[68]

Holmes did look back on it, of course, and with some frequency, as was evident by his reference to one of his "periodic wallows in Scott . . . the old order in which the sword and the gentleman were beliefs," he admit-ted in 1911, "is near enough to me to make this their last voice enchanting in spite of the common sense of commerce." Yet even as a young man at Harvard, it was already clear to Holmes, in the words of another author whom he admired, that the "old order changeth, yielding place to new." And although Alfred, Lord Tennyson did not write this until after the Civil War—the version of *Idylls of the King* that Holmes and his contemporaries enthused over in 1859 did not yet include "The Passing of Arthur"—nev-ertheless the sense of change was, as Holmes later described it, already "in the air" when he was at college. It takes no great leap of the imagination to realize how readily, for the New England youth of his class and genera-tion, wallowing as they were in the tales of Arthur and his knights, inspired by Harriet Beecher Stowe's *Uncle Tom's Cabin*, the abolitionist imperative might appear not just a moral cause worthy of taking up arms for, but almost a mandatory one. The dragon they would slay was slavery, but they would slay it, in some senses, more for their own sakes than for those of the enslaved. "Resistance to something was," as Henry Adams argued, "the law of New England nature."[69]

In some ways, therefore, even before he arrived at Harvard, Holmes was primed to look for a cause that would conform to his own internalized imperative toward duty that was an integral aspect of his Brahmin heritage. In abolition, arguably, he found it. At the same time, he may have been influ-enced neither by deeply-held personal convictions, far less maternal expec-tations, nor even by a romantic yearning for a mythical medieval England, but by simple peer pressure. Clearly, his involvement with Higginson, his cousin Wendell Phillips, and other abolitionists, and his close friendship with the Quaker abolitionist Pen Hallowell, played no small part in his decision to enlist. Yet even here, it is doubtful that Holmes acted in concert with his peers because of the desire for comradeship, as such. For him, the prospect of conflict offered something rather different.

In later years, Holmes recalled a time long before the Civil War, long before Harvard, when he had seen a parade wending its way through the streets of Boston. "I was most impressed," he remembered, "by the part played by a carload of veterans. I got the notion, which has persisted, that the glory of life was to be carried in a civic procession, in a barge, as a survivor—I did not inquire too curiously of what." To conceive of oneself as a survivor, of course, is quite normal. Few wars would be fought absent that assumption. And yet to see oneself as a survivor carries its own particular sense of isolation. The adolescent Holmes may have been striving, of course, for a sense of self-reliance. It may be that, in his final year at Harvard, having written his *Books* essay emulating Emerson, along with those on Plato and Dürer, Holmes had reached that "time in every man's education," as Emerson described it, "when he arrives at the conviction that envy is ignorance; that imitation is suicide; that he must take himself for better, for worse, as his portion."[70] In this sense, on the verge of adulthood, and even as he set off for war in the company of his Harvard comrades, Holmes was, arguably, a man who, in his own mind, was already alone.

NOTES

1 G. Edward White, *Justice Oliver Wendell Holmes: Law and the Inner Self* (New York and Oxford: Oxford University Press, 1993) 8–14.

2 Louis Menand, *The Metaphysical Club* (New York: Flamingo, 2002) 69.

3 John T. Morse, *Life and Letters of Oliver Wendell Holmes*, 2 Vols. (London: Sampson Low, Marston and Company, 1896) I, 210; William Dean Howells, *Literary Friends and Acquaintances: A Personal Retrospect of American Authorship* (New York and London: Harper Brothers, 1911) 148.

4 Robert C. Winthrop, *Life and Letters of John Winthrop*, 2 Vols. (Boston: Ticknor and Fields, 1864, 1867) II, 19.

5 Walt Whitman, *Complete Prose and Poetry of Walt Whitman*, ed. Malcolm Cowley, 2 Vols. (New York: Pellegrini and Cudahy, 1948) II, 402; and for examples of nineteenth-century New England historians' perspectives, see, e.g., Francis Parkman's multi-volume work, *France and England in North America* (1865–1892); and George Bancroft, *History of the United States of America* (1854–1878).

6 Henry Adams, *The Education of Henry Adams*, ed. Ernest Samuels (Boston: Houghton Mifflin Company, 1973) 32, 43.

7 Paul Goodman, "Ethics and Enterprise: The Values of a Boston Elite, 1800–1860," *American Quarterly*, 18:3 (Autumn 1966) 437–451, 437; Morse, *Life and Letters*, I, 3. It should be noted that in using the term "racial," Morse meant Anglo-Saxon Protestant but in a purely cultural and religious sense, as opposed to, e.g., Latin Catholicism, not in the sense of pseudo "scientific racism."

8 Goodman, "Ethics and Enterprise," 441. For a study of the mercantile elites, in particular, see Robert F. Dalzell, *Enterprising Elite: The Boston Associates and the World They Made* (1987. Reprint. New York and London: W.W. Norton, 1993).

9 *Boston's Growth. A Bird's Eye View of Boston's Increase in Territory and Population from Its Beginning to the Present* (Boston: State Street Trust Company, 1910) 5.

10 Edward Pessen, "Did Fortunes Rise and Fall Mercurially in Antebellum America? The Tale of Two Cities: Boston and New York," *Journal of Social History*, 4:4 (Summer 1971) 339–357, 356;

see also Peter R. Knights, *The Plain People of Boston: A Study in City Growth, 1830–1860* (New York: Oxford University Press, 1971) 33–34; Richard A. Meckel, "Immigration, Mortality, and Population Growth in Boston, 1840–1880," *The Journal of Interdisciplinary History*, 15:3 (Winter 1985) 393–417, 394; Heather D. Curtis, "Visions of Self, Success, and Society among Young Men in Antebellum Boston," *Church History*, 73:3 (September 2004) 613–634, 613.

11 David E. Stannard, *The Puritan Way of Death: A Study in Religion, Culture, and Social Change* (New York and Oxford: Oxford University Press, 1977), 168–171.

12 Aaron Sachs, "American Arcadia: Mount Auburn Cemetery and the Nineteenth-Century Landscape Tradition," *Environmental History*, 15:2 (April 2010) 206–235, 211. The literature on this subject is considerable, but specific discussions of Mount Auburn can be found in: Blanche M.G. Linden, *Silent City on a Hill: Picturesque Landscapes of Memory and Boston's Mount Auburn Cemetery*, New Edition (Amherst: University of Massachusetts Press, 2007); Stanley French, "The Cemetery as Cultural Institution: The Establishment of Mount Auburn and the 'Rural Cemetery Movement,'" *American Quarterly*, 26:1 (March 1974) 37–59; Mark Schantz, *Awaiting the Heavenly Country: The Civil War and America's Culture of Death* (Ithaca, NY: Cornell University Press, 2008); and Susan-Mary Grant, "Patriot Graves: American National Identity and the Civil War Dead," *American Nineteenth Century History* 5:3 (Fall 2004) 74–100. Mount Auburn was not the first Rural cemetery. That was Grove Street Cemetery in New Haven, which dated to 1796, but Mount Auburn was the more famous and the more ambitious, and its reputation quickly eclipsed that of Grove Street Cemetery. See French, ibid., pp. 43–44, 53. For a valuable introduction to early-nineteenth-century attitudes toward cemeteries, see Garry Wills, *Lincoln at Gettysburg: The Words that Remade America* (New York: Simon and Schuster, 1992), Chapter 2, "Gettysburg and the Culture of Death," esp. pp. 63–69.

13 Nathaniel B. Shurtleff, *A Topographical and Historical Description of Boston* (Boston: Boston City Council, 1871) 187, 190, 216; Thomas Wentworth Higginson, *Cheerful Yesterdays* (1898. Reprint. Boston: Houghton Mifflin, 1901) 31–32; Levi Lincoln quoted in French, "The Cemetery as Cultural Institution," pp. 48–49.

14 Goodman, "Ethics and Enterprise," 443.

15 Oliver Wendell Holmes, *The Autocrat of the Breakfast-Table* (Boston: Phillips, Sampson and Company, 1858). Earlier essays with that title had appeared in *The New England Magazine* in 1831 and 1832, but the 1858 version was a reworking of the idea of conversational essays. It was followed by *The Professor of the Breakfast-Table* (1859) and, almost two decades later, *The Poet at the Breakfast-Table* (1872).

16 Oliver Wendell Holmes, Jr., to Clara Stevens, July 26, 1914, quoted in G. Edward White, *Justice Oliver Wendell Holmes: Law and the Inner Self* (New York and Oxford: Oxford University Press, 1993) 10.

17 White, *Law and the Inner Self*, 10; Howells, *Literary Friends*, 146, 181.

18 Goodman, "Ethics and Enterprise," 444–445; the Saturday Club is sometimes described as being the organizing group behind *The Atlantic Monthly*, but although many of its members regularly wrote for the magazine, this was not the case; there was a distinct Atlantic Club; see Higginson, *Cheerful Yesterdays*, 176; Morse, *Life and Letters*, I, 240–241; and for descriptions and recollections of the Saturday Club, see Sarah Forbes Hughes (ed.), *Letters and Recollections of John Murray Forbes*, 2 Vols. (Boston: Houghton, Mifflin and Company, 1899) I, 33–34; and Carlos Baker, *Emerson Among the Eccentrics: A Group Portrait* (New York: Penguin Books, 1997) 494–495.

19 Forbes Hughes, *Letters and Recollections*, 33; Brooks quoted in Howard M. Wach, "'Expansive Intellect and Moral Agency': Public Culture in Antebellum Boston," *Proceedings of the Massachusetts Historical Society*, Third Series, 107 (1995) 30–56, 30–31; Peter Gibian, *Oliver Wendell Holmes and the Culture of Conversation* (New York and Cambridge: Cambridge University Press, 2004) 5.

20 Morse, *Life and Letters*, I, 158.

21 Oliver Wendell Holmes, *Elsie Venner: A Romance of Destiny* (New York: Grosset and Dunlap, 1861) vii–viii. For a detailed and sophisticated analysis of *Elsie Venner* see Michael Weinstein, *The Imaginative Prose of Oliver Wendell Holmes* (Columbia; Missouri University Press, 2006) 67–70.

22 See, for example, the discussion of Dr. Holmes' views on hereditary tendencies in Morse, *Life and Letters*, I, 274–278.

23 Abraham Lincoln, "Speech at Springfield, Illinois," June 16, 1858 in Roy Basler (ed.), *The Collected Works of Abraham Lincoln*, 11 Vols. (New Brunswick, NJ: Rutgers University Press, 1953) II, 461. This biblical phrase, of course, was a common one and had often been used by others before, in the context of American slavery most notably by abolitionist leader William Lloyd Garrison in 1855; see William E. Cain (ed.), *William Lloyd Garrison and the Fight against Slavery: Selections from the Liberator* (Boston: Bedford Books, 1995) 20, quoted in David W. Blight, "William Lloyd Garrison at Two Hundred: His Radicalism and His Legacy for Our Time," in James Brewer Stewart (ed.), *William Lloyd Garrison at Two Hundred* (New Haven, CT and London: Yale University Press, 2008) 11, n.1.

24 Adams, *Education*, 9, 27; William James quoted in Albert W. Alschuler, *Law without Values: The Life, Work, and Legacy of Justice Holmes* (Chicago and London: University of Chicago Press, 2000) 15.

25 Oliver Wendell Holmes, "Reflections on the Past and Future: Remarks at a Dinner of the Alpha Delta Phi Club, Cambridge, September 27, 1912," in Mark DeWolfe Howe (ed.), *Oliver Wendell Holmes: Occasional Speeches* (Cambridge, MA: The Belknap Press of Harvard University Press, 1962) 165; and Holmes to Frederick Pollock, August 2, 1923, Mark DeWolfe Howe (ed.), *Holmes-Pollock Letters: The Correspondence of Mr. Justice Holmes and Sir Frederick Pollock, 1874–1932*, Second Edition: Two Volumes in One (Cambridge, MA: The Belknap Press of Harvard University Press, 1961) II, 120.

26 Oliver Wendell Holmes to Harold Laski, January 14, 1920, Mark DeWolfe Howe (ed.), *Holmes-Laski Letters: The Correspondence of Mr Justice Holmes and Harold J. Laski*, 2 Vols. (Cambridge, MA: Harvard University Press, 1953) I, 232.

27 Grant Gilmore, *The Ages of American Law* (New Haven, CT: Yale University Press, 1977) 41.

28 Henry Cabot Lodge, *Early Memories* (New York: Charles Scribner's Sons, 1913) 16–17.

29 Forbes Hughes, *Letters and Recollections*, I, 144.

30 Ralph Waldo Emerson, "The Fugitive Slave Law" (1851), in Edward Waldo Emerson (ed.), *The Complete Works of Ralph Waldo Emerson*, Vol. 11, *Miscellanies* (Boston and New York: Houghton Mifflin, 1901) 180; on this subject see also Harold Schwartz. "Fugitive Slave Days in Boston," *The New England Quarterly*, 27 (1954) 193–211; and Susan-Mary Grant, *North over South: Northern Nationalism and American Identity in the Antebellum Era* (Lawrence: University Press of Kansas, 2000) 124–129.

31 Adams, *Education*, 48; Thomas Wentworth Higginson, sermon preached in Worcester, June 4, 1854, published as *Massachusetts in Mourning* (Boston, 1854) 5; for his description of his involvement in several fugitive slave cases, see Higginson, *Cheerful Yesterdays*, 139–166; Forbes, *Letters and Recollections*, I, 143. On the legal issues surrounding Burns see Paul Finkelman, "Legal Ethics and Fugitive Slaves: The Anthony Burns Case, Judge Loring, and Abolitionist Attorneys," 17 *Cardozo Law Review* 1793–1858 (1996).

32 Higginson, *Cheerful Yesterdays*, 117–118.

33 Higginson, *Cheerful Yesterdays*, 196–234; Thomas H. Gladstone, *The Englishman in Kansas: Or, Squatter Life and Border Warfare* (New York: Miller and Company, 1857) 69; Paul Finkelman, "Manufacturing Martyrdom: The Antislavery Response to John Brown's Raid," in Finkelman (ed.), *His Soul Goes Marching on: Responses to John Brown and the Harpers Ferry Raid* (Charlottesville: University of Virginia Press, 1994) 41–66, 59. For an assessment of the propaganda surrounding "Bleeding Kansas" in 1856, see Dale E. Watts, "How Bloody Was Bleeding Kansas?" *Kansas History: A Journal of the Central Plains*, 18:2 (Summer 1995) 116–129.

34 Emerson, *The Complete Works of Ralph Waldo Emerson*, Vol. 7, *Society and Solitude*, 107.

35 White, *Oliver Wendell Holmes*, 15; Adams, *Education*, 26, 53, 7. See also Sheldon M. Novick, *Honorable Justice: The Life of Oliver Wendell Holmes* (New York: Dell Publishing, 1990) 11–14; and White, *Law and the Inner Self*, 7–8.

36 Adams, *Education*, 7, 54; Holmes to Laski, May 8, 1918, in *Holmes-Laski Letters*, I, 154.

37 Frederick C. Fiechter, J., "The Preparation of an Aristocrat," *New England Quarterly*, 6:1 (March 1933) 3–28, 7; Lodge, *Early Memories*, 19; Adams, *Education*, 41–42.

38 Adams, *Education*, 35.

39 Fred Somkin, *Unquiet Eagle: Memory and Desire in the Idea of American Freedom, 1815–1860* (Ithaca, NY: Cornell University Press, 1967) 9.

40 Betty G. Farrell, *Elite Families: Class and Power in Nineteenth-Century Boston* (New York: State University of New York Press, 1993) 2; Gibian, *Culture of Conversation*, 6.

41 Adams, *Education*, 26; Lodge, *Early Memories*, 16.

42 Holmes to Morris Cohen, February 5, 1919, Felix S. Cohen (ed.), "Holmes-Cohen Correspondence," *Journal of the History of Ideas*, 9:1 (January 1948) 3–52, 14–15.

43 Oliver Wendell Holmes, Sr. to James Russell Lowell, November 29, 1846, in Morse, *Life and Letters*, I, 300–301. The context, and hence the reference to war, was the Mexican War of 1846–1848, a war that many in Dr. Holmes' intellectual circle regarded as prompted by the expansionist ambitions of southern slaveholders.

44 Amelia Jackson Holmes to Emily Hallowell, February 1, 1863, extract in Novick, *Honorable Justice*, 15; see also White, *Law and the Inner Self*, 14.

45 Robert Gould Shaw to Sarah Shaw, March 19, 1858, Russell Duncan (ed.), *Blue-Eyed Child of Fortune: The Civil War Letters of Colonel Robert Gould Shaw* (Athens and London: University of Georgia Press, 1999) 13.

46 Holmes to Laski, May 8, 1918, in *Holmes-Laski Letters*, I, 154; White, *Law and the Inner Self*, 13.

47 William H. Seward, Senate, March 11, 1850, *Congressional Globe*, 31st Congress, 1st Sess., *Appendix*, 260–269, 265; Holmes, Jr. to Laski, January 29, 1926, in *Holmes-Laski Letters*, II, 822–823.

48 Holmes to Laski, 5 November 1926, *Holmes-Laski Letters*, II, 893; and see also Higginson, *Cheerful Yesterdays*, 240–243; Richard F. Miller, *Harvard's Civil War: A History of the Twentieth Massachusetts Volunteer Infantry* (Hanover and London: University Press of New England, 2005) 13; Finkelman, "Manufacturing Martyrdom," 59; James Brewer Stewart, *Wendell Phillips: Liberty's Hero*, New Edition (Baton Rouge: Louisiana State University Press, 1998) 214; White, *Law and the Inner Self*, 32. On attitudes in Boston generally at this time, see Barbara F. Berenson, *Boston and the Civil War: Hub of the Second Revolution* (Charleston, SC: The History Press, 2014).

49 Bowen, *Yankee from Olympus*, 115.

50 Don E. Fehrenbacher, *The Dred Scott Case: Its Significance in American Law and Politics* (New York and Oxford: Oxford University Press, 1978) 1, 5; see also Paul Finkelman, *Dred Scott v. Sandford: A Brief History with Documents* (Boston and New York: Bedford Books, 1997).

51 Harold Holzer (ed.), *The Lincoln-Douglas Debates* (New York: Harper Collins, 1993) 1, 359.

52 Higginson, *Cheerful Yesterdays*, 124–125, 245; Thomas H. O'Connor, *Civil War Boston: Home Front and Battlefield* (Boston: Northeastern University Press, 1997) 35–36.

53 William H. Seward, *Speech at Rochester, 25 October 1858* (New York: *New York Tribune*, 1860) 2.

54 Higginson, *Cheerful Yesterdays*, 47.

55 Adams, *Education*, 55; White, *Law and the Inner Self*, 22–23, 24–25.

56 Holmes to Miss Lucy Hale, April 24, 1858 quoted in Novick, *Honorable Justice*, 4.

57 Fiechter, "The Preparation of an American Aristocrat," 8; White, *Law and the Inner Self*, 36, 38.

58 White, *Law and the Inner Self*, 36, 12; Oliver Wendell Holmes, *The Poet at the Breakfast-Table* (London: Walter Scott, Ltd., 1897) 217–218, 131.

59 Holmes, *Poet*, 131.

60 Bowen, *Yankee from Olympus*, 149; Higginson, *Cheerful Yesterdays*, 202; White, *Law and the Inner Self*, 36; Holmes to Lady Pollock, September 6, 1902, in Mark DeWolfe Howe (ed.), *Holmes-Pollock Letters: The Correspondence of Mr. Justice Holmes and Sir Frederick Pollock, 1874–1932*, Second Edition: Two Volumes in One (Cambridge, MA: The Belknap Press of Harvard University Press, 1961) I, 105.

61 Fiechter, "The Preparation of an American Aristocrat," 10–11; Holmes to Felix Cohen, September 14, 1920, "Holmes-Cohen Correspondence," 25; see also Novick, *Honorable Justice*, 28.

62 Holmes to Pollock, February 20, 1925, *Holmes-Pollock Letters*, II, 156; see also Wolfgang Stechow, "Justice Holmes' Notes on Albert Durer," *The Journal of Aesthetics and Art Criticism*, 8:2 (December 1949) 119–124, 124; Holmes' essay on Dürer is replicated in this article.

63 Holmes, "Notes on Albert Dürer," in Stechow, "Justice Holmes' Notes," 123.

64 Fiechter, "The Preparation of an American Aristocrat," 13; White, *Law and the Inner Self*, 34, 41–42.

65 Walton H. Hamilton, "On Dating Mr. Justice Holmes," *The University of Chicago Law Review*, 9:1 (December 1941) 1–29, 6; Liva Baker, *The Justice from Beacon Hill: The Life and Times of Oliver Wendell Holmes* (New York: Harper Collins, 1991) 22–23.

66 Richard Maxwell Brown, *No Duty to Retreat: Violence and Values in American History and Society* (New York and Oxford: Oxford University Press, 1991) 31; Baker, *Justice from Beacon Hill*, 105.

67 Edmund Wilson, *Patriotic Gore: Studies in the Literature of the American Civil War* (1962. Reprint. London: The Hogarth Press, 1987) 747–748.

68 Novick, *Honorable Justice*, 22–23; Sir Walter Scott, "Essay on Chivalry," in Scott, *Miscellaneous Prose Works*, 28 Vols. (Paris, 1837 edn.), II, 261.

69 Holmes to Baroness Moncheur, quoted in Wilson, *Patriotic Gore*, 747; Alfred, Lord Tennyson, *Idylls of the King*, ed. J.M. Gray (Harmondsworth: Penguin Books, 1983) 299; Holmes, n. 61, above; Adams, *Education*, 7; see also White, *Law and the Inner Self*, 22–23.

70 Holmes, "Reflections on the Past and Future," 163; Holmes recalled the same event to Morris Cohen, January 30, 1912, "Holmes-Cohen Correspondence," 27; Ralph Waldo Emerson, "Self-Reliance," 1841, in *The Essential Writings of Ralph Waldo Emerson*, ed. Brooks Atkinson (New York: Random House, 2000) 133.

CHAPTER 2

CITIZEN SOLDIER

THE BRAHMIN ON THE BATTLEFIELD

"not only all society but most romance rests on the death of men and where the most men have died there is the most interest."

(Oliver Wendell Holmes to Harold Laski, 1927)[1]

In hindsight, the decision to hang their great coats with their striking red linings on the trees behind them was a bad one. They offered a conspicuous target for the Confederate troops hidden in the woods to aim at. Yet waving, in effect, a red rag at the enemy was hardly the cause of the tragedy that followed. For on the afternoon of October 21, 1861, Union forces fighting in Virginia found themselves, quite literally, between a rock and a hard place. Numerically overwhelmed by an enemy concealed in the woods ahead, and trapped between them and a steep bluff at the base of which lay the Potomac behind them, they were, as the official record acknowledged, "cut off alike from retreat and re-enforcements." The Union's almost inevitable defeat that afternoon quickly turned into disaster. The men, and one of them was Wendell Holmes, scrambled, stumbled, or were carried back over the bluff they had struggled up only hours before. Some fell and died instantly on the treacherous rocks below, others drowned attempting to reach the safety of the Maryland shore, and many succumbed to the steady stream of gunfire that rained down on them from the bluff above as they fled.[2]

The Battle of Ball's Bluff was a relatively minor engagement in the American Civil War, but it was a microcosm of the longer war to come. From the irony of descriptions of "the gallant dead" colonel, Edward D. Baker, a close friend of Lincoln's, who "fell gloriously in battle," through the accounts of surgical procedures undertaken to try and save the wounded, to the official reports designed to defend individual actions as much as describe the military action on the field, all the elements that would come to define the conflict were present.[3] In time these would fill volumes: official records and private reminiscences, newspaper columns and magazine articles, court cases and correspondence, and books both factual and fictional. Whatever psychological impact the war had on Holmes, it was certainly a brooding presence in the nation's life throughout his long career.

And yet it had all been, in many respects, so unexpected. Some form of limited military confrontation between Union and Confederate forces was certainly anticipated in the aftermath of the secession winter of 1860/1861. "Although no one believed in civil war," Henry Adams recalled, "the air reeked of it." But at the same time many assumed, with Adams, that the secessionists were simply "unbalanced in mind—fit for medical treatment, like other victims of hallucination," not to mention "stupendously ignorant of the world" as well as "mentally one-sided, ill-balanced, and provincial to a degree rarely known." They posed no real threat. The war itself, indeed, seemed to pose no real threat, at least to its officer class. Many would have concurred with Robert Gould Shaw's assurance to his mother that "there is not much more danger in war than in peace at least for officers. There are comparatively few men killed," he wrote, in the summer of 1861, and by "far the greater number die of diseases, contracted by dirt & neglect of all laws of health." Officers, he believed, were not susceptible to such risks.[4]

No one, in short, anticipated four long years of conflict in 1861; nor over 600,000 dead, and as many, if not more, suffering from disease and wounds, both psychological and physical that would plague them, in many cases, for the rest of their lives. That was not at all the kind of war that Northerners expected in 1861. It was certainly not the kind of war that the adolescent abolitionist Holmes enlisted for. What kind of war they had signed up for, indeed, was far from clear; what was clear was that, for many, what it was not was a war for the abolition of slavery.

From the perspective of 1861, secession offered a challenge to national integrity, but not necessarily an opportunity to terminate chattel slavery: for some, of course, in seceding the Southern states, had handed the government that opportunity on a plate. But even then their language, in 1861, focused on federal power. In part this was a pragmatic political response. It derived from the need to secure support on the part of an administration that had received less than half the popular vote and by awareness on the part of abolitionists that not all Northerners shared their sense of slavery as a moral wrong. It was in this context that the radical Republican and vehement opponent of slavery Charles Sumner told businessman John Murray Forbes that he wished "to try the strength of the government now. Surely it is not worth having," he argued, "on the condition that any one State may at any time break it up."[5] To Sumner's dismay, however, since secession was regarded by the Lincoln administration as a rebellion in, not of the South, securing the Union might never require, and indeed might preclude, the abolition of slavery. Loyal Southerners, loyal slaveholders, were protected by a Constitution that itself protected their property rights. And some of those rights inhered in their ownership of slaves.

It is no surprise, therefore, that in 1861 the issue was widely understood to revolve not around anti-slavery but rather how best to defend the legitimacy and define the legality of the federal system. "Rebellion smells no sweeter because it is called Secession," James Russell Lowell argued, "nor does Order lose its divine precedence in human affairs because a knave may nickname it Coercion." Secession, as historian John Lothrop Motley saw it, was nothing more than "the return to chaos." The right of revolution, he emphasized, was "indisputable," but secession was not revolution; it was rebellion. The Constitutional scholar Francis Lieber summed up such sentiments best; the Union, he argued, was not "a sort of political picnic to which the invited guest may go and carry his share of the viands or not, as he thinks fit."[6]

The enthusiasm expressed by many Northerners in 1861, in short, was, in the words of Holmes' fellow soldier Elisha Hunt Rhodes, "all for the Union." And it was an enthusiasm shared by those closest to Holmes. Writing to the English poet Frederick Locker-Lampson, Dr. Holmes described "the sense of national life and unity throughout the free states" that followed the fall of Fort Sumter in Charleston Harbor to Confederate forces in April 1861. It was, he noted, "the most exulting, joyous triumphant feeling that our nation has ever known." There was now "a complete unity of purpose throughout the whole north." For Dr. Holmes, the outbreak of civil conflict represented the commencement of "the great battle of law and liberty," by which he meant national liberty, not emancipation. Emerson, too, exulted in the "sentiment mightier than logic, wide as light, strong as gravity" that he saw penetrating "the college, the bank, the farm-house, and the church" alike. "We are wafted into a revolution," he declared, "which, though at first sight a calamity of the human race, finds all men in good heart, in courage, in a generosity of mutual and patriotic support." With both father and intellectual mentor expressing such fluent *rage militaire*, it may be no surprise that Wendell Holmes felt that volunteering was the better part of valor.[7]

★★★

Holmes' brief military career, however, generally understood to represent "the key formative phase" in his life, got off to a rather slow start even as the martial momentum gathered force around him. In the aftermath of the fall of Fort Sumter, the newly-inaugurated Republican president Abraham Lincoln called for 75,000 troops, to be raised through the state militias. Holmes, along with many of his fellow students including Pen Hallowell, Henry L. Abbott, his brother William, James Jackson Lowell, William Lowell (Willie) Putnam, and William Francis (Frank) Bartlett, signed up for duty in the

Boston unit of the Massachusetts Volunteer Militia, the New England Guards or Fourth Battalion. But the mix of motives in this small, self-selected band was already indicative of the confusion of sentiment that Southern secession inspired in the North.

Hallowell was a devoted abolitionist, as was Willie Putnam. For Putnam, a "century of civil war [was] better than a day of slavery," and he prayed "that every river in this land of ours may run with blood, and every city be laid in ashes rather than this war should come to an end without the utter destruction of every vestige of this curse so monstrous." At the same time, he knew "full well that all is not yet as it should be, and that a union man and an abolitionist do not mean the same thing." Holmes may to some degree have shared Putnam's perspective, but not everyone did. Frank Bartlett, for one, was not convinced that he was pursuing the right course of action at all. He viewed secession as the inevitable outcome of "the interference of the North" in Southern affairs, and considered it "sad to think that we must break so many of our social ties and part with our best friends all on account of a lot of *damned Niggers*." Even as he signed up for the Fourth Battalion, Bartlett wondered whether taking up arms in the cause of Union would not be "fighting rather against my principles, since I have stuck up for the South all along. We shall see," he concluded, somewhat indecisively.[8]

Bartlett was not alone in his struggle to balance the patriotic imperative with personal sentiment, especially when that sentiment was so antipathetic to the abolitionism espoused by some of his fellow volunteers. In several crucial respects, Boston Brahmins may have "marched together in lockstep" but that did not mean that they marched to the same internal beat. In this regard, one solution—possibly an obvious one given the mid-nineteenth-century fascination with all things medieval—was to present the war for the Union as a modern-day crusade. This served a dual function. It resonated with young men like Holmes whose imaginations had already been fired by the novels of Walter Scott or the poetry of Tennyson. And it facilitated the formation of a coherent response to secession on the part of Northerners whose opinions, especially on abolition, differed widely. In short, it accommodated those who saw the war from the outset as one to destroy slavery, those who saw it as one to save the Union, and, above all, those who over time came to believe that these might actually be flip sides of the same coin.[9]

For non-combatants such as Motley, who saw the conflict as a challenge to national legitimacy, the idea that volunteering represented an expression of the "genuine chivalry of the Free States" akin to that of the crusades was certainly a constructive, if somewhat contrived, one. It enabled him to locate Wendell Holmes' willingness to fight within what he described to Dr. Holmes as "a noble cause like ours," despite the fact that father and son held very different perspectives on the cause in question in 1861. Dr. Holmes, indeed, was fairly consistent in his sentiments throughout the war. As late as 1863, he still stressed the political value of the national compact over any emancipatory imperative. "We say to those who would take back their several contributions to that undivided unity which we call the Nation," he declared in a speech delivered in Boston that year, the "bronze is cast; the statue is on its pedestal; you cannot reclaim the brass you flung into the crucible!" His son's opinion by that point, of course, informed as it was by war's realities, was rather less sanguine.[10]

In the spring of 1861, however, the entire question of motivation was moot for Wendell Holmes. Toward the end of April, the Fourth Battalion was finally called up for garrison duty, which mainly consisted of drilling and training at Fort Independence in Boston Harbor. Holmes was enthusiastic at this gentle introduction to the art of war. "I'm in bully condition," he told his mother, "and have got to enjoying the life much." He drew a little sketch of his new, short haircut and the early incarnation of what, in his later life, would be cultivated as a quite considerable military moustache. And he sounded like many soldiers in the war's early stages in his request for provisions. Butter, "fresh meat," and olives were what he desired, along with a carpet bag and some handkerchiefs. Yet although Holmes wrote as if he were already very far from home, to his intense frustration in the spring of 1861 he had got no further than Boston Harbor.[11]

By the end of May, indeed, it seemed as if Holmes' military career was over before it had even begun. On the 25th of the month, the Fourth Battalion retraced its steps back to Boston and paraded through the city's streets before being reviewed on the Common and then officially disbanded. What was especially galling for Holmes was that his peremptory withdrawal from Harvard to join up had cost him his relatively high ranking in his year group, although the university did permit him and Hallowell to return, complete their degrees, and graduate. Graduation offered Holmes the opportunity to deliver the Class Poem in which, according to one journalist covering the ceremony, he compared "the student leaving college to a steamer leaving port." Even as he delivered it, however, Holmes must have wondered if he was ever going to launch himself on the high seas of military adventure that his month at Fort Independence had offered him a brief glimpse of, but that had terminated so abruptly.[12]

Holmes had hoped to join Pen Hallowell and Frank Bartlett in one of the newly formed volunteer regiments, specifically the Twentieth Massachusetts Volunteer Infantry, known as the Harvard Regiment since its officer class was mainly drawn from the college. But whilst the others were quick to find a commission in a regiment in which the "rank of the line officers" was "arranged in accordance with the estimate formed of their soldierly capacity and efficiency," the tall and lanky Holmes' progress in this regard was slow. Not until the summer, and after some considerable intervention from his father, did Holmes receive his commission; even then, he was not immediately sent South with the regiment. Instead, he was charged with a recruitment drive, along with Bartlett, and spent a month at his old summer stamping ground, Pittsfield, drumming up support for the regiment and the war, which had begun badly for the Union with the defeat, in late July, at what is now known as the first battle of Bull Run (Manassas).[13]

"Recruiting was slow and difficult at this time," Frank Palfrey recalled, "as the regiments with lower numbers had exhausted the first enthusiasm of the community." By early September, however, having successfully persuaded eleven men to sign up for the regiment Holmes was back at Camp Massasoit near Boston. On the 4th of that month he was finally on his way South: first to Camp Kalorama in Washington, then Camp Burnside close to the Capitol, and finally onwards to Camp Benton in Maryland.[14]

From Camp Kalorama Holmes wrote again to his mother, reporting on the dinner he and his fellow officers had enjoyed at the famous Delmonico's in New York en route for Washington, and advising her that, so far, he was in little danger. "There is expectation of a fight very soon," he wrote, "but we I do not believe run any chance of service except as reserve." The following week found Holmes at Camp Burnside, and in the midst of rather more activity; "all sorts of camps around us," he reported, "military discipline—and a regular soldier's life." The bustling life that Holmes was seeing was just part of the Union's main force, the Army of the Potomac, in the process of organizing itself, albeit slowly, for what became known as the Peninsula Campaign, under the overall command of General George B. McClellan. Holmes' regiment formed part of the Third Brigade of General Charles P. Stone's Corps of Observation that comprised twelve infantry regiments, including the Forty-Second New York (Tammany) regiment, a cavalry regiment, and four batteries.[15]

The Twentieth Massachusetts was relatively fortunate among Civil War volunteer regiments in having as its commanding officer Colonel William Raymond Lee, a graduate of West Point and a professional soldier, when so many other regiments were led by inexperienced and untrained officers who were often politically connected. "The appointment of political generals" and other political officers, as Civil War historian James McPherson has emphasized, was "an essential part of the process by which a highly politicized society mobilized for war." At the same time, it did not bode especially well for the regiments concerned. But even with the benefit of experience at the helm, the Twentieth Massachusetts was under-strength when it left Boston—hence Holmes' and Bartlett's recruitment efforts—with only around two-thirds the men it should have had. It also seemed to some a rather rarefied regiment: too full of Harvard's privileged graduates to con-stitute a truly effective fighting force. As Colonel Charles Devens, com-manding the Fifteenth Massachusetts, told Frank Palfrey, the "sooner you get this blue-blooded notion out of your head, the better for yourself and the Regiment."[16]

The idea that neither the Twentieth Massachusetts as a unit nor its offi-cer class was especially suited to combat was not an entirely alien one to some of the officers concerned, including Holmes. This had little to do with the fact that the Harvard Regiment was something of a blue-blooded Brahmin band, however, and more to do with timing. It applied to virtually everyone involved in the Union war effort in 1861, volunteer soldiers and non-combatants alike. In his memoirs of the Civil War, completed just over thirty years after the fall of Fort Sumter, Union surgeon John H. Brinton looked back to the chaos that was the autumn of 1861. "In the exigencies of our national strife," he recalled, "from the magnitude and pressure of its demands, officers fresh from civil life were called upon at a moment's notice, and without previous training, to discharge these high duties; how to do so properly they had yet to learn, and that in the face of pressing events."[17]

In respect of its medical support, and this would be important for Holmes as for others, the Twentieth Massachusetts was also a relatively fortunate regi-ment. Its three regimental surgeons were also all Harvard graduates, and two of them, Henry Bryant and Edward Hutchinson Robbins Revere, had, like Dr. Holmes, trained in Paris. Bryant had, in addition, at least some experi-ence as a battlefield surgeon from serving with the French Army during the Algerian War. His informed perspective, however, was unlikely to have been shared by the volunteers on the frontline, far less the Northern public at home, whose confidence in the Union's ability to wage war was matched only by their complete naïveté about the nature of nineteenth-century warfare. Ultimately, the Civil War was a venture for which civilian life had provided little preparation but one accompanied, crucially, by a widespread assumption that professional competence, be it martial or medical, would be achieved, and that in pretty short order. Most Americans thought the war would be fast and not very bloody, like the Mexican War fought a decade and a half earlier. Virtually no one, North or South, could anticipate the magnitude of the change in warfare that lay ahead.

"At the battle of Cherubusco, in Mexico," *Scientific American* noted in May, 1861, two months before First Bull Run/Manassas, "125 American balls were fired for every Mexican that was killed . . . better firing than that of the enemy, who fired 800 balls for every man killed on our side. This, however," the journal warned, 'will not do now." If in "olden times, the solid column and the desperate charge generally won the battle," modern weaponry, and specifically the rifle, "would soon slaughter the best drilled columns in the world."[18] With the benefit of his experiences in Kansas and his pre-war preparatory reading, a more hardened hand like Tom Higginson might have been at least aware of this; Holmes and his comrades in the Twentieth Massachusetts—and almost all other soldiers and officers—were largely oblivious.

Holmes and his fellow students had read of war, and they had imagined war, but imagination, and a competent commander, could only marginally prepare them for the reality. And the reality, at least as Holmes first found it, was frustrating on several levels. Although its officer class gave the Harvard Regiment its blue-blood reputation, the rank and file comprised a heterogeneous mix of Massachusetts' men; laborers, porters, seamen, farmers, and industrial workers accounted for well over 50 percent of the regiment. Holmes sometimes found it hard to control the men under his command, many of whom showed no particular interest, at this early stage in the war, in following orders or comporting themselves with anything approximating military discipline. This was a widespread problem. Higginson, too, recalled that discipline in the new regiments "was not easy, especially in the case of some newly arrived company, perhaps in a high state of whiskey." We had, he remembered, "to learn to bear and forbear."[19]

Disciplinary difficulties were exacerbated by the general absence of action. "It seems so queer to see an encampment & twig men through a glass & think they are our enemies," Holmes admitted to his mother. He had seen, he told her, "one man in a straw hat sitting unconcernedly on his tail apparently a guard on duty for the secesshers. Men and horses," too, he wrote, "are seen from time to time from the tops of the trees," but as "firing across the river is forbidden," all that Holmes could do at that point was "sit & look & listen to their drums." Largely all this inactivity derived from McClellan's tendency to overestimate Confederate numbers—he assumed some 150,000 Confederate troops awaited him across the Potomac when in fact there were only some 45,000. Hence Holmes and his regiment were consigned to play a waiting game, during which the opposing sides were as likely to exchange newspapers as shots across the lines. Holmes reported hearing "some of our pickets talking across" the river to their Confederate counterparts. All of this lent some "reality to the life" of a soldier, he noted, but it was hardly the full frontal confrontation with the enemy that he had been anticipating.[20]

★★★

For Holmes, as for his regiment, it turned out to be very much a case of being careful what one wishes for. Frank Bartlett had reported that the men of the Twentieth Massachusetts "were quite elated at the idea of having a brush" with the enemy, but when that brush came, at Ball's Bluff in late October, it was rather more than they had anticipated. In its aftermath, the Battle of Ball's Bluff drew comparisons with the famous Charge of the Light

Brigade. Both, certainly, resulted from confusion over orders; in the case of Ball's Bluff the suggestion offered by McClellan to General Stone on October 20 that "perhaps a slight demonstration on your part" would suffice to test the resolve of Confederate forces then positioned at Leesburg. "My telegram did not," McClellan later reported, "contemplate the making [of] an attack upon the enemy," but an attack nevertheless was made, with disastrous results for the Union forces involved.[21]

Under the overall command of Colonel Edward Baker, then senator for Oregon with only limited military experience gained during the Mexican War (1846–1848), Holmes' regiment, together with the Fifteenth Massachusetts and a New York and Pennsylvanian regiment, was detailed to cross to the western bank of the Potomac. They had to navigate the narrow strip of land—Harrisons's Island—mid-river, scale the bluff, and engage the enemy in what was expected to be a minor skirmish.

Bartlett, writing to his mother after the battle, described the ascent by Union forces on October 20 and 21 up a "steep bank one hundred and fifty feet high with thick wood on it," on which there was "not room enough to form ten men." The "banks were so slippery," he recalled, "that you could not stand." Positioned as support for the Fifteenth Massachusetts, the men of the Twentieth were told that "they *must stand fast* if the Fifteenth came running down the road" in order to cover their retreat. "It looked rather dubious," Bartlett commented with a degree of understatement. "The Fifteenth might get across, but we must check the advance of the enemy and get cut to pieces."[22]

The Twentieth Massachusetts was positioned, as Holmes' closest friend in the regiment, Henry Abbot, described it, in "one of the most complete slaughter pens ever devised." At around nine o'clock the sound of a "splendid volley," in the words of Bartlett's official report, alerted the Twentieth Massachusetts to action. "*We knew we were in for it then*," Bartlett noted, and he was not wrong. "The whizzing of balls was a new sensation" that, he admitted, he had been "curious to experience." He acknowledged that Ball's Bluff had afforded him that opportunity in abundance, and even expressed his admiration for Confederate accuracy. "They fired beautifully," he reported, and his men "began to drop around me" as the minor skirmish turned into a massacre of the poorly placed, inexperienced, and inadequately supported Union troops, around half of whom were killed, wounded, or taken prisoner. Among the dead was Sergeant John Merchant, one of the men that Holmes had recruited from Pittsfield. Among the captured was Colonel Lee. And among the wounded was Wendell Holmes.[23]

The letters that Civil War soldiers wrote home may not, of course, have conveyed the full picture, either of events or of the writer's sentiments on the battlefield. And Holmes was no exception in this respect. "Here I am flat on my back after our first engagement," he wrote to his mother, "wounded but pretty comfortable." He had "felt and acted very cool," he told her, "and did my duty I am sure." What Holmes' letter did make evident was that, although addressed to his mother, it was a letter intended for family consumption and in particular directed at his father. Most soldiers described their wounds up to a point, but Holmes gave what amounted to a medical diagnosis based on the trajectory and emergence of the bullet—a Minié ball that he retained in his personal possessions to the end of his life—that assured him, and his family, that he would likely recover.[24]

In his diary entry detailing the battle, composed well after the event, Holmes adopted a more intellectual approach to injury, and attempted to analyze "the intensity of the mind's action and its increased suggestiveness, after one has received a wound." His physical description of being shot was overlaid by a literary recollection—a childhood book about the English Civil War, Frederick Marryatt's *Children of the New Forest*—in which a central character "died with terrible haemorrhages & great agony," that he thought might apply to his own case. He considered taking the laudanum that his father had given him before he left for the front, but held off, "determined," he recalled, "to wait until pain or sinking strength warned me of the end being near."[25]

When it became apparent that Holmes was going to survive, his mind—at least that part of it he confided to his diary—swiftly snapped back into the track pursued by the young who imagine they will live forever. "I thought for awhile that I was dying," he wrote, "and it seemed the most natural thing in the world." And yet the "moment the hope of life returned," he admitted, "it seemed as abhorrent to nature as ever that I should die." Removed from Camp Benton to Pen Hallowell's home in Philadelphia, Holmes spent just over a week there recuperating before being escorted back to Boston by his father; the first of several trips Dr. Holmes would take to retrieve his heir and namesake. By January of 1862 Holmes was well enough to return to recruitment duty, and found himself in Pittsfield once again; but he would not rejoin his regiment until almost the end of March.[26]

For both father and son, the safety and security of Boston made Ball's Bluff seem almost a bad dream, but one they frequently replayed, for different reasons, over the winter of 1861/1862. Dr. Holmes took the opportunity of relaying the entire experience at second hand to his friend John Lothrop Motley. And the story he told became a familiar one, reiterated by countless individuals and reprinted in any number of publications between 1861 and 1865. It was one that simultaneously critiqued and consecrated the conflict; it condemned "the stupid sacrifice" even as it urged that this serve as a source of national pride. Dr. Holmes' own pride in his son's "honorable wounds" was certainly palpable. "He is now thriving well, able to walk, but has a considerable open wound," Dr. Holmes advised Motley; it was a "most narrow escape from instant death!" Now, Dr. Holmes reported, his son was basking in the attention, much of it female, that the role "of young hero with wounds in his heart" afforded him.[27]

Yet Holmes' experiences at Ball's Bluff, and the contradictions between his reactions to these and the response both of the wider culture and, indeed, his own father, highlight the distance between home-front and battlefield during the Civil War. The hyperbole of home-front representations of that battle, of most battles, bore little relation to the battlefield realities as Holmes and his fellow soldiers experienced them. For Union troops, indeed, it was not so much the battle but its aftermath that often proved the most problematic, especially if they had sustained any injury. When one of the regimental surgeons of the Twentieth Massachusetts, Henry Bryant, hastened to Ball's Bluff after the battle, it was in the anticipation of treating a limited number of casualties. Instead, a scene of carnage confronted him.

"Many of the wounded were crying and shrieking and the whole floor was covered with blood," Bryant recalled: "one man had three balls through his head, one taking off his nose and one of his eyes—another man was lying near him with brain projecting from a wound in the side of his head," and "poor Lieutenant [William Lowell] Putnam was lying near the fireplace with his intestines projecting from a wound in his abdomen." Putnam, whom his mother designated the "martyr-boy" of Massachusetts, would not survive his devastating injuries. Captain John C. Putnam, whose right arm had to be amputated (it was accorded a decent burial on Harrison's Island, alongside the leg of Colonel George H. Ward), did survive, both the battle and the war; but he carried the reminder of it all his life in the form of his missing arm. Suffering from phantom limb syndrome, Putnam expended "constant mental effort" trying "to move the fingers of his missing hand," Pen Hallowell later recorded, an effort that both "perplexed his mind and wore away his life."[28]

By contrast, Holmes had a far better time of it, although he may not always have appreciated this. He recalled being transported to Camp Benton in "one of the two wheeled ambulances which were then in vogue as one form of torture." Not only was the ambulance broken, he reported, but "the horse baulked and the man didn't know how to drive." His experience was more typical than not, and in this respect revealed one of the major logistical shortcomings of the Union war effort in its early stages: the removal of the wounded from the field. As George Templeton Strong, New York lawyer and treasurer of the United States Sanitary Commission (USSC), the main voluntary civilian body for the support of Union troops, charged, in the war's early stages the Union's Medical Department was "utterly unequal to [its] present work." This was somewhat inevitable given that, as Strong acknowledged, it had fallen into "routine habits acquired in long dealing with an army of ten or fifteen thousand" rather than field armies, such as the Army of the Potomac, of which Holmes' regiment was just one small part, in excess of 120,000 men.[29]

At the time of Ball's Bluff, Union medical support in Virginia was under the control of Charles S. Tripler, who was hardly inexperienced in military medical matters, having served in the Mexican War. Nevertheless, Tripler was ultimately felled by his frustration at being unable "to get together ambulances and wagons to have these trains properly and economically conducted, to have boats prepared and in position, to procure buildings for hospitals, to get subsistence for the sick and wounded, and, in short, doing the duty assigned to quartermasters and subsistence officers." His first official report comprised a catalogue of complaints concerning the general ineptitude he encountered. "The surgeons of regiments in the field are intended for service," he sniped in 1861, "and not for ornament." Tripler was especially irked that many of the officers used any available transport to convey themselves to and from Washington, rather than ensuring that wounded men, like Holmes, could be safely and swiftly removed from the field. By the time that his replacement, Jonathan Letterman, arrived in the summer of 1862, matters had not improved; indeed, they had worsened.[30]

So, although in the war's early years there were very pressing pragmatic and patriotic reasons for the Northern press to report its battles in a positive light, nevertheless the enthusiasm of those far from the front sometimes rankled with those who ended up in the firing line and, sometimes, on the front pages. The Twentieth Massachusetts found itself in that position in the aftermath of Ball's Bluff, although Henry Abbott, for one, regarded much of the coverage as "all blow and poppycock," and described himself as "completely disgusted with these newspaper notices." But they kept appearing, most notably in the form of an especially fulsome editorial in *Harper's Weekly*, in which Holmes was mentioned by name and held up as evidence of the fact that, as the title of the editorial put it, "New England Never Runs."[31]

Deploying almost every available cliché relating to combat, *Harper's Weekly* urged its readers to smile through their tears at "the steadfast bravery of the Massachusetts boys. In the front of a fearful fire, with no means of retreat, with every chance against them," *Harper's* reported, "those young men stood serene, each man a hero—each man showing the quality of which invincible armies are made." And Holmes, in particular, was singled out as evidence of New England steadfastness on the grounds that he had sustained a wound to his chest: "not in the back," *Harper's* emphasized, "no, not in the back. In the breast is Massachusetts wounded, if she is struck. Forward she falls, if she fall dead."[32]

Holmes may well have been flattered by this invocation of himself as the personification of his state. Many years later he still recalled how "flamboyant" the *Harper's* editorial had been, but in the context of the Battle of Antietam (1862). On that later occasion he had been "hit in the back," which was, he noted wryly, "not so good for the newspapers." At the same time, in the disjunction between what *Harper's* reported and what Holmes experienced, lay the potential for much deeper disillusionment, almost, perhaps, a sense of betrayal: betrayal by his government, who had sent its armies into the field without adequate medical support; up to a point betrayal by his parents, who had inculcated such a strong sense of duty in him and whose expectations he struggled to fulfill; but above all a much more fundamental betrayal of his antebellum, adolescent view of war. In Holmes, arguably, this had very little to do with the shock of combat as such, far less the reality of the death and physical destruction around him. It derived rather from the realization that war need not be just to be justified, that individual ideals do not determine its outcome; that right, in short, did not mean might, neither in a military context nor any other. This can, of course, be interpreted as a skepticism born of battle, but this interpretation says more about popular representations of the Civil War's meaning than it explains Holmes' personal response to conflict.[33]

In the aftermath of Ball's Bluff, for example, *Harper's* expressed its confidence that Union soldiers marched to war with "every rifle . . . loaded and rammed down with an idea. They are not machine-soldiers," it enthused, "they are men soldiers." This was a perspective that Union commander Ulysses S. Grant would later echo in his memoirs of the war. "The armies of Europe are machines," Grant opined, comprising men "who are not very intelligent and who have little interest in the contest in which they are called upon to take part." Union armies, by contrast, consisted of "men who knew what they were fighting for," Grant argued, men who "could not be induced to serve as soldiers, except in an emergency when the safety of the nation was involved." Such men, Grant asserted, "must have been more than equal to men who fought merely because they were brave and because they were so thoroughly drilled and inured to hardships."[34]

It is doubtful that Holmes would have concurred. Much later in life, he had been asked by Alexander W. Kinglake, author of *The Invasion of the Crimea* that Holmes claimed to have read during the Civil War, if the men of the Twentieth Massachusetts had fought in line. Holmes had replied in the affirmative adding, however, that he "believed you could make baboons do it if you had the right sort of officers." He had tried to explain his thinking to his parents at the time. "I never I believe have shown, as you seemed to hint, any wavering in my belief in the right of our cause," Holmes wrote, "it is my disbelief in our success by arms in wh. I differ from you." His parents failed to appreciate either "the unity or the determination of the South," Holmes believed, because they trusted in the superiority of Northern civilization and anti-slavery ideology, but this, he averred, was a mistake. "I think you are hopeful," he advised them, "because (excuse me) you are ignorant."[35]

For Holmes, writing at the end of 1862, it was no longer a certainty that the Union would win. He already perceived the parallels between civilization in the North and the South; both were "diffusive and aggressive," and if Northern "civ[ilization] & progress are the better things," he suggested, "why they will conquer in the long run," but faster through peace than through war. War, he asserted, in one of the few direct invocations of abolitionist language that he left to posterity, was not merely "the brother of slavery," it was "slavery's parent, child and sustainer at once." Holmes was writing this, of course, at the end of the worst year for the Union, and one of the worst for him personally on the battlefield. And yet it seems likely that he had arrived at the conclusions he expressed in December 1862, well over a year previously, at Ball's Bluff.

Thinking then that he was dying prompted Holmes to reflect "that the majority vote of the civilized world declared that with my opinions I was *en route* for Hell," but he decided that the "deathbed recantation" was not for him. Whatever awaited him in the great hereafter was probably for the best, "for it is in accordance with a general law," Holmes concluded, "and *good & universal* (or *general law*) are synonymous terms in the universe." Having clearly given the matter some thought in the interim between the memory and the memoir, he qualified his sentiments in a way that foreshadowed some of his later legal arguments: "I can now add," he wrote, "that our phrase *good* only means certain general truths seen through the heart & will instead of being merely contemplated intellectually—I doubt if the intellect accepts or recognizes that classification of good and bad."[36]

Ball's Bluff is generally recognized as a turning point for Holmes: the moment that he realized that he "had denied God and still survived." That, the literary critic Edmund Wilson asserted, "was the end of God in the cosmology of Oliver Wendell Holmes, who was never again tempted to believe and who lived to be over ninety." This secular epiphany is often identified as the start of a process whereby Holmes ceased to think "through the heart," and turned toward the colder climes of an intellectual life uncluttered by faith but also, his critics would charge, by feeling. Certainly, partly thanks to *Harper's Weekly*, Ball's Bluff was the origin of what might be termed the Holmes' legend, in both its public and private manifestations. And yet Holmes' individual baptism of fire at Ball's Bluff was, in the end, about neither fame nor faith. As Henry Adams pointed out, "the profoundest lessons are not the lessons of reason; they are sudden strains that permanently warp the mind." For Holmes, arguably the most important lesson of his life was learned on that muddy bluff in Virginia in October of 1861: almost precisely at that point, indeed, when he grasped that his fellow Americans really were trying to kill him.[37]

★★★

By the time Holmes returned to his regiment, now stationed in Washington, in March, 1862, it was rather different from the one he had left in October the previous year. The capture of, among others, its colonel William Lee and one of its surgeons Edward Revere, together with the death or wounding of so many of its most committed abolitionist officers, not only necessitated a change in command structure but produced a significant shift in the regiment's outlook. But it was not only the regiment that had changed; the whole tone of the war, by the start of 1862, was transforming, as the scale of the conflict gradually became apparent, its human cost more visible.

Even as Holmes recuperated from his wounds, the creation of "Northern Martyrology" had begun to gather momentum, and perhaps nowhere more forcibly than in Massachusetts, as the state, and especially the city of Boston, tried to come to terms with the very high-profile loss of several members of its Brahmin class. On the Sunday prior to Holmes' arrival back in Boston, the Rev. Cyrus Bartol preached an emotive sermon in commemoration of Willie Putnam, whose funeral had taken place the week before. Taking his text from the Book of Samuel ("The beauty of Israel is slain upon thy high places"), Bartol emphasized the value of sacrifice. "It is the law of our life," he declared, "that all earthly progress in every good cause starts in sacrifice, lives on sacrifice, and without ever-new sacrifice would faint and die."[38]

As far as Putnam himself was concerned, Bartol noted that he, in common with Holmes, had intended to practice law after the war, "if he survived." Unlike Holmes, however, Bartol suggested that Putnam had never anticipated surviving; he "offered himself," Bartol proclaimed, "as though less to slay than be slain." Much of Bartol's sermon, of course, was designed both to commiserate with and consecrate one family's loss, and in its language it was a precursor of any number of similar sermons preached over the course of the conflict. At the same time, in the search for meaning in the face of terrible tragedy, and in their location of sacrificial death in the nation's name as the core of that meaning, such sermons necessarily elevated the idea of death in battle above that of survival. Holmes had once imagined the "glory" of being a war veteran, paraded "in a civic procession" as a survivor, but as he must have begun to realize while he was away from the battlefield, on the home-front it was sacrifice, not survival, that Northerners were being urged to value as the second year of the Civil War began in earnest.[39]

What was most notable about Bartol's sermon, however, with its emphasis on "sacrifice for a worthy object" was its absolute silence on the one object that Willie Putnam had believed was worth fighting for, worth dying for: emancipation. Bartol had a great deal to say about "that dream of liberty for which our sires crossed the sea," fleeing from "a slavery they would have shuddered to foresee," but this was political liberty he was talking about: the liberty of a republican nation, fighting then for its existence, not the liberty of those held in bondage in the South. As Willie Putnam had feared, support for the Union, anti-slavery, and abolition did not yet march together in the Twentieth Massachusetts. "I haven't seen any men or officers in this part of the loyal army who are willing to fight for abolitionists," Henry Abbott advised his aunt toward the end of 1861. Whatever their various views, however, for the men of his regiment, the subject of slavery already threatened a reputation hard-won at Ball's Bluff.[40]

In the time that Holmes was absent from the regiment, and with Colonel Lee languishing as a prisoner-of-war, temporary command had passed to Frank Palfrey, with Frank Bartlett as his second-in-command. Although Holmes, on his return, expressed some hesitation about this—"Don't like the look of things under Palf," he told his parents, "wish Lee was here"—in general both Holmes and Henry Abbott were content with the arrangement, even if Abbott felt that Palfrey's was a personality "undisturbed in any strong passions" and that the "necessary infusion of vigor" was supplied by Bartlett. Yet they worked well together, largely because, as Holmes and Abbott agreed, Palfrey's "desire of popularity never allows him to interfere with Frank [Bartlett] carrying out the proper discipline." However, before too long, Palfrey proved very unpopular indeed, through no real fault of his own.[41]

The problem arose with a rumor that one of the regiment's officers, George Nelson Macy, had, under Palfrey's orders but contrary to official Army policy, arrested, and returned to their owners, two fugitive slaves who had entered Camp Benton. The resulting flurry of outraged correspondence that flew between Palfrey, the strongly abolitionist Governor of Massachusetts John A. Andrew, the Secretary of War Simon Cameron, and George B. McClellan provided a master-class in crossed wires, poor communication, and the perils of putting pen to paper prematurely. But the entire affair really boiled down to one main question: was the Harvard Regiment complicit in slave-catching, as some Northern publications, including *The Liberator* and the *Boston Journal*, charged? Worse, were its officers, at the end of 1861, proud "of their pro-Slavery opinions and purposes," as one anonymous source claimed? Andrew sought clarification from the Secretary of War himself that Massachusetts' troops were not expected "to become the hunters of men," and trusted that he would take steps to "save our soldiers and our State from such dishonor."[42]

In many respects, this all had much more to do with Army politics and personal rivalries within the Twentieth Massachusetts than with slavery, *per se*. It did, however, highlight the growing divisions between those, like

Andrew, whose views on slavery were more radical, and who felt that the Union army should at the very least facilitate the efforts of those slaves seeking to escape to freedom across Union lines, and those like McClellan, who personally was not opposed to slavery and whose conservative position was that slaves were Southern property, and Southern property was sacrosanct. McClellan's response to Andrews' concerns was inevitable, given his views, which may have reflected, at least up to a point, the perspective then prevalent in the Twentieth Massachusetts. The entire affair was none of Andrew's business, McClellan ruled, since volunteer troops were now "a portion of the Federal Army" and "entirely removed from the authority of the governors of the several States." This was as bureaucratic as it was blinkered, however, in the context of a conflict much more dependent than most on the continuing support of the home-front. In early 1862, however, with McClellan finally readying to launch his spring campaign, the home-front was still largely behind him and his view of the war as solely one to save the Union.[43]

★★★

Within days of Holmes' return, the Twentieth Massachusetts sailed from Washington for Hampton Roads, Virginia, along with the rest of the 120,000 men in the Army of the Potomac. Holmes' regiment was now just one small part of McClellan's attempt to push toward Richmond up the James Peninsula with enough speed, he hoped, to take the Confederates by surprise. The extent of the undertaking, however, combined with the fact that McClellan had invited several journalists, including the British reporters Edward Dicey and William Howard Russell, rather undermined any notion of either surprise or speed. The sheer scale of operations and the general air of martial pageantry surrounding the affair was impressive. The "scene before my eyes," Dicey reported, "was one of war":

> An endlessly military panorama seemed to be unrolling itself ceaselessly. Sometimes it was a line of artillery struggling and floundering onward through the mud—sometimes it was a company of wild Texan cavalry, rattling past, with the jingle of their belts and spurs. Sometimes it was a long train of sutlers' wagons, ambulance vans, or forage-carts, drawn by the shaggy Pennsylvania mules. Orderlies innumerable galloped up and down, patrols without end passed along the pavements, and at every window and doorstep and street corner you saw soldiers standing.

And this was just the center of the action in the city. All around Washington, as Dicey saw, "every hillside seemed covered with camps," whose "white tents caught your eye on all sides," whilst across the river, "the great army of the Potomac stretched miles away, right up to the advanced posts of the Confederates south of the far-famed Manassas. The numbers were so vast," he commented, "that it was hard to realize them."[44]

What Dicey's description highlighted was the fact that the Army of the Potomac did not travel light. Holmes reported that the officers of his regiment "have reduced baggage to a very few portables," but that hardly signified in the context of the army as a whole: an army, furthermore, comprising regiments that fairly dwarfed, in size but also in ability, Holmes' relatively small Brahmin band. "I had no idea before," Holmes' comrade Henry Ropes commented, "how good the other Regiments were compared with ours. I had thought the 20th was a long way ahead of all," he admitted, "but this is not so. Many other Regiments are our equals in every respect, and perhaps our superiors." Certainly, most regiments were far bigger, which brought its own problems. "The Federal armies are not handled easily," Russell observed, and were especially "luxurious in the matter of baggage, and canteens, and private stores." The mild spring weather and the accumulated paraphernalia of war, oddly enough, combined to lend the entire enterprise a rather unmilitary air. The "scene is delightful," Elisha Hunt Rhodes of the Second Rhode Island Volunteers noted; the "ships are gaily decorated with flags, and it looks more like a pleasure excursion than an army looking for the enemy."[45]

If Holmes shared Rhodes' sense of excitement, on reaching the James Peninsula he was soon disabused of any notion that he was engaged in a "pleasure excursion." Blocked at Yorktown, the Union Army settled in to besiege the town. It was not a promising start to the campaign; even the weather turned against them. For over half the month that the Twentieth Massachusetts was encamped in front of Yorktown's defenses it rained, heavily. To make matters worse, the tents were delayed, and when they did arrive were of a design that offered little protection from the elements. This is "a campaign now & no mistake," Holmes told his parents. "No tents, no trunks—no nothing—it has rained like the devil," he reported, and everyone was soaked through, up to their knees in mud, and had been enduring "volleys and scattering shots from the enemy" for days. "I am in good spirits," he advised them, "though of course I despise the life in itself outside of special circumstances & principles."[46]

Holmes' disillusionment, then, was clear, but only with the trials and tribulations, not to say the terrors, of life so close to the enemy; he "fairly trembled" when his friend Henry Abbott led an advance toward Confederate lines, fearful that he would "see some bowled over every minute." For much of his time, however, Holmes found himself on picket duty, whiling the hours away with Pen Hallowell; "sitting on a stump smoking our pipes & reading old letters," was how he described it. Exhibiting the kind of "coolness" that was the traditional expression of approval among the men of the Twentieth, he noted that "[n]ow and then a bullet would whizz high over our heads from the other side."[47]

Yet although Holmes made picket duty sound, at best, an opportunity for conversation with a friend or, at worst, tiresome and, usually, cold and wet, it could be much more dangerous than that, as Frank Bartlett found out when he lost a leg to a Confederate sharpshooter. Being measured for his crutches, Bartlett observed, was akin to "being measured for a coffin." He knew he was fortunate to have survived, but at the same time, had to come to terms with the fact that he had left part of himself, psychologically as well as physically, on the peninsula. And, like John Putnam, Bartlett's brain retained the memory of what the body had lost. He sought assurance that his leg had received a "Christian burial, for my foot torments me," he reported, "as if it were ill at rest."[48]

Holmes reported the incident to his parents, but said no more than that Bartlett "bore it bravely." By this point, Holmes himself was rather unsettled. He knew that, health-wise, he had no cause for complaint, but the combined effects of the relentless rain, the constant Confederate sniping, and the removal from the regiment—although he returned to the war, Bartlett never returned to the Twentieth Massachusetts—of a man whose leadership he trusted was taking its toll. Bartlett had been, as Henry Abbott emphasized, the *de facto* commander of the Twentieth Massachusetts, "the one officers & men looked to for preservation whenever we should get into battle." The loss of Bartlett was a huge blow to morale in the regiment. And personally it deeply affected Holmes.[49]

Both Abbott and Holmes may have taken some comfort from the fact that, in May, Colonel Lee returned, just in time to enter Yorktown with the regiment at the termination of the siege. Abbott was elated. "Col. Lee is enormously popular," he told his mother; "[h]e certainly has a charm of conciliating every body about him." Yet despite Abbott's assurances that the "old cliques" cohered around Lee, regimental politics remained problematic; nothing seemed settled, neither the regiment, nor the course of the campaign, nor even Holmes himself had a clear sense of where they were in the greater scheme of things. After several weeks of maneuver, in what was, for him, an unusually lengthy letter home, Holmes attempted to describe the Battle of Fair Oaks (Seven Pines) at the end of May and start of June, 1862 with the aid of a hastily drawn sketch that obscured as much as it illuminated. The same could be said of the battle, the most extensive engagement in the Eastern Theatre up to that point, but as inconclusive in its outcome as it was costly in terms of casualties; about 6,000 men were lost on each side, and both sides claimed the victory.[50]

Holmes was not alone in his disenchantment with the war. It was at Fair Oaks that McClellan described himself as "tired of the sickening sight of the battlefield, with its mangled corpses & poor suffering wounded." Holmes, by contrast, tried to sound less concerned at its human cost. "It is singular," he observed, "with what indifference one gets to look on the dead bodies in gray clothes wh. lie all around," but then promptly contradicted himself by describing these quite graphically. Although the survivors were burying the dead "as fast as we can," Holmes reported that there was a danger, especially at night, on picket duty, of treading "on the swollen bodies already fly blown and decaying, of men shot in the head, back or bowels—Many of the wounds," he told his parents, "are terrible to look at—especially those fr. fragments of shell."[51]

On one level, Holmes' description of the battlefield at Fair Oaks was hardly unusual. And yet when contrasted with that provided by Henry Abbott, the differences are noticeable. For Abbott, Fair Oaks was all about "the most tremendous volleys," and the "wonderful discipline" of the men. It was about the "terribly frightened" Confederate prisoners, who expected to be killed, but who were treated with kindness and offered food and blankets. Abbott did acknowledge that this last was largely "to show that we were 'generous as well as brave,'" but Fair Oaks nevertheless left him "elated," even if it was the elation of adrenalin talking.[52]

Holmes' reaction was very different. Above all, and in contradiction to Abbott's version, the destruction of the human individual was juxtaposed, in Holmes' description, with the destruction of the humane imperative. Clearly Holmes still, in 1862, held some notion of how wars should be fought, if they must be fought at all. He was shocked that his own side should come under fire whilst attempting to bury the dead: not even their own dead, but the Confederate dead. His naïveté at this point was productive of an admixture of martial pride at his regiment's being "masters of the field," moral outrage at the targeting of burial parties, and barely muted horror at the reality of the corpses. Ultimately, Fair Oaks was, for Holmes, a military cliché: both "splendid and awful to behold." In contrast to Abbott, words failed even Holmes, in the end.[53]

★★★

After Fair Oaks, the Twentieth Massachusetts remained in camp, suffering from the combined effects of the battle and malnutrition. Holmes reported suffering "scorbutic symptoms," and well knew the cause: "want of *fresh food.*" By this point medical support had passed from the control of Charles Tripler to Jonathan Letterman, who arrived in Virginia in the summer of 1862. The sheer scale of the medical problem, largely, as Letterman recalled, the result of scurvy plus the effects of "marching and fighting in such a region, in such weather, with lack of food, want of rest, great excitement, and the depression necessarily consequent upon it," was immediately apparent to him. But it would take several months before he managed to establish what became known as the "Letterman System"—an arrangement of forward field hospitals, a more effective ambulance corps, and the efficient distribution of both food and medical supplies—in the Army of the Potomac. His efforts were not facilitated by the fact that the Army was now in retreat in the face of a Confederate counter-offensive against the Union front in Virginia that became known as the Seven Days' Battles.[54]

In their weakened state, fighting the series of rear-guard actions that represented the essence of the Seven Days as the Army of the Potomac moved back toward Harrison's Landing on the James River proved a dismal, depressing, and enervating experience for the men of the Twentieth Massachusetts. Holmes reported the destruction of the Union's stores and the abandonment of the wounded at Savage Station, the main Federal supply depot; and marching, marching, marching, in intense heat with no water, straight into battle, past "a deserted battery the dead lying thick around it." On the penultimate day of the Seven Days, 30 June, 1862, and almost exhausted, the Twentieth Massachusetts had ceased marching at a crossroads, Glendale, formed a line of battle, and began to advance.[55]

Glendale was, as Holmes described it, "a deuce of a time . . . The guns got so hot and dirty," he recalled, that "we could not load or fire more than 2/3 of 'em." It was a costly action for his regiment. Pen Hallowell was slightly wounded. Henry Abbott received a more debilitating wound in his right arm that put him out of action until early August. Holmes emerged unscathed, but the "anxiety" he endured during the Battle of Glendale had, he wrote, "been more terrible than almost any past experience." And it was one awful moment from that afternoon in June 1862, just as the Union advance began, that would remain with Holmes for the rest of his life: the moment he glanced down the line and caught the eye of his cousin, James Jackson Lowell, saluted, looked back a moment later, and Lowell was gone.[56]

The Battle of Glendale, indeed, even more than Ball's Bluff, may be regarded as a turning-point for Holmes: the point at which he started to sound more like a soldier, but also the moment when he decided what kind of soldier he wanted to be. What had only been implicit in his correspondence home became explicit during the Seven Days. Like all Civil War soldiers, the sense of being supported by the home-front was crucial for Holmes, for morale but also for reinforcement of the war's meaning, of what he was fighting for. After the Battle of Glendale, Holmes made clear, really for the first time, that it was his family that had "sustained" him through his "terrible trials." At the same time, in listing the actions, "Allen's Farm, Savage's Station, Nelson's Farm, Malverton," that he had been engaged in, Holmes was starting to locate himself more firmly in a martial narrative. In time it would become a survivor's story, and a veteran's one. And it was a narrative that owed a very great deal to his father, and to the Civil War's single bloodiest battle: Antietam.[57]

★★★

"In the dead of the night which closed upon the bloody field of Antie-tam, my household was startled from its slumbers by the loud summons of a telegraphic messenger. The air had been heavy all day with rumors of battle, and thousands and tens of thousands had walked the streets with throbbing hearts, in dread anticipation of the tidings any hour might bring." So began Dr. Holmes' published account of his search, in the aftermath of Antietam, for his son, wounded on the field. When it appeared in *The Atlantic Monthly* at the end of 1862, it provided a powerful confirmation of the earlier *Harper's Weekly* public presentation of Oliver Wendell Holmes, Jr. as a Civil War hero.[58]

The hero in question, however, was suffering. He was suffering because he had been shot through the neck at Antietam, but he had been suffering for some time before that with dysentery: the scourge of many Civil War soldiers and a death sentence for some 50,000 of them. "Never since the terrible exposures of Fair Oaks have I been myself," Holmes wrote home mournfully; "I can digest hardtack or tacks or shingles but one damp night recalling those dreary times plays the deuce with me." Clearly, the problem was not entirely due to the "spasmodic pain in bowels & constant diarrhea," that he complained of, but his situation was about to get a lot worse.[59]

Over the summer, Holmes' regiment had been recuperating and recruit-ing at Harrison's Landing in Virginia, the latter facilitated by the Militia Act passed that year that sought to raise 300,000 new troops for nine months' service. Moved to Aquia Creek at the end of August, by September 17, 1862 it was camped near Antietam Creek, Maryland. From there, Holmes wrote to his parents in the middle of the night, 3.00a.m., to tell them that his regi-ment was being held in reserve, but might be engaging the enemy later that day. We'll "lick 'em if we do," he wrote. Only three hours later, and the Battle of Antietam had begun in earnest, with the Twentieth Massachusetts in the midst of the action, literally. Flanked by Confederate forces, the Twentieth suffered heavy losses; and it was on being ordered to retreat that Holmes, fleeing the field as fast as he could—as he later recalled—was shot in the back of the neck.[60]

"*Through* the neck," Dr. Holmes later wrote, "no bullet left in the wound." He reconsidered the telegram he had received; "thought not mortal," it had read. As might have been expected from a literary man and a parent, he began to parse the possibilities. "*Thought not* mortal, or *not thought* mortal,— which was it? The first," he decided, "that is better than the second would be." He set off at once for the battlefield, accompanied at first by a medi-cal colleague, Dr. George H. Gay, but was soon joined by other travelers, including the poet Walt Whitman, all headed Southward in search of family or simply seeking to help. On the very day he left, Wendell had written to assure his parents that all was well. "Usual luck," Holmes noted, "ball entered at the rear passing straight through the central seam of coat & waistcoat collar coming out towa [*sic*] the front on the left hand side—yet it don't seem to have smashed my spine or I suppose I should be dead or paralysed or something." Hallowell, too, was fortunate; although Holmes had assumed that, with the "bone smashed above the elbow" his friend would lose his arm, he did not.[61]

By the time Dr. Holmes' account appeared, of course, not only was he aware that his son was safe, but most of his readership would have been fully familiar with events at Antietam the previous September. Many of them might already have seen Matthew Brady's famous photographic exhibition in New York, "The Dead of Antietam," with its graphic images of corpses on the field. Reviewing the exhibition, the *New York Times* observed that if Brady had "not brought bodies and laid them in our door-yards and along the streets, he has done something very like it," and in the process brought "home to us the terrible reality and earnestness of war." They might not, of course, have been fully familiar with such aspects of the treatment of those dead, or the images of the war, as Dr. Holmes provided them with. "The slain of higher condition," Dr. Holmes could not help but notice, were being embalmed and sent home, whereas "the dead of the rank-and-file were being gathered up and committed hastily to the earth." And as for what Dr. Holmes termed the "great caravan of maimed pilgrims," these were so numerous as to "make a joint-stock of their suffering; it was next to impossible to individualize it," he observed, "and so bring it home as one can do with a single broken limb or aching wound."[62]

For Dr. Holmes, of course, it was precisely his search for one individual that brought home to him the full gravity and implications of the conflict. And it was through that one individual that he sought to bring it home to the Northern public. It has been suggested that Holmes took from this published narrative the sense that "he was no ordinary Civil War enlistee," but that may have been contrary to his father's intentions. Dr. Holmes effectively made his son, for the benefit of his readers, a form of everyman, the universal Union soldier, whose personal trials, and whose family's fears, were replicated across the North. In its biblical allusions of the prodigal "son and brother [who] was dead and is alive again, and was lost and is found," Dr. Holmes was striving for a more national sense of return, rebirth, and regeneration; on one level he was writing about his son, on another, arguably, he was writing about the nation.[63]

After Antietam, Dr. Holmes became much more concerned about the war's material cost, but also its moral implications. How "idle it is to look for any other cause than slavery as having any material agency in dividing the nation," he announced the following year. "Match the two broken pieces of the Union," he proposed, "and you will find the fissure that separates them zigzagging itself half across the continent like an isothermal line, shooting its splintery projections, and opening its re-entering angles." And the fissure was slavery. Developing the reflections on hereditary tendencies that he had explored in *Elsie Venner*, Dr. Holmes delineated a nation torn between "the hereditary character of the Southern people" and "the awakened conscience of the North." And yet the "new truth" that was the moral imperative to eradicate slavery was not recognized by his son, who no longer believed that moral change was achievable by military means: a suspicion he had probably already entertained after Ball's Bluff but only fully articulated in the months after Antietam. For Dr. Holmes the war became a fluid entity, capable of altering its course from one to save a Union to one to improve a nation; for his son it became fixed as no more than duty almost from the start. Further, it was a duty that in some respects, despite his many assertions to the contrary, he felt he had failed to fulfill.[64]

Perhaps as a form of compensation for this feeling, Holmes would return often to the Battle of Antietam over the course of his life, the battle at which, he frequently reminded himself and others, he "was nearly killed." In so doing he located himself in the larger story not just of the Civil War but of that moment when the war for the Union became something bigger, because it was the Union victory at Antietam that gave the Lincoln administration the confidence to issue the Preliminary Emancipation Proclamation and, on January 1, 1863, the final Emancipation Proclamation. But at the time, Holmes chose not to be part of that larger story. Instead, he selected to remain with his regiment, a regiment that was not universally supportive of the new direction that the war had taken: that was, indeed, quite strongly opposed to it. "The president's proclamation is of course received with universal disgust," Henry Abbott observed, "particularly the part which enjoins officers to see that it is carried out. You may be sure," he stressed, "that we shan't see to any thing of the kind, having decidedly too much reverence for the constitution." In Hallowell's absence, and having forged a stronger friendship with Abbott over the winter of 1862/1863, Holmes' earlier abolitionist enthusiasm may have seemed to him a distant dream. Certainly it was not one he could share with Abbott.[65]

★★★

In their respective shifts of sentiment on the meaning of the Civil War, father and son were, in some respects, reflecting the respective perspectives of home-front and battlefront over the course of the conflict. Even before Antietam, Boston's perspective on the war was changing. As he watched events on the battlefield unfold, the journalist Edward Dicey tracked the emergence of "the conviction that the Union could not be preserved consistently with slavery" across New England in 1862. This, he noted, "was beginning to make way rapidly." By the summer, even Dr. Holmes had noticed "that the spirit of hostility to slavery as the cause of this war is speedily and certainly increasing." He had attended a talk at Tremont Temple the previous evening given by John C. Frémont, former Commander of the Department of the West, whose unilateral and illegal attempt to emancipate slaves in Missouri had resulted in his being relieved of command by Lincoln in November 1861. Despite this official censure, Dr. Holmes was struck by how receptive the audience was to Frémont's views on slavery. These "would never have gained a little while ago," he noted, but "a miscellaneous Boston audience would be more like to cheer any denunciation of slavery now than any other sentiment."[66]

By this time, however, his son was less inclined toward such sentiments. And although it cannot be said with any certainty that Holmes became disenchanted with abolitionism even as his father became enthusiastic about it, Holmes' silence on the matter strongly suggests a case of the dog that didn't bark. In this instance, it is very much a case of actions having to speak louder than words, because the clue to his thinking lies only partly in what Holmes said—since he said so very little—but in what he did.

The Lincoln administration already had more radical plans in train as far as emancipation was concerned. The path toward the issuance of the Emancipation Proclamation in 1863 was necessarily convoluted, but the first steps along it were being taken even as Holmes and the Twentieth Massachusetts fought their way through Virginia. In the middle of June, Congress passed legislation prohibiting slavery in all future United States' territories. Whilst this did nothing to affect slavery in those states where it existed, this ruling was nevertheless a repudiation of the ruling in *Dred Scott v. Sandford* (1857) that Congress had no power to legislate on slavery.

In fact, Congress was already able to legislate on slavery via the First Confiscation Act (1861) that permitted the seizure of rebel property, including slaves. Meanwhile the Secretary of War notified commanders they were free to provide refuge for any slaves escaping Southern masters. The passage of the Second Confiscation Act in July 1862 extended this remit to facilitate the emancipation of slaves in those areas that came under Union control. Another statute prohibited U.S. Army officers from returning fugitive slaves, while the Militia Act of 1862 allowed for the enlistment of black troops. By July 1862 perhaps 100,000 slaves had already escaped to Union lines, and unbeknownst to Holmes or indeed to anyone outside of the Cabinet, President Lincoln had drafted the Emancipation Proclamation and was waiting only for the appropriate moment to issue it.

With the passage of the Militia Act in August 1862 and the announcement that Emancipation would take place on January 1, 1863, Governor Andrew began organizing an African American regiment in Boston. Holmes' close friend and vehement abolitionist Pen Hallowell was, perhaps unsurprisingly, quick to offer his services. In less than a year Hallowell would join one of the most famous African American regiments of the war, the Fifty-Fourth Massachusetts Volunteer Infantry, first mustered into service in May 1863; and later would accept the colonelcy of its sister regiment, the Fifty-Fifth Massachusetts, mustered into service the following month, June 1863.

But Holmes, who, many scholars argue, effectively followed Hallowell to war in 1861 did not follow him out of the Twentieth Massachusetts in 1863, although Hallowell asked him directly to do so; "your name," he urged, "would command attention." But Holmes refused: then, and again a year later in 1864, when Pen's brother, Ned, offered him the chance to reconsider following the Fifty-Fourth's famous assault on Fort Wagner, in Charleston Harbor, where so many of the regiment, including its colonel, Robert Gould Shaw, had fallen.[67] It was, in more than one respect, a parting of the ways.

★★★

In November 1862 Holmes had returned, together with Henry Abbott, to a rather dispirited Twentieth Massachusetts, then commanded by Ferdinand Dreher and Alan Shepard: "the crack brained Dreher & obstinate ignoramus Shepherd [sic]" as he described them. The regiment, in Holmes' view, was "going to H—L as fast as ever it can," and the Union's chances of success were fading. "The Army is tired with its hard, & its terrible experience & still more with its mismanagement," he advised his sister Amelia. Before long, Holmes believed, "the majority will say that we are vainly working to effect what never happens—the subjugation (for that is it) of a great civilized nation." His disenchantment may have had a physical cause. Holmes was, as he wrote home, still "stretched out miserably sick with dysentery, growing weaker each day from illness and starvation." Kept from the field at Fred-ericksburg at the end of 1862, his suffering was psychological as much as physical; "what self reproaches I have gone through," he told his mother, "for what I could not help and the doctor, no easy hand, declared necessary."[68]

By the spring of 1863, Holmes was in rather better spirits, but at the start of May, just outside Fredericksburg and approaching Mayre's Heights, the regiment found itself under fire from Confederates located on the heights. It was here that Holmes received what appeared, at first, to be a minor injury—he was shot in his heel—but that proved more debilitating than either of his previous two wounds. He avoided amputation but, in later life, Holmes recalled wishing that he might have lost his foot, and thereby been honorably discharged from a war that held no more meaning for him. As it was, he was out of action for much of the summer and fall of 1863. As his regiment fought at Gettysburg, the Massachusetts Fifty-Fourth stormed the ramparts at Fort Wagner, and his father delivered his stirring July 4 oration in support of a Union, a nation now fully committed to equality, Holmes sat in Boston in a state of what now might be diagnosed as depression. The war came home for him, as for others, through the newspapers and in the coffins: bearing back to Holmes the good news and the bad, but above all the bodies of his comrades from the front.[69]

"We know now what War means," Dr. Holmes declaimed, "and we cannot look its dull, dead ghastliness in the face unless we feel that there is some great and noble principle in it." This, he stressed, "is our Holy War," a view in which his cultural circle concurred. The Emancipation Proclamation had initiated, according to, among others, businessman John Murray Forbes, "the greatest act in American history, the emancipation of 3,000,000 of blacks and of 5,000,000 of whites from the power of an aristocratic class." Holmes knew what Forbes and his father meant. And he tried, so very hard, to recall that crusading zeal of the spring of 1861, to return to that moment and that mindset. We "need all the examples of chivalry to help us bind our rebellious desires to steadfastness in the Christian Crusade of the 19th century," Holmes observed to his father's friend, the author Charles Eliot Norton. "If one didn't believe that this war was such a crusade, in the cause of the future of the whole civilized world," he added, "it would be hard indeed to keep the hand to the sword."[70]

Yet even as he wrote this, Holmes, battling through the Wilderness in Virginia as part of Ulysses S. Grant's relentless Overland Campaign, was already considering leaving the Twentieth Massachusetts, and the war. By this point the Civil War, in its relentless attrition, more closely resembled the battlefields of the Western Front of the First World War half a century later. It had, for Holmes, become just too much to bear. Just over two weeks later, Henry Abbott was dead. Toward the end of May, Holmes only narrowly escaped death himself when his pistol misfired. His days were spent burying the dead, dealing with exhaustion, absorbing the sight of "the dead of both sides . . . piled in the trenches 5 or 6 deep—wounded often writhing under superincumbent dead." Even the trees, he noticed, "were in slivers from the constant peppering of bullets." Union losses were running at over a thousand per day; "nearly every Regimental off—I knew or cared for," Holmes despaired, "is dead or wounded." On July 18, 1864, the three-year enlistment period for the Twentieth Massachusetts expired; some of the few remaining men would reenlist, and the war itself would last for another year; but for Holmes, the battle was over.[71]

At the end of his term of service, therefore, Holmes chose not to reenlist. He left that option open, but he was exhausted. He had observed that there was "a kind of heroism in the endurance," but he could no longer find that heroism in himself, and he could no longer endure. "I started in this thing a boy," he told his mother; "I am now a man." But, as he had already stressed to both parents, he was "not the same man (may not have quite the same ideas) & certainly am not so elastic as I was." In particular, he emphasized,

"I *will not acknowledge the same claims upon me under those circumstances* that existed formerly." Holmes still worried about his "soldierly honor," and he continuously emphasized the imperative of duty, but by this stage he was simply searching for an honorable exit: to placate his parents, in part, but mainly for his own peace of mind. In later years, Holmes would reiterate his belief that "young men who live through a war in which they have taken part will find themselves different." Yet arguably, what haunted Holmes, and what made the Civil War a continuous presence in his life, was his suspicion that it had not changed him at all; it had simply revealed who he really was.[72]

NOTES

1 Oliver Wendell Holmes to Harold Laski, July 28, 1927, in Mark DeWolfe Howe (ed.), *Holmes-Laski Letters: The Correspondence of Mr Justice Holmes and Harold J. Laski*, 2 Vols. (Cambridge, MA: Harvard University Press, 1953) II, 966.

2 Henry Abbott to father, October 22, 1861, in Robert Garth Scott (ed.), *Fallen Leaves: The Civil War Letters of Major Henry Livermore Abbott* (Kent, OH: The Kent State University Press, 1991) 60–66, and esp. 62; Report of S. Williams (General Orders No. 32), October 25, 1861, in *The War of the Rebellion: A Compilation of the Official Records of the Union and Confederate Armies*, 128 Vols. (Washington: Government Printing Office, 1880–1901), hereinafter ORA, Series 1, Vol. 5, 291; for a detailed account of the battle of Ball's Bluff, although obviously largely from the perspective of the Twentieth Massachusetts, see Richard F. Miller, *Harvard's Civil War: A History of the Twentieth Massachusetts Volunteer Infantry* (Hanover and London: University Press of New England, 2005) 51–83.

3 Report of S. Williams (General Orders No. 31), ORA, Series 1, Vol. 5, 291.

4 Henry Adams, *The Education of Henry Adams*, ed. Ernest Samuels (Boston: Houghton Mifflin Company, 1973) 99–100; Robert Gould Shaw to mother, June 9, 1861, in Russell Duncan (ed.), *Blue-Eyed Child of Fortune: The Civil War Letters of Colonel Robert Gould Shaw* (Athens and London: University of Georgia Press, 1999) 107.

5 Charles Sumner to John Murray Forbes, January 13, 1861, in Sarah Forbes Hughes (ed.), *Letters and Recollections of John Murray Forbes*, 2 Vols. (Boston: Houghton, Mifflin and Company, 1899) I, 186.

6 James Russell Lowell, "E Pluribus Unum," *Atlantic Monthly*, 7:40 (February 1861) 235–246, 238; John Lothrop Motley, "The Causes of the American Civil War: A Paper Contributed to the London *Times*," in Frank Freidel (ed.), *Union Pamphlets of the Civil War, 1861–1865*, 2 Vols. (Cambridge, MA: The Belknap Press of Harvard University Press, 1967) I, 29–54, 31–32, 36. Motley's letter appeared in the London *Times* on May 23 and 24, 1861; Francis Lieber, *What is Our Constitution – League, Pact, or Government? Two Lectures on the Constitution of the United States . . . to which is Appended an Address on Secession* (New York: Columbia Law School, 1861) 41.

7 Elisha Hunt Rhodes, *All For the Union: The Civil War Diary and Letters of Elisha Hunt Rhodes*, ed. Robert Hunt Rhodes (New York: Vintage Books, 1991) 57; Oliver Wendell Holmes, Sr. to Frederick Locker-Lampson, May 13, 1861, quoted in Carroll A. Wilson, *Thirteen Author Collections of the Nineteenth Century and Five Centuries of Familiar Quotations*, eds. Jean C. S. Wilson and David A. Randall, 2 Vols. (New York: Charles Scribner's Sons, 1950) II, 535–536; Ralph Waldo Emerson quoted in James Elliot Cabot, *A Memoir of Ralph Waldo Emerson*, 2 Vols. (Boston, n.p., 1887) II, 600–601; for further discussion see Susan-Mary Grant, *North over South: Northern Nationalism and American Identity in the Antebellum Era* (Lawrence: University Press of Kansas, 2000) 150–152; on the dominance of northern Union sentiment in 1861, see Gary Gallagher, *The Union War* (Cambridge, MA: Harvard University Press, 2011) 2.

8 Bartlett quoted in Sheldon M. Novick, *Honorable Justice: The Life of Oliver Wendell Holmes* (New York: Dell Publishing, 1990) 33; Francis William Palfrey, *Memoir of William Francis Bartlett* (Boston: Houghton, Mifflin and Company, 1881) 2; Putnam quoted in Duncan, *Blue-Eyed Child of Fortune*, 156.

9 Liva Baker, *The Justice from Beacon Hill: The Life and Times of Oliver Wendell Holmes* (New York: Harper Collins, 1991) 22–23.

10 Motley quoted in Novick, *Honorable Justice*, 34; Oliver Wendell Holmes, Sr., "Holmes," *Oration Delivered before the City Authorities at Boston* (Philadelphia: 1863) 27.

11 Richard Maxwell Brown, *No Duty to Retreat: Violence and Values in American History and Society* (New York and Oxford: Oxford University Press, 1991) 31; Novick, *Honorable Justice*, 33; Holmes to Amelia Holmes, May 1, 1861, in Mark DeWolfe Howe (ed.), *Touched with Fire: Civil War Letters and Diary of Oliver Wendell Holmes, Jr., 1861–1864* (Cambridge, MA: Harvard University Press, 1946) 3–4.

12 Baker, *Justice from Beacon Hill*, 98–100; Catherine Drinker Bowen, *Yankee from Olympus: Justice Holmes and His Family* (Boston: Little, Brown and Company, 1944) 144.

13 Palfrey, *Memoir of Bartlett*, 5.

14 Palfrey, *Memoir of Bartlett*, 5; Miller, *Harvard's Civil War*, 32.

15 Holmes to mother, September 8 and 11, 1861, in Howe, *Touched with Fire*, 4–5, 6–7.

16 Palfrey, *Memoir of Bartlett*, 6–7; Robert Garth Scott (ed.), *Fallen Leaves: The Civil War Letters of Major Henry Livermore Abbott* (Kent, OH: The Kent State University Press, 1991) 4; James M. McPherson, *Battle Cry of Freedom: The Civil War Era* (New York and Oxford: Oxford University Press, 1988) 329; Devens quoted in Novick, *Honorable Justice*, 38.

17 John H. Brinton, *Personal Memoirs of John H. Brinton, Civil War Surgeon, 1861–1865* (1891. Reprint. Carbondale and Edwardsville: Southern Illinois University Press, 1996) 54.

18 *Scientific American*, 4:19 (May 11, 1861) 292; Edward Hagerman, *The American Civil War and the Origins of Modern Warfare: Idea, Organization, and Field Command* (1988. Reprint. Bloomington and Indianapolis: Indiana University Press, 1992) 16–17.

19 Miller, *Harvard's Civil War*, 34–37; Bowen, *Yankee from Olympus*, 151; Thomas Wentworth Higginson, *Cheerful Yesterdays* (1898. Reprint. Boston: Houghton Mifflin, 1901) 250.

20 Holmes to mother, September 23, 1861, in Howe, *Touched with Fire*, 11–12; for a description of this period, see also Palfrey, *Memoir of Bartlett*, 7–11.

21 Palfrey, *Memoir of Bartlett*, 9; A.V. Colburn to Stone, October 20, 1861, and *Report of Geo. B. McClellan*, November 1, 1861, ORA, Series 1, Vol. 5, 290.

22 Palfrey, *Memoir of Bartlett*, 17.

23 Henry Abbott to father, October 22, 1861, in Scott, *Fallen Leaves*, 60; Palfrey, *Memoir of Bartlett*, 21–23; Miller, *Harvard's Civil War*, 70.

24 Holmes to mother, October 23, 1861, in Howe, *Touched with Fire*, 13–19.

25 Holmes, Diary entry in Howe, *Touched with Fire*, 23–24.

26 Holmes, Diary entry in Howe, *Touched with Fire*, 32.

27 John T. Morse, *Life and Letters of Oliver Wendell Holmes*, 2 Vols. (London: Sampson Low, Marston and Company, 1896), II, 157–159.

28 Bryant quoted in Miller, *Harvard's Civil War*, 80–81; Mary Trail Spence Lowell Putnam, *William Lowell Putnam* (1862. Reprint. Cambridge, MA: Riverside Press, 1864) 9; Norwood P. Hallowell, *Reminiscences Written for My Children* (Boston: Little, Brown and Company, 1896) 6–7.

29 Holmes, Diary entry in Howe, *Touched with Fire*, 29–30; Allan Nevins and Milton Halsey Thomas (eds.), *The Diary of George Templeton Strong*, 4 Vols. (New York: The Macmillan Company, 1952) III, 181.

30 Charles A. Tripler to U.S. Surgeon General William A. Hammond, quoted in Francis M. Wafer, *A Surgeon in the Army of the Potomac*, ed. Cheryl A. Wells (Montreal and London: McGill-Queen's University Press, 2008) xxxiv; *Report of Surgeon Charles S. Tripler, Medical Director of the Army of the Potomac, of the Operations of the Medical Department of that Army from August 12, 1861, to March 17, 1862*, ORA, Series 1, Vol. 5 (XIV) 86–89; support for troops in the field was still an

issue, and the subject of a lengthy exchange in the *Christian Examiner*, in the latter stages of the war (January 1864); and see *Have We the Best Possible Ambulance System?* (Boston: Walker, Wise and Company, 1864). For an overview of the subject, see John S. Haller, Jr., *Farmcarts to Fords: A History of the Military Ambulance, 1790–1925* (Carbondale: Southern Illinois University Press, 1992).

31 Henry Abbott to father, November 7, 1861, in Scott, *Fallen Leaves*, 74.

32 *Harper's Weekly*, November 9, 1861.

33 Holmes to Sir Frederick Pollock, June 28, 1930, in Mark DeWolfe Howe (ed.), *Holmes-Pollock Letters: The Correspondence of Mr. Justice Holmes and Sir Frederick Pollock, 1874–1932*, Second Edition: Two Volumes in One (Cambridge, MA: The Belknap Press of Harvard University Press, 1961) II, 269–270.

34 *Harper's Weekly*, November 9, 1861; Ulysses S. Grant, *Personal Memoirs* (1885, 1886. Reprint. New York and London: Penguin Books, 1999) 627.

35 Novick, *Honorable Justice*, 55; although Holmes did later state that he had read Kinglake whilst he was in the Army, the first volume of *The Invasion of the Crimea* (there were eight in total) only came out in 1863; Holmes to Pollock, June 9, 1930, *Holmes-Pollock Letters*, II, 267; Holmes, Jr. to father, December 20, 1862, in Howe (ed.), *Touched with Fire*, 80.

36 Holmes, Diary entry in Howe, *Touched with Fire*, 27–28.

37 Edmund Wilson, *Patriotic Gore: Studies in the Literature of the American Civil War* (1962. Reprint. London: The Hogarth Press, 1987) 747; Holmes, Jr. to father, December 20, 1862, in Howe (ed.), *Touched with Fire*, 80; Adams, *Education*, 108.

38 Miller, *Harvard's Civil War*, 495: C.A. Bartol, *Our Sacrifices: A Sermon Preached in the West Church, November 3, 1861* (Boston: Ticknor and Fields, 1861) 3.

39 Bartol, *Our Sacrifices*, 20; Holmes, "Reflections on the Past and Future" (1912), in Richard A. Posner (ed.), *The Essential Holmes: Selections from the Letters, Speeches, Judicial Opinions, and Other Writings of Oliver Wendell Holmes, Jr.* (1992. Reprint. Chicago and London: The University of Chicago Press, 1996) 4.

40 Bartol, *Our Sacrifices*, 11; Henry Abbott to Aunt Lizzy, December 21, 1861, in Scott, *Fallen Leaves*, 92–93.

41 Holmes to parents, March 25, 1862, in Howe, *Touched with Fire* 37; Henry Abbott to father, December 31, 1861, in Scott, *Fallen Leaves*, 94, 96; Holmes to parents, April 7, 1862, and April 23, 1862, both in Howe, *Touched with Fire*, 41, 45–46.

42 This controversy is covered in careful detail in Miller, *Harvard's Civil War*, 96–100, and the official correspondence relating to the charge can be followed through the ORA, Series 2, Vol. 1, 784–799 in the correspondence between Governor Andrew, Secretary of War, Simon Cameron, and McClellan; John A. Andrew to Simon Cameron, December 7, 1861, ORA, Series 2, Vol. 1, 784.

43 George B. McClellan to Andrew, December 20, 1861, ORA, Series 2, Vol. 1, 791; Novick, *Honorable Justice*, 54.

44 Edward Dicey, *Spectator of America* (Athens and London: The University of Georgia Press, 1989) 142–143.

45 Holmes to parents, March 25, 1862, in Howe, *Touched with Fire*, 38; Henry Ropes quoted in Miller, *Harvard's Civil War*, 111; William Howard Russell, *My Diary North and South* (Boston: T.O.H.P. Burnham, 1863) 546; Rhodes, *All For the Union*, 53.

46 Miller, *Harvard's Civil War*, 112–113; Holmes to parents, April 7, 1862, in Howe, *Touched with Fire*, 39–42.

47 Holmes to parents, April 7 and 23, 1862, in Howe, *Touched with Fire*, 41, 43–44.

48 Miller, *Harvard's Civil War*, 115; Palfrey, *Memoirs of Bartlett*, 45, 48.

49 Holmes to parents, April 17, 1862, in Howe, *Touched with Fire*, 43; Henry Abbott to mother, April 26, 1862, in Scott, *Fallen Leaves*, 112.

50 Henry Abbott to Arthur, May 8, and to mother, May 18, 1862, in Scott, *Fallen Leaves*, 115, 119; Holmes to parents, April 25, 1862, in Howe, *Touched with Fire*, 47.

51 McClellan quoted in David J. Eicher, *The Longest Night: A Military History of the Civil War* (2001. Reprint. London: Pimlico, 2002) 279; Holmes to parents, June 2, 1862, in Howe, *Touched with Fire*, 48–50, 51–52; Henry Abbott to father, June 6, 1862, in Scott, *Fallen Leaves*, 127–129.

52 McClellan quoted in Eicher, *The Longest Night*, 279; Holmes to parents, June 2,1862, in Howe, *Touched with Fire*, 48–50, 51–52; Henry Abbott to father, June 6, 1862, in Scott, *Fallen Leaves*, 127–129.

53 Holmes to parents, June 2, 1862, in Howe, *Touched with Fire*, 48–50, 51–52.

54 Jonathan Letterman, *Medical Recollections of the Army of the Potomac* (New York: D. Appleton and Company, 1866) 6–7, 9; for an extended discussion of the "Letterman System" see Frank R. Freemon, *Gangrene and Glory: Medical Care During the American Civil War* (Urbana and Chicago: University of Illinois Press, 2001) 67–76; Eicher, *Longest Night*, 280.

55 Holmes to parents, July 5, 1862, in Howe, *Touched with Fire*, 58–59.

56 Holmes to parents, July 5, 1862, in Howe, *Touched with Fire*, 59–60; the Battle of Glendale is also known as the Battle of Nelson's Farm and often, in Confederate memoirs, Frazier's Farm; Holmes recalled the death of Lowell in his Memorial Day Address of 1884: Oliver Wendell Holmes, Jr., "Memorial Day Address, May 30 1884," Mark DeWolfe Howe (ed.), *Oliver Wendell Holmes: Occasional Speeches* (Cambridge, MA: The Belknap Press of Harvard University Press, 1962) 9.

57 Holmes to parents, July 5, 1862, in Howe, *Touched with Fire*, 61.

58 Oliver Wendell Holmes, Sr., "My Hunt after 'The Captain,'" *The Atlantic Monthly*, 10:62 (December 1862) 738.

59 Holmes to parents, September 5, 17, and 18, 1862, in Howe, *Touched with Fire*, 61–62, 63.

60 Holmes to parents, September 17, 1862, in Howe, *Touched with Fire*, 63; Miller, *Harvard's Civil War*, 174–175.

61 Holmes, Sr., "My Hunt," 738; Holmes to parents, September 18, 1862, in Howe, *Touched with Fire*, 64–65.

62 *New York Times*, October 20, 1862; Holmes, Sr., "My Hunt," 743–744.

63 G. Edward White, *Justice Oliver Wendell Holmes: Law and the Inner Self* (New York and Oxford: Oxford University Press, 1993) 58; Holmes, Sr., "My Hunt," 752.

64 Morse, *Life and Letters*, I, 43–44; Oliver Wendell Holmes, Sr., *Oration Delivered before the City Authorities at Boston* (Boston: Farwell and Company, 1863) 17, 23.

65 See, e.g., Holmes to Lady (Ellen) Askwith, September 18, 1914 and September 17, 1919, in OWH Papers, Harvard Law School (HLS); Henry Abbott to Aunt Lizzie, January 10, 1863, in Scott, *Fallen Leaves*, 161.

66 Dicey, *Spectator of America*, 76; Dr. Holmes to Motley, August 20, 1862, in Morse, *Life and Letters*, II, 167. For a detailed analysis of the complicated legal road toward emancipation, see Paul Finkelman, "Lincoln, Emancipation, and the Limits of Constitutional Change," 2008 *Supreme Court Review*, 2008, 349–387.

67 Miller, *Harvard's Civil War*, 135; Novick, Hallowell quoted in Novick, *Honorable Justice*, 75, 79.

68 Holmes to Amelia Holmes, November 16, 1862; to mother December 12, 1862, in Howe, *Touched with Fire*, 70–73, 74–76.

69 Holmes to mother, May 3 and 4, 1863, in Howe, *Touched with Fire*, 92–93; Holmes to Ellen Askwith, March 3, 1915, OWH Papers, *op.cit.*; Novick, *Honorable Justice*, 78–79.

70 Holmes, Sr., *Oration*, 55, 62; Sarah Forbes Hughes (ed.), *Letters and Recollections of John Murray Forbes*, 2 Vols. (Boston: Houghton, Mifflin and Company, 1899) I, 347; Holmes to Charles Eliot Norton, April 17, 1864, OWH Papers, HLS.

71 Holmes diary entry, May 12, 1864; Holmes to parents May 16, 1864, in Howe, *Touched with Fire*, 115, 122.

72 Holmes to parents, June 24, 1864; to mother, June 24, 1864; and to parents May 30, 1864, in Howe, *Touched with Fire*, 149, 142–143, 135; Holmes to Ellen Askwith, September 18, 1914, OWH Papers, *op.cit.*

CHAPTER **3**

THE DOUBTS OF CIVIL LIFE,
LAW AND LOGIC

*"The life of the law has not been logic: it has been experience . . . The law embodies the
story of a nation's development through many centuries, and it cannot be dealt with as if it
contained only the axioms and corollaries of a book of mathematics."*
(Oliver Wendell Holmes, Jr., *The Common Law*, 1881)[1]

The Civil War was, for Oliver Wendell Holmes, unfinished business. That
was not entirely due to the trauma of the experience, although it certainly was
traumatic. In later life, Holmes sometimes used its physical trauma as a psychological prop, a means of "converting misfortune into a source of satisfaction." When he recalled what he had been through as a young man, he was
able, he admitted, to "pretend" to himself that any "discomforts came from"
the war, "and inwardly swagger." At the time, however, he had little sense of
swagger. As the war progressed, and as more of the Twentieth Massachusetts
fell, it came to seem to Holmes what it actually was: a more brutal conflict
than he, than anyone had imagined in 1861. By the end of his service, in
July 1864, he had internalized what he had neither the will nor the words
to express; "I have not been & am not likely to be in the mood for writing
details," he observed in the midst of the Wilderness Campaign.[2] But he never
did provide the details.

Holmes' apparent silence on the subject was partly because his Civil War
experiences were so disjointed. Over the three years that he was with the
Twentieth Massachusetts, almost a third of that time was spent away from
it, either recovering from injury or on recruitment drives. He had ample
opportunity, therefore, to discuss in person with friends and family back in
Boston at least some of the issues that other soldiers committed to paper
and thereby to posterity. Exacerbating the difficulty for scholars searching
for evidence of Holmes' thinking is the fact that Holmes undertook some

fairly rigorous post-war editing of his correspondence from the front and his diary, both already brief to the point of terseness in comparison with the lengthy, literary letters that many of his comrades sent to their families. All this can prove problematic for those seeking to trace his development, and that of his ideas, over the course of the conflict and its immediate aftermath.[3]

The solution most often arrived at is to sift Holmes' later voluminous correspondence and speeches for such gleanings from the Civil War years and after as may be found. These, of course, refract, and likely distort the young Holmes through the lens of the older version's perspective, and shine little light on the months immediately following his departure from the Twentieth Massachusetts, when his future seemed so uncertain. The diary he began almost two years later during a visit to Europe offers little more than a summer snapshot of Holmes effectively on holiday, although in this, at least, some sense both of his philosophical attitudes and his physical determination is conveyed. Holmes' 1866 trip has been described as a "grand tour," which in a sense it was; but few wealthy nineteenth-century Americans undertaking such a tour took sightseeing to the quite literal heights that Holmes did when he went climbing in the Bernese Alps with his friend the famous mountaineer Leslie (later Sir Leslie) Stephen, author of *The Playground of Europe* (1871) and father of Virginia Woolf.[4]

The experience did not make a life-long mountaineer out of Holmes, and so this particular achievement is often swiftly passed over by those heading purposively toward the peaks and precipices of his legal cases during his years on the Supreme Court. Yet it was one that, along with the Civil War, remained with him all his life, and, in time, constituted a crucial component of the Holmes myth. His ascents of, among others, the Balmhorn and the Mönch, and traverse of the Col du Géant in the Mont Blanc Massif, all of which involved climbing far in excess of 3,000 meters (over 12,000 feet), were enough to accord him membership in the recently-formed but already prestigious Alpine Club (UK).

At the time, and rather in common with his Civil War experiences, Holmes' diary conveyed merely a glimmer of the emotions these ascents produced in him; but he admitted to fear on the Gemmi Pass—an "unpleasant creeping in my backbone"—and traversing part of the Balmhorn was "like going along the edge of an oyster shell." At the time, he wrote, the Alps were "the finest sight I ever saw," and years afterwards they lived still in his mind's eye. Almost half a century later, he included his ascents in the Alps in his list of the few external events in his life to have stirred "great emotions" in him (the others were a storm at sea, a solar eclipse, and battle). For Holmes, as indeed for many others, the Alps conjured up the infinite, "the arête of the past, beyond whom articulate history is silent."[5]

Back home in Boston, and as with Holmes' childhood and adolescence, glimpses of him in these early years can also be found in the writings of others; in fiction, for example, specifically in the work of Henry James whose contact with Holmes, largely brokered through Holmes' friendship with his brother William James, one of Dr. Holmes' students at Harvard Medical School, began in the months immediately after Holmes returned from the front.

Scholars disagree over how close Henry and Wendell ever actually were. What can be said with some certainty is that Holmes proved attractive to the young James partly because, as a Union soldier, he served as a sort of wish-fulfillment figure for a man who had not fought, and partly because, as a war veteran, he provided suitable literary fodder: more suitable, perhaps, than Henry's own brother, "Wilky" (Garth Wilkinson), who had fought with Pen Hallowell in the Fifty-Fourth Massachusetts but whose traumatic war experiences were perhaps too close to home, too troubling, to permit of fictional treatment.

What impact Holmes' appearance in fictionalized form in James' Civil War story, "A Most Extraordinary Case," had on him in later life can only be surmised. Yet just as *Harper's Weekly* and Holmes' father in *The Atlantic Monthly* had presented him in their pages as the epitome of the Union soldier during the war, so James portrayed him as the valiant veteran after it. "For the past three years," James wrote of his literary creation, "he had been stretched without intermission on the rack of duty. Although constantly exposed to hard service, it had been his fortune never to receive a serious wound," until that is, "his health broke down." James might, of course, have been describing any number of Civil War soldiers; but it was in the details that he distinguished his hero from the herd, and outlined aspects of Holmes' character that seemed to James, even on his brief acquaintance, already obvious. He was "in his innermost soul a singularly nervous, over-scrupulous person," James observed, and the "sense of lost time" was "his perpetual bugbear,—the feeling that precious hours were now fleeting unaccounted, which in more congenial labors would suffice almost for the building of a monument more lasting than brass."[6]

The Holmes that James hinted at in his story suffered from a sense of life being squandered. This was the Holmes that his family knew well, and worried about. "Now do take time enough & not try to crowd everything into 4 or 5 months," his mother wrote to him during his trip to Europe; "don't feel as you did at home that you must accomplish just so much each 24 hours." He had been, as he had told her, "uncommon busy," which was hardly true; it was common enough for him. And the fact that so many of his comrades had died at the start of their lives only reinforced his awareness not just of life's brevity but of the role chance played in it. "But how luck has followed me," he admitted later, "I shaved through wounds with my life when 1/8 inch difference would have finished me." Even apparently bad luck had saved him at times. Henry Abbott had died, after all, when Holmes himself was bedbound with dysentery. It could have been him who perished in the Wilderness. Possibly Holmes felt that it should have been him. Earlier, while Holmes was still recuperating from his heel injury, Abbott had written to him. "Why the deuce aren't you more careful?" Abbott had grumbled. "You will be maimed for life if you don't look sharp." In some ways, of course, Holmes already was maimed for life.[7]

It is important, however, not to exaggerate this. The Civil War was surely "pivotal in the development" of Holmes' "mature philosophical beliefs," but it was more psychological than philosophical for him, and would, in many respects, remain so. In common with many Civil War soldiers, as Holmes matured, so the character of the war veteran fitted him more comfortably. But it was a role he only fully grew into over time. As he became the aged figure that, at the start of the war, he had assumed a soldier to be, increasingly he consciously conformed to the image of him presented to the world, first by *Harper's*, then by his father, and later by James: an idealized soldier/veteran of the Civil War. He was hardly alone in doing this, although he was rather more successful at it than some. Civil War hero did not always easily translate into civilian exemplar in post-war America. And even in Holmes' case the transition would hardly have been as effective had he not proved so successful in his chosen career.[8]

Toward the end of that career, in the preface to a collection of his legal papers, Holmes described himself as "an old warrior who cannot expect to bear arms much longer," and expressed his pride "that the brilliant young soldiers" of the legal profession still accorded him "a place in their councils of war." It was an astute acknowledgment of how others saw him; an accurate summation of how he saw the law; and possibly an insight into how he actually saw himself. Because if the Civil War informed Holmes' professional role as Supreme Court Justice, ultimately it was his legal career that confirmed his public persona of Civil War veteran.[9]

★★★

Holmes' legal career had, of course, first been mooted in 1861, when he had contemplated his future prospects in his autobiographical entry for the Harvard Class Album. "If I survive the war," he had written, "I expect to study law as my profession." But Holmes was undecided, in 1861 and still three years later, whether law or philosophy, or perhaps even medicines, was to be his focus. In later years he described himself as having been "shoved into the law," but whether by his father or his better instincts was a little unclear, especially since Dr. Holmes was not at the time convinced that the legal profession was the best one for his son to pursue. Possibly Holmes meant "shoved" in the sense that, whatever direction his father recommended, he would have been likely to go in the opposite one. He certainly seemed to have had a life-long inclination to present many of his decisions as having derived from a sense of duty, made under duress; or possibly, in maturity, he simply saw more clearly the contours of the path he had followed and the possible detours he might have taken.[10]

Yet in one element Holmes was consistent. Both in youth and in maturity, he was driven, rather as his father had been, to try and find order amidst chaos, to stabilize "the dash and recoil, of the unceasing tide" that he perceived within himself as much as in the world around him. Unsurprisingly the Civil War had done nothing to correct that tendency: quite the opposite. In this, he was fully in tune with his age, not simply in the sense of being the consummate product of it, but also as one of its creators.[11]

Holmes was "characteristic of the male members of his generation and class . . . in delaying his professional commitments after the conclusion of the Civil War." But the days of "versatility and gentlemanly amateurishness," although they had suited his father, would not suit him. Although the professions were, like Holmes himself, less clearly defined in 1864 than they would become later in the nineteenth century, when Holmes was contemplating his future, subjects such as law, medicine, and science were on the cusp of the kind of professional organization that is taken for granted today. The entire process of professionalization, indeed, was "an extended and sometimes painful and turbulent" one for the nation as much as for Holmes. In that sense, the professional really was personal for him.[12]

Over the summer of 1864, Holmes clearly sought advice from a range of people on his future prospects, including his long-term mentor, Ralph Waldo Emerson. But his focus remained on the law, and in the fall of 1864 he finally settled on Harvard Law School. In selecting the path of the law, Holmes was following a familial, national, and legal tradition that stretched back to his maternal grandfather, Justice Charles Jackson. His return to that tradition may have proved of some comfort to Holmes over the first few years of his legal studies and later practice. Indeed, it may have provided a very necessary sense of security in the aftermath of conflict, one that led, in time, to real satisfaction with a subject that, as he frequently admitted, had initially seemed to comprise only "a ragbag of details," not obviously "worthy of the interest of an intelligent man." He quite quickly changed his mind.[13]

Shortly after starting law school, Holmes reported that his first taste of legal studies was already proving greatly satisfying. "Certainly it far exceeds my expectation," he declared, "both as [mental] gymnastics and for its intrinsic interest." Although he felt that "[truth] sifts so slowly from the dust of the law," that there was truth to be uncovered he was certain. "Law, of which

I once doubted," he observed a year later, "is now my enthusiastic pursuit," not least because, as he saw it, the law made "play of what would otherwise be work." In correspondence with the philosopher Morris Cohen many years later, Holmes expressed his delight "that a philosopher is interested in the law—I should hardly be interested in it," he averred, if "it did not open a wider door to philosophizing."[14]

At the very start of his career, indeed, the idea that the law might function in this way for him was rather a leap of faith on Holmes' part—the faith of youth embarking on a new venture. Holmes' friend William James expressed a similar enthusiasm for his subject, medicine, and in much the same language. There "is no occupation on earth," James announced at the start of his medical studies, "from which men of very different temperament and gifts can get more life and growth of character and wisdom than this." Over time, however, both Holmes and James would vent their frustration at the disorganized nature of their respective professions; and both would seek to effect reform within them. And, in part, their growing sense of frustration derived from the lack of professional educational structure that both encountered at the start of their careers. Holmes made the problem clear in a short piece penned, anonymously, for the *American Law Review* when he was its editor. In an echo of Henry Adams' general critique of Harvard's teaching methods, the notice dismissed the education bestowed upon fledgling lawyers at Harvard as "almost a disgrace," and one that did real damage to "the profession throughout the country."[15]

The format of a legal education at Harvard in 1864 provided a liberal degree of flexibility in terms of how one approached the law, which Holmes appreciated. Later in life, he claimed to have reveled in the "black gulf of solitude more isolating than that which surrounds the dying man." However, he also admitted that the flexibility of the curriculum forced him to struggle to make sense of the law. He had to trust in "his own unshaken will." There was precious little else to hang on to at the time. Six years after he enrolled, of course, the first and most famous dean of the law school, Christopher Columbus Langdell, would alter radically Harvard's teaching methods by introducing the case, or Socratic system of teaching law, possibly as much for economic reasons as for educational efficacy. Holmes thoroughly approved of this development, mainly because he had endured, even if he claimed partly to have enjoyed, a more traditional, not to say turgid method of instruction.[16]

The three professors teaching law when Holmes arrived at Harvard—former Chief Justice of New Hampshire and Royall Professor Joel Parker, legal scholar Theophilus Parsons, and former Governor of Massachusetts Emory Washburn—largely expected the students to educate themselves through reading legal textbooks, not studying individual appellate decisions under the guidance of the professoriate. Holmes and his fellow students were therefore introduced to such seminal texts as *Commentaries on the Constitution of the United States* (1833) by Associate Justice Joseph Story, the first Dane Professor of Law at Harvard; his successor, Simon Greenleaf's *Treatise on the Law of Evidence* (1842–1853); and Parson's own *Law of Contracts* (1857).

Together, these works offered a fairly comprehensive interpretation of the development of the law in America. And although such reading was in no sense intended to be narrowly legal, its density had quite the opposite effect. "The Law of Contracts," as Parsons announced in the opening sentence of his two-volume, nearly 2,000-page tome that analyzed some 6,000 cases, "may be regarded as including nearly all the law which regulates the relations of human life. Indeed, it may be looked upon as the basis of human society." Whether his work served as the basis for a solid grounding in the law for such novices as Holmes was another matter.[17]

Human society, in any case, is a flexible construction, and, in legal terms, hardly a static one. Although Holmes and his fellow students inherited the results of many of the landmark legal rulings that men such as Story and Greenleaf had been instrumental in, they may only have been vaguely, and possibly not at all, aware of some of these prior to their arrival at Harvard. Story, for example, had ruled on the famous *Amistad* case the day after Holmes was born. And both he and Greenleaf had been involved in the contentious, and somewhat attenuated, ruling that was *Charles River Bridge v. Warren Bridge* (1837), a case revolving around tolls and transport that impacted on both Harvard college finances and on the development of Boston as a city. For Holmes, therefore, the names on his textbooks were in theory far from distant figures; they were those of a proximate world, but it was no longer his world.

The expectation entertained by Parker, Parsons, and Washburn, therefore, "that legal education should follow the course which earlier generations had found effective," was as out of date as it was frustrating to their students. Their system required no prior knowledge, set no examinations, and, despite the fact that all three had extensive practical legal experience, deliberately privileged theory over practice. And by effectively putting the cart before the horse, it too often left the students floundering amidst "a throng of glittering generalities, like a swarm of little bodiless cherubs fluttering at the top of one of Correggio's pictures," as Holmes poetically put it. Henry James, who had dipped his toe into Harvard's legal waters, only to withdraw it again with some alacrity, famously critiqued the "dryness and hardness, prose unrelieved, at their deadliest" of Parker's lecturing style. Holmes, in later life, was more circumspect in his comments, although possibly equally as critical. He simply noted that Parker "showed in the chair the same qualities that had made him famous on the bench." It was, after all, as Holmes said in the same speech, a "combination of tact and will which gives a man immediate prominence among his fellows," and whatever else Holmes was, he was almost always tactful.[18]

Not everything that Holmes read at Harvard was impenetrable. At least one of the textbooks he had studied as a student, pedagogically designed as it was, he clearly found more approachable than some of the rest since he echoed it in many of his later speeches: Timothy Walker's *Introduction to American Law* (1837). Walker offered more to Holmes than simply the opportunity to test himself against the rigorous academic requirements of the law, although for the "Young Astronomer" that aspect of the undertaking undoubtedly appealed to him. "We are trying the greatest political experiment the world ever witnessed," Walker advised his students, "and the experience of all history warns us not to feel to secure ... if our liberty is to be ultimately preserved, it is at the price of sleepless vigilance. I refer not to foreign aggression," he explained, "for of this we have nothing to fear; our only enemies" he asserted "are those of our own household."[19]

If that particular sentence resonated with Holmes, it was perhaps not just because of his recent military experiences. His upbringing in Cambridge and Boston in the 1840 and 1850s had already revealed to him a world in turmoil: riven by racial and class distinctions, defined by abolitionist, economic, and intellectual agitation, it was a world cast adrift from the religious and social certainties of an earlier age. The law, Holmes believed, would provide him with an intellectual harbor, and enable him to make sense of the war, and the world; but first, he had to make sense of the law.

★★★

It is important, however, to locate the point at which Holmes entered the legal world. As his military narrative ended, the legal one began, but the two inevitably overlapped. In 1841 when Holmes was born, and John Quincy Adams had invoked the "inalienable right" that was life and liberty in support of the *Amistad* captives, so the United States in 1865 was forced to confront the most basic tenets of its commitment to the idea that all men are created equal. The result took the form of the Civil Rights Act of 1866 and, more importantly, the Thirteenth, Fourteenth, and Fifteenth Amendments, the three so-called "Reconstruction" amendments to the Constitution that together ended slavery, established citizenship for everyone born in the United States, including former slaves, and prohibited racial discrimination in voting rights.[20]

In the short term, of course, the Reconstruction amendments achieved only a qualified equality: politically, personally, and legislatively limited as far as the newly-emancipated African American population was concerned. Nevertheless, as constitutional amendments they were the most prominent, but hardly the only examples of long-reaching transformative legislation to emerge from the Civil War. As historians who have studied the legislative legacy of the conflict have shown, the exigencies of waging war fundamentally altered traditional understandings of "the way the economy and society worked," or rather signally failed to work absent a degree of government intervention unimaginable in the *laissez-faire* Antebellum Era. The result was a raft of "agricultural policies, transcontinental railroad legislation, and eventually even the Thirteenth Amendment," all designed "to foster a wealthy populace and a strong nation," to draw up, in effect, a "blueprint for modern America."[21]

The common law was not part of that blueprint, and had never been devised to deal with the kinds of national institutions that emerged in the post-war era. Worse, grounded as it was in precedents produced in the distant past, it seemed to many not simply an amorphous mass of contradictory interpretative imperatives but potentially "antidemocratic." The law in the mid-nineteenth century was dangerously susceptible, as Liva Baker puts it, to "judicial manipulation through misrepresentation." Clarification through codification of the law was consequently advocated by reformers who sought not just clarity but security through "judicial conformity to firmly established principles."[22]

It was this reform impulse, together with the impact of much of the legislation drawn up during the war and in the decades after, that created the context for Holmes' early career. His career as a whole, in fact, was positioned in the period between two transformative eras: the Civil War, and the Reconstruction amendments, which were added to the Constitution just as Holmes became a lawyer; and the New Deal that reframed American politics and constitutional interpretations just as Holmes was leaving the Bench. In the middle of this was the Progressive Era—through which Holmes lived and worked.

The transition from the *laissez-faire* world of the late nineteenth century and the progressive response to the excesses of that period, all of which led to the New Deal and the explosion of "rights" after the Second World War, determined, to a great extent, scholarly interpretations of Holmes. The first few decades of that career, indeed, can be located within what might be regarded as something of an intellectual interregnum for America's legal profession as it wrangled over reform. The problem was largely the result of a combination of overconfidence and complacency. Even as the nation dramatically changed, socially, politically, and economically, it was the apparently slow pace of technological change that encouraged the idea that the law could be coherently codified, that "a stable body of law was not only a theoretical possibility but an accomplished fact." In the fifty years between the Civil War and the First World War, lawyers, judges, and law professors alike were "convinced beyond the shadow of a doubt, that they were serving not only righteousness but truth." In this context, the law began to be regarded "as the ultimate salvation of a free society—a government not of men but of laws," and Holmes himself became the "embodiment" of this "dream."[23]

Whether presented as hero or villain of the piece, Holmes is often positioned at the very center of "a (complex) story about the fall from grace—wherein most of the Justices," with the exception of Holmes, "strayed from the path of righteousness and imposed their *laissez-faire* philosophy on the nation through the pretext of constitutional interpretation." The law, or rather the judges who interpreted it in this era, was frequently perceived as "at odds with more democratic institutions, which acutely perceived the failure of *laissez-faire* to do justice to an increasingly interdependent world." In this brave new world the courts "became the apostles of reaction and the guardians of a romanticized, oversimplified past." They dealt with the later nineteenth-century realities of railroads, industrial accidents, and worker unrest via a convoluted and confusing legal language devised for a more feudal age. Constrained by its own precedents, the legal profession itself can be viewed as little more than a "camp follower" in the nation's inexorable march toward a modernity that extended beyond its legal lineaments, one defined by a particularly exploitative form of "capitalist enterprise" driven by a "grasping and predatory industrialism" after 1865. The social and economic game had changed, in other words, but the legal rules remained the same.[24]

There is no doubt that the legal landscape of post-Civil War America was littered with a certain amount of antediluvian detritus, and set fair to create still more. As lawyer and future British Ambassador to the United States James (later Viscount) Bryce observed, during and just after the Civil War there had "sprung up a perfect forest of judicial constructions," a process that "shows no sign of stopping; nor can it, for the new conditions of economics and politics bring up new problems for solution." For Holmes, however, it was not simply the "unwieldy system of precedents and forms," nor even the challenge of the changing economic and political landscape that frustrated him. The law, he came to believe, had "to be started over again."[25]

Determined by a combination of scientific principles and "philosophical speculation," the law should, Holmes argued, be designed to establish general principles in terms fixed enough for its rubric to constitute a coherent conceptual system, yet fluid enough for its rules to apply "in an actual system." One has to be careful with Holmes' thoughts in this regard, of course, since as he also frequently observed, while some believed the proposition that "the chief end of man is to frame general ideas" in fact "no general idea is worth a straw." To some extent he was simply being provocative in this respect; in others he was deadly serious in his own particular search for order, a search that would result, ultimately, in the work that would establish his reputation and that would in time "take on a life of its own": *The Common Law* (1881).[26]

Even if its composition was the result of a sudden flash of inspiration on Holmes' part, he spent some twenty years developing the ideas in *The Common Law*. How far back one wishes to go depends to a great extent, again, on how central one perceives the Civil War to have been, and how much of a break from Holmes' antebellum assumptions it represented in philosophical as in psychological terms for him. Certainly the interpretation of the law defined his life. But assessing the record of the Supreme Court Justice he eventually became also revolves around the extent to which his life defined his interpretation of the law.

★★★

From 1864 to 1882, Holmes developed an "intense professional regime."[27] In philosophical as in temporal terms, however, it was a protracted process, with the end result far from certain or even predictable. Nevertheless, and despite the frustrations Holmes experienced at Harvard Law School, the fall of that year promised a fresh start, for him and for the nation. Lincoln had been safely elected once again, and the war, now clearly going the Union's way, was reaching its endgame. The Republican administration was looking forward, fighting to secure the ratification of the Thirteenth Amendment that would finally and forever terminate slavery in the United States.

Holmes was looking forward, too, to a life beyond the battlefield. But by the end of 1865 he had exhausted all that Harvard Law School had to offer, or possibly Harvard had exhausted him. He wanted practice, not theory, and left to work at the Boston law firm of his friend Robert M. Morse. His decision may not have derived entirely from frustration at the college curriculum.

In throwing himself wholeheartedly into the legal world, Holmes was quite clearly relieved to have found a distraction from the Civil War. He may have left the battlefield behind, but the battlefield still regularly came back to Boston in the form of the many funerals he had to attend, the eulogies he heard, and the images that both conjured up for a man who had, arguably, abandoned the Army just at the point when the Union cause was at its most critical: on the battlefield but also at the polls. Although Holmes left little tangible evidence behind him of any particular interest in the politics of that period, the 1864 election really was the decision point for a nation, when it had to choose between the continuance of a war whose outcome was not yet certain and a compromise peace with the Confederacy. As Holmes, in the fall of 1864, began to tackle Story on constitutional law and Parsons on contracts, Union propagandists strove to persuade the Northern population that the Union created by the Constitution was still worth fighting for, that to compromise now was to negate the value of the sacrifice of men such as Henry Abbott, who had given their all for that republican ideal.

Holmes himself published a very personal poem in memory of Abbott in the *Boston Transcript* that fall. "He steered unquestioning nor turning back,/ Into the darkness and the unknown sea," Holmes wrote; "He vanished in the starless night, and we/Saw but the shining of his luminous wake." In the same month, the Rev. Cyrus Bartol took to his pulpit yet again to commemorate another of Holmes' former comrades, his cousin Charles Russell Lowell, Jr., who had died at the Battle of Cedar Creek in October. "Blood, shed in testimony to any truth or principle," he preached, "is the chief riches of mankind." And what "do we contract for with this blood?" he asked. "I said for our life," he declared, "I add, for our Union."[28]

And just as Bartol utilized the language of the law to sanctify the sacrifices made in the nation's name, so Holmes used the language of the war to sanctify legal study. The law, as Holmes described it, offered its practitioners a "masculine diet," calling for almost as much, possibly more bravery than the battlefield. In Holmes' version, what Theodore Roosevelt would later famously term the "strenuous life" could as readily consist in a scholarly one as any other. A "man may live greatly in the law as anywhere else," Holmes asserted, and "there as elsewhere he may wreak himself upon life, may drink the bitter cup of heroism, may wear his heart out after the unattainable." But there was a cost. "No man has earned the right to intellectual ambition," Holmes warned, "until he has learned to lay his course by a star which he has never seen,—to dig by the divining rod for springs which he may never reach. In saying this," he advised an undergraduate audience at Harvard in 1886, "I point to that which will make your study heroic. For I say to you in all sadness of conviction, that to think great thoughts you must be heroes as well as idealists."[29]

And Holmes had been, above all, an idealist. But the world that had housed his ideals had changed dramatically when Lincoln was assassinated in April. In July of 1865, Holmes had attended Harvard's Commemoration Day, an occasion that combined relief at the ending of the war with overly ostentatious outpourings of grief at its cost. It was, as the New York *Tribune* described it, "the largest gathering of the Alumni ever known in the annals of the College," brought together "to twine the wreaths of oratory and song around the brows of the surviving heroes, to sing dirges and pronounce eulogies upon the illustrious dead." The paper's language echoed what Holmes' own had been in its invocation of "chivalric knights" and "departed heroes," but possibly the memories conjured up by the "wreaths of oratory" had become just a little too tangled by that point for him.[30]

The day was filled with, for Holmes, familiar faces. Emerson spoke. Frank Bartlett tried to, but could not. Holmes' father spoke. And Dr. Holmes' poem "Union and Liberty," set to music, was sung afterwards. It was also the occasion of the delivery of James Russell Lowell's famous, twelve-stanza "Ode," praised by some at the time as "full of spirit and pathos," and damned by others since as a piece of "dated doggerel" that "must have been only slightly less painful than battle itself" for its audience to endure. Overtly nationalist in its invocation of the "new imperial race" to have emerged from the war, and probably not to everyone's taste even in 1865, it is impossible to assess what impact, if any, it had on Holmes; save to note that its language, like that of the New York *Tribune*, like that of Holmes himself before the war, would creep back in to Holmes' rhetoric decades later, when the memory of the Civil War was not so raw, when its meaning had changed. In 1865, however, Holmes wanted to move forward, away from the past, from the war, and from the college.[31]

Holmes' actions were not precipitate, however. Leaving law school before completing the course of instruction was quite a normal step for law students at the time, and in no sense jeopardized Holmes' degree, which he received in the summer of 1866 just before he left for Europe. On his return from his adventures in the Alps, he left Morse's offices to take up a post at the firm of Chandler, Shattuck, and Thayer, and his legal work began in earnest. To George O. Shattuck, Holmes was later to acknowledge, he owed "more than I have ever owed any one else in the world, outside my immediate family."[32]

Possibly not the least of the reasons for Holmes' admiration for a man who had done so much to launch his career was the fact that, as Holmes later recalled, Shattuck's "great vitality found only a partial outlet and expression in the law." Holmes, in 1866, was still determined to combine the scholarly and legal life. To this end, the following year when he was admitted to the Massachusetts Bar, he began contributing book reviews, and later writing summaries of the decisions of state courts for the *American Law Review*. Founded by two of his legal colleagues, John Gray and the military historian and lawyer John Ropes, whose brother, Henry, had fought with Holmes in the Twentieth Massachusetts, the *Review* was designed to contribute to what was, at the time, a relatively limited range of professional literature. Holmes' work for the *Review* was exhausting, but it offered him the opportunity of delving deeply and widely into the many facets of his chosen profession. Only a few years later, in 1872, the year in which Holmes also got married, he became its editor.[33]

Holmes' career was taking off. And outside the law he had also made new friends in the form of William and Henry James, recently moved to Boston, friends who shared his interests and his intellectual curiosity. Like Holmes, William James was uncertain about his future prospects. He was studying medicine, but had toyed with the idea of becoming an artist. He was equally invigorated by the philosophical and scientific questions of the

age and, like Holmes, sought some sense of intellectual security in a changing world, some system that would, as he put it, "evolve cosmos out of
chaos."[34]

With such similarity of outlook, it was perhaps inevitable that William
and Wendell would develop an intense, if brief, friendship. Indeed, if the
Civil War stands as the central psychological experience in the development of Holmes' later judicial and personal philosophy, the intellectual
influence of William James often runs a close second. Their friendship was
an extremely convoluted one, couched within the context of the complex,
not to say rarefied religious, moral, and philosophical universe inhabited by
the nineteenth-century's educated elite. And Holmes, raised as he was in the
intensely combative intellectual atmosphere that Dr. Holmes' household
afforded, was primed almost from birth to confront, head on, some of the
most contentious and challenging social, philosophical, and scientific questions of his age. These questions, of course, had already been "in the air"
while he was still an undergraduate at Harvard.[35]

While it lasted, the relationship between Holmes and James was undoubtedly a mutually supportive one. And the letters they exchanged whilst James
was abroad over the summer of 1865 and again two years later foreshadowed
much of Holmes' style. Yet although they spent many hours in discussion
when together, when apart Holmes hesitated to set his thoughts down on
paper. "Writing is so unnatural to me," he told James, that "I have never
before dared to try it to you unless in connection with a subject." As far as
the serious metaphysics went, the effort was largely all on James' side. Holmes
could get to the point, and often, as James acknowledged, it was as pertinent
as it was pithy, but there had to be a point; shared soul-searching was not
really in Holmes' repertoire. "In spite of my many friends," Holmes admitted to James, "I am almost alone in my thoughts and feelings." And although
he assured James that he could "never fail to derive a secret comfort and
companionship from the thought of you," and would "always respect and
love you whether we see much or little of each other," with Holmes there
always was a sense of distance. Ultimately the friendship floundered in the
resultant gap.[36]

Part of the difficulty was Holmes' growing commitment to the law.
Although happy to discuss the idea that "all experience to be thought must
be thought through concepts," Holmes' own experiential range was narrowing, perceptibly so, to the point where the concepts he thought about were
largely all "law—law—law . . . and nothing but law." And with the best will
in the world, there was a limit to how much James wanted to hear about
that. Holmes did try to defend himself to his friend. If "a man chooses a
profession he cannot forever content himself in picking out the plums with
fastidious dilettantism and give the rest of the loaf to the poor," he explained.

Holmes clearly felt defensive on the whole subject; he sensed James' disapproval. "Such has been my cowardice that I have been almost glad that you weren't here," he wrote, "lest you should be disgusted to find me inaccessible to ideas and impressions of more spiritual significance but alien to my studies." Holmes was hopeful that James would not "turn away from one in whom you discerned the possibility of friendship because his vigils were at a different shrine."[37]

But Holmes was wrong. That was precisely what James did. Largely he did so out of his own sense of isolation whilst abroad, his hankering after the "ghosts of the past," but especially "the tall and lanky one of Charles Street . . . I should like to have you opposite me in any mood," James wrote Holmes at the start of 1868, "whether the facetiously excursive, the metaphysically discursive, the personally confidential, or the jadedly cursive and argumentative . . . I feel as if a talk with you of any kind could not fail to set me on my legs again for three weeks at least." By the end of that year, his views had shifted. He confided to another friend his dismay that Holmes "should be getting more and more absorbed in legal business and studies whereby the sympathies we have in common are growing very narrowed."[38]

In the end, James' betrayal of Holmes went even further than disappointment or disapproval; it slipped into dismissal. "The more I live in the world," William observed to his brother Henry, "the more cold-blooded, conscious egotism and conceit of people afflict me . . . All the noble qualities of Wendell Holmes, for instance, are poisoned by them," James charged, and "the good he has done me is more in presenting me something to kick away from or react against than to follow and embrace."[39] And this was a dismissal in which James' family became complicit. Although Holmes was a regular visitor to the James' household, increasingly the Jameses found him bemusing and their response could be patronizing.

Holmes had, at the start of his career, been commissioned to revise Chancellor James Kent's *Commentaries on American Law*, a standard text but one that, by the 1860s, was in need of updating. He became slightly paranoid about the task, it is true, but in the days before computer backups, possibly not unreasonably so. History is, after all, littered with accounts of missing manuscripts, abandoned on trains, destroyed by fire, or otherwise misplaced by their frantic or forgetful authors. The James family, however, simply could not understand why Holmes carted his manuscript of the *Commentaries* about everywhere he went. Writing to Henry, Mrs. James observed, critically if not unkindly, that Holmes was "life, body and soul . . . absorbed in his *last* work upon his Kent. He carries about his manuscript in his green bag and never loses sight of it for a moment," she reported. He even took it to the bathroom with him, which Mrs. James, not entirely irrationally, found rather odd. "His pallid face, and this fearful grip upon his work," she observed, "makes him a melancholy sight."[40]

The date of Mrs. James' missive, 1873, suggests, however, that she rather rushed to judgment. It was not the first time she had commented on Holmes' "egotism" and her letters doubtless simply reflected the conversational slant in the James family when the topic of Holmes came up. In 1873, however, Kent was hardly the sole source of Holmes' melancholy. George Shattuck was leaving his firm. He and Holmes would soon join forces in a new one, but it was nevertheless an unsettled time. Holmes' wife, Fanny, whom he had married the previous year, had been seriously ill for many months, and was only just recovering her health sufficiently to help with the proofs of her husband's work. The fact that the *Commentaries* were by that point almost at the printing stage, combined with Fanny's protracted illness, and Holmes recently taking on the editorship of the *American Law Review* may well explain his apparently distracted air. Both his work and wife were taking their emotional toll. And this was a man, after all, who had only a few years before seen many of his friends perish. When his new bride fell ill within weeks of their marriage, it may be no surprise that Holmes held on, so very tightly, to what was at that time possibly the only secure point in his life. But the James family was famously unforgiving: famously because its combined judgment contributed to the image of Holmes as a man driven almost beyond reason by his ambition.[41]

Holmes undoubtedly was ambitious and sought professional recognition. But William James was uncharitable in his description of Holmes as "a powerful battery, formed like a planing machine to gouge a deep self-beneficial groove through life." James' ultimate critique of Holmes, of course, lay in his accusation that Holmes was in some senses an incomplete man, "composed of at least two and a half different people rolled into one." From James' perspective, this was doubtless true. Holmes was two people: the man he really was, and the man that James wanted him to be. To a great extent, that duality has defined contemporary assessments of Holmes. But it may have derived from the one thing that James did not want Holmes to be, and that was Fanny's husband. James had long admired Fanny Dixwell, and had made overtures in her direction when Holmes was in Europe in 1866. A decade later, and several years after Holmes and Fanny were married, James spent a holiday with them, and admitted to Henry that he had fallen "quite in love with she." This was disingenuous. He had been smitten since the summer of 1865.[42]

Holmes and James had more in common than love for the same woman, of course. Like Holmes, James set himself a reading regime that he struggled to sustain. The books "weigh on me like a haystack," he complained. "I loathe the thought of them; and yet they have poisoned my slave of a conscience so that I can't enjoy anything else. I have reached an age," he admitted, "when practical work of some kind clamors to be done."[43] Holmes, too, struggled with his own expectations but, unlike James at this stage, he believed that the law was the system within which he could organize his thoughts and his life. He may have been aware that there would be a cost, even at the start. But in later life he still argued that the choice he made had been, for him, no choice at all. As he wrote to Harold Laski some fifty years later:

> It is a comment on man when he absorbs himself in a system or an atmosphere Catholicism Hegel Spiritualism it doesn't matter what, he soon loses all relation to outside standards, and becomes a satellite of the sun around which the system turns. I don't see how we can help smiling at ourselves so arbitrary, irrational and despotically given are our ultimates. I feel as if I were wasting my patrimony when I am not producing articulate words and merely receiving impressions that lose their form when I turn my back. An artist would feel just the opposite each yielding to a compulsion of nature as he yields to the outside world, and having no better justification than that he desires to live. Why? Why do I desire to win my game of solitaire? A foolish question, to which the only answer is that you are up against it. Accept the inevitable and do your damnedest.[44]

Holmes had found his purpose, and his path, even if James believed it was a narrow one. "I don't expect anything from you," James told him, although clearly he did. "I suppose you are sinking ever deeper into the sloughs of the law," he complained, "yet I ween [think about] the Eternal Mystery still from time to time gives her goad another turn in the raw she once established between your ribs. Don't," he urged Holmes "let it heal over yet." James proposed the formation of a "philosophical society" on his return to Boston, one devoted to the discussion of "the very tallest and broadest questions," and "composed of none but the very topmost cream of Boston manhood." Such a society, he believed, "may grow into something important after a sufficient number of years."[45]

★★★

Such a society, comprising, among others, Holmes, James, and philosopher and mathematician Chauncey Wright, and subsequently dubbed "The Metaphysical Club," was formed, and disbanded, in 1872. Although short-lived, its influence on Holmes has often been cited as significant, particularly in the development of his jurisprudential theory. Yet it was hardly the only opportunity Holmes had to hone his ideas. The Metaphysical Club, in some respects, had only ever been an offshoot of an earlier club, founded in 1868 and modeled on the Saturday Club begun a decade earlier and still going strong; both Dr. Holmes and William James' father were regular attendees. Their philosophical progeny, the next generation of clubbable conversationalists, included Holmes, John Ropes, Henry Adams, author William Dean Howells, and literary critic Thomas Sergeant Perry. All were intellectual heavyweights in hindsight, but mostly still young men at the time: ambitious young men who believed, with Adams, and indeed with youth in general, that their generation was uniquely challenged, and that to navigate the post-Civil War world it "needed something quite new."[46]

It may well have been the case that, as author Herman Melville put it in his novel, *Redburn*, "the thing that had guided the father could not guide the son." But in Holmes' life there was a paternal pattern of sorts that he followed in its iconoclastic imperative. Dr. Holmes' generation had struggled against its Calvinist constraints, and the battle was largely won by the time Wendell reached maturity, even if echoes of the Puritan past remained in his personality. Wendell's generation did have Charles Darwin to contend with, but it is important not to over-emphasize the significance of this. *On the Origin of Species* (1859) did not turn the world upside down overnight. And it did not inculcate in Holmes a robust Reform Darwinism that informed his decisions and dissents on the Supreme Court.[47]

Holmes later admitted to having read neither Darwin nor the equally influential philosopher Herbert Spencer's writings on society, psychology, and evolution that had, he commented, promised "to put the universe into our pockets," whilst an undergraduate. But he was doubtless familiar with the arguments. His famous refusal to read newspapers did not mean that he was isolated from current events. There were a great many things "in the air" in the 1870s and 1880s, many of which were given a thorough airing at the intense intellectual gatherings Holmes attended, even if his professional duties permitted him to do so only sporadically. But to attempt to differentiate decisively between the various philosophical permutations pursued in the course of these discussions may be a fruitless task. In working toward what would become *The Common Law*, and developing his mature legal philosophy, Holmes extracted from the whole what resonated most closely with his own ideas. Many of these predated his involvement with Chauncey Wright or even James.[48]

Holmes' philosophical outlook, in effect, evolved along the same lines and in the same direction as the society that had produced him. In many respects, too, it was located less on the level of elite intellectual debate but rather more prosaically grounded in the process of post-war professionalization, and not just as that affected the law. The search for the symbiosis between the physical and the philosophical, at base, revolved around the search for the security of scientific certainties. This was, after all, the "age of railroads, telegraphs, science," but it was only in the latter part of the nineteenth century that science fully entered the equation. *On the Origin of Species* contributed to the debate, but it was not in and of itself a transitive or transformative element in it. Indeed, the remarkable thing about Darwinism was "not the conflict it inspired, but—considering its implications—the lack of conflict."

This derived from the essential "similarity between scientific and religious values" that enabled "most Americans to move fluidly from one intellectual and emotional realm to another." Both "could legitimate the needs of particular individuals to achieve and control" and both proffered the possibility of progress. Moral and scientific advances, in short, could be seen as "parallel and complementary."[49]

That, at least, was the theory. In practice, and especially in legal practice, Holmes perceived that progress was hampered by the absence of theory. This insight rather set Holmes apart from both his legal colleagues and his intellectual circle, because the many ideas "in the air" in the post-Civil War era could be as practically enervating as they were potentially exciting. Not the least of the contributions of science in the decades after the Civil War was the medicalization of whole swathes of the population, but especially the elites, via the identification of a new nervous ailment: neurasthenia, a complex complaint that could be summed up as presenting in a "paralysis of the will," leading to an "immobilizing introspection." And many of Holmes' circle seemed especially susceptible to this peculiar post-war malady, including Henry Adams, William James, and Charles Eliot Norton. But not Holmes, who rejected, to James' dismay, the tendency, as he put it later to Laski, merely to receive "impressions that lose their form when I turn my back."[50]

Holmes had reached this conclusion long before composing the series of lectures that became *The Common Law*. Although he wrote to Emerson in 1876 that he had "learned, after a laborious and somewhat painful period of probation, that the law opens a way to philosophy as well as anything else, if pursued far enough, and I hope to prove it before I die," in fact he had arrived at that point a decade before.[51] As early as the spring of 1867 he had enthused to William James that

> the winter has been a success, I think, both for the simple discipline of the work and because I now go on with an ever increasing conviction that law as well as any other series of facts in this world may be approached in the interests of science and may be studied, yes and practised, with the preservation of one's ideals. I should even say that they grew robust under the regimen, more than that I do not ask. To finish the search of mankind, to discover the ne plus ultra which is the demand of ingenuous youth, one finds is not allotted to an individual. To reconcile oneself to life to dimly apprehend that this dream disturbing the sleep of the cosm is not the result of a dyspepsy, but is well to suspect some of the divine harmonies, though you cannot note them like a score of music these things, methinks, furnish vanishing points which give a kind of perspective to the chaos of events.[52]

In the law, in effect, Holmes had identified an external outlet for the ideas that exercised, to no immediately obvious end, many of his contemporaries: where they floundered, he focused.

★★★

Holmes' determination almost paid off sooner than he had anticipated. Within the legal profession, his scholarly profile was high, partly through his editorial work for the *Law Review* and partly through Kent's *Commentaries*, the revised edition of which was well received when it came out in 1873. The opportunity, when it came, however, had almost as much to do with Holmes' war record as with his rising professional status. When in 1878 a vacancy appeared on the District Court it seemed, for a time, that Holmes might be offered a federal judgeship. Holmes described himself as "in a mild excitement" about the possibility although, as usual, he expressed ambivalence; "if I were appointed," he commented, "I should hardly know whether to be glad or sorry." For a time it looked promising. The president, Rutherford B. Hayes, was not only a lawyer himself but, more crucially, was a former general who had seen combat in the Civil War. As Holmes' colleague John Gray noted, in this respect "Holmes' wounds and sufferings in the war ought to help his chances." In the end, these were not enough to secure Holmes the judgeship, but it had clearly been a near miss, and indicative of the ongoing influence that the Civil War had in directing the post-war careers of Holmes and his contemporaries.[53]

With the chance for a judgeship gone, Holmes consoled himself, as he rationalized it, "by studying toward a vanishing point which is the center of perspective in my landscape." In other words, he returned to his intellectual interrogation of the law, his search for its "fundamental notions and principles" in essays he penned for the *Law Review* and pursued through his intensive reading regime. Less than two years later, however, his chance to pull all his scholarly work and his ideas together presented itself when he was invited by the trustees of the prestigious Lowell Institute in Boston to deliver the Lowell Lectures for 1880.[54]

Out of these lectures emerged *The Common Law*, and a thesis that revealed that, in philosophical terms, the law was for Holmes a combination of compromise in determining and classification in defining the development of what was, by the mid-nineteenth century, a confusing collection of decisions, particularly related to civil grievances, or torts, and more especially to the question of when liability might be imposed. Understanding the history of the law was the key for Holmes: that, and uncovering some of its erroneous assumptions, especially its moral ones. "The law of torts abounds in moral phraseology," he noted. "It has much to say of wrongs, of malice, fraud, intent, and negligence. Hence it may naturally be supposed," Holmes argued, "that the risk of a man's conduct is thrown upon him as the result of some moral short-coming." This was the theory. The practice, however, the "more popular opinion," and the more common ruling, was that man "acts at his peril always, and wholly irrespective of the state of his consciousness upon the matter."[55]

Holmes illustrated his argument by invoking what he termed the "average man, the man of ordinary intelligence and reasonable prudence. Liability," Holmes asserted, "is said to arise out of such conduct as would be blameworthy in him." But the focus on the act and not its outcome was a mistake, Holmes argued. This "average man" was simply "an ideal being, represented by the jury when they are appealed to, and his conduct is an external or objective standard when applied to any given individual." And this man "may be morally without stain, because he has less than ordinary intelligence or prudence; but," Holmes stressed, "he is required to have these qualities at his peril. If he has them, he will not, as a general rule, incur liability without blameworthiness." The injury, and not the impulse behind it, determined cases.[56]

In his separation of the moral theory from the practical practice, Holmes almost seemed be echoing, or at least reacting to, not just the written documents of the law but the central question posed by his father's novel, *Elsie Venner*. "It is very singular," Dr. Holmes had pointed out in that novel, "that we recognize all the bodily defects that unfit a man for military service, and all the intellectual ones that limit his range of thought, but always talk at him as if all his moral powers were perfect. I suppose." Dr. Holmes mused, "we must punish evil-doers as we extirpate vermin; but I don't know that we have any more right to judge them than we have to judge rats and mice, which are just as good as cats and weasels, though we think it necessary to treat them as criminals."[57]

The focus of Dr. Holmes' concerns, of course, was the extent and nature of pre-natal influence. But his point was, as his son surely realized, as pertinent in the legal as in the medical world; and much of it revolved around the question of self-determination, or free will. Holmes frequently asserted that his generation differed from his father's in its conception of and reaction to this particular metaphysical conundrum, but in *The Common Law* we see the continuation of a conversation probably first begun around a dinner-table in Boston in the antebellum period. "I would not give much for men's judgments of each other's character," Dr. Holmes had written. His son sought to show that the law need not try to do so.[58]

Holmes may not have been fully aware of the extent to which he was still debating what was for him and his family a very old argument. He never directly acknowledged that he was. Much later in life, he did acknowledge the intellectual debt he owed to Chauncey Wright, by then "a nearly forgotten philosopher of real merit" as Holmes described him. For Wright, whose brother had died from wounds sustained at Cold Harbor, the only certainty was uncertainty. And it was from Wright, Holmes later claimed, that he had learned not to "say *necessary* about the universe, that we don't know whether anything is necessary or not. So I describe myself as a *bet*tabilitarian." Holmes explained: "I believe that we can bet on the behaviour of the universe in its contact with us. We bet that we can know what it will be. That," he observed, "leaves a loophole for free will—in the miraculous sense—the creation of a new atom of force, although I don't in the least believe in it." When "one thinks coldly," Holmes observed, there is "no reason for attributing to man a significance different in kind from that which belongs to a baboon or to a grain of sand." In this respect, Holmes, like Wright, "took satisfaction in the notion that values are epiphenomenal—that beneath all the talk of principles and ideals, what people do is just a fancy version of what amoebas do."[59]

Logic, in short, had little to do with it. "The life of the law has not been logic," Holmes famously asserted in the opening paragraph of *The Common Law*, "it has been experience."

> The felt necessities of the time, the prevalent moral and political theories, intuitions of public policy, avowed or unconscious, even the prejudices which judges share with their fellow-men, have had a good deal more to do than the syllogism in determining the rules by which men should be governed. The law embodies the story of a nation's development through many centuries, and it cannot be dealt with as if it contained only the axioms and corollaries of a book of mathematics.[60]

What Holmes meant by "experience," in legal terms, derived both from his own recent experience and from what he believed that of the law had always been. On one level, he believed that there was no fixed, theoretical framework for legal rulings; the law meant what judges said it meant, and only having arrived at a decision did the judges in question decide on a rationale for it. Further, they did so in light of those "considerations of what is expedient for the community concerned." Rather than representing fixed and essentially immutable rules, for Holmes the law was an evolutionary, organic system: a social, context-sensitive construction. In this respect, it simply reflected life. "All acts," he argued, "taken apart from their surrounding circumstances are indifferent to the law." Crooking a finger is no crime; it is only the proximity of a loaded pistol to the finger and, further, the additional proximity of an individual "as to be manifestly likely to be hit, that make the act a wrong." At the same time, and although no weaponry need be involved, Holmes believed that a single imperative had consistently comprised the core business of the courts: revenge.[61]

"It is commonly known," Holmes asserted, "that the early forms of legal procedure were grounded in vengeance." From that premise, the law had evolved as societies became more complex to encompass the idea of liability for loss or injury, be it actively or passively effected; indeed, intent became irrelevant in Holmes' view. Although, as he put it, "even a dog distinguishes between being stumbled over and being kicked," Holmes promoted an essentially permissive perspective on the law, such that the moral intention behind the act was hardly the business of a mature legal system in the same way that, for example, railroad legislation had become the business of the post–Civil War federal government.[62]

This was not to say that Holmes perceived the law as amoral, simply that he argued that it was subjective and should, perhaps, seek to be objective. There was a moral imperative toward justice, but it was rooted in the "thought that some one was to blame." That, too, however, had evolved into the rather more nebulous notion of fairness, not as this applied to people, but to procedure. Utilizing the example of Admiralty law, he explained that the tendency to accord a ship a gender illustrated how the law operated through both a process of succession and substitution; individuals were interchangeable with other individuals, but also with inanimate objects. In a mature legal system, the inanimate became animated, the corporation became corporeal, both alike endowed with a living personality susceptible to legal process. Once one grasped all that, Holmes proposed, many of the law's apparent peculiarities made perfect sense.[63]

One might consider that, had *The Common Law* made perfect sense, either at the time or since, it would be as susceptible as it has proved to be to such a multiplicity of contradictory interpretations. Many of these revolve around Holmes' perceived lack of originality in some of his arguments. Yet Holmes was never promising originality as such. He was striving for coherence. And he would likely not have been surprised at the long-term reception of his work, nor even the criticisms of it. He was, as one biographer has argued, essentially "an evolutionary historian, deriving fundamental principles from the change of legal doctrine over time."[64]

And Holmes had, after all, made his position clear enough in *The Common Law*. "In order to know" what the law is, Holmes had argued, "we must know what it has been, and what it tends to become. We must alternately consult history and existing theories of legislation. But the most difficult labor," he warned, "will be to understand the combination of the two into new products at every stage." He reached for an example with sufficient contemporary relevance to a generation then debating Darwin to illustrate what he meant. "In form," he explained, the law's "growth is logical."

> The official theory is that each new decision follows syllogistically from existing precedents. But just as the clavicle in the cat only tells of the existence of some earlier creature to which a collar-bone was useful, precedents survive in the law long after the use they once served is at an end and the reason for them has been forgotten. The result of following them must often be failure and confusion from the merely logical point of view.[65]

At the same time, the law was not condemned simply to circumnavigate the ever-decreasing circles of past precedents, since, Holmes assured his audience, "in substance the growth of the law is legislative."

> And as the law is administered by able and experienced men, who know too much to sacrifice good sense to a syllogism, it will be found that, when ancient rules maintain themselves in the way that has been and will be shown in this book, new reasons more fitted to the time have been found for them, and they gradually receive a new content, and at last a new form, from the grounds to which they have been transplanted.

"The truth is," Holmes pointed out, "that the law is always approaching, and never reaching, consistency. It is forever adopting new principles from life at one end, and it always retains old ones from history at the other. It will become entirely consistent," he concluded, "only when it ceases to grow." He could have been writing about himself.[66]

★★★

Accepting that Holmes argued for an evolutionary perspective on the law, even if this was not the most original of insights at the time, it is important to emphasize that he, too, evolved. The law, he asserted, was of its time; but so was he. There is a natural tendency to confine debate over Holmes' views to the precedents found in legal history, to highlight, as he did, the parallels between feudal legislation designed to deal with individuals and farms and its industrial intellectual progeny devised to deal with corporations and railroads. But the wider world around him echoed what he argued. Only a decade later, the noted historian Frederick Jackson Turner proposed that each "age tries to form its own conception of the past. *Each age writes the history of the past anew with reference to the conditions uppermost in its own time.*"[67] In his evolutionary approach to the law, Holmes was fully in step with his age, even if, over the years since, he has sometimes been rejected by subsequent jurisprudential interpretation.

Holmes' emphasis on liability, or blame, in the law's development may also have carried elements of his environment at the time of the composition of *The Common Law*. Holmes lived in what was, in effect, a blame culture. The 1870s and 1880s were marked by economic uncertainty and labor unrest and massive disparities of wealth, and the early years of what became known, after the title of an 1873 social critique composed by Mark Twain and Charles Dudley Warner, "The Gilded Age." The financial panic of 1873, prompted by the collapse of Jay Cooke and Company, the nation's leading investment bank, led to a nationwide depression and a series of labor strikes, especially in the textile industry in Massachusetts and in northeastern Pennsylvania's anthracite mining region. By far the most serious labor crisis, however, occurred in 1877 when, in the wake of an announcement that railroad workers' wages would be cut, the nation's railroads ground to a halt.

The violence that erupted when federal troops attempted to break the strike shocked a nation traditionally fearful that European revolutionary ideas might cross the Atlantic. The French Revolution had introduced such concerns in the eighteenth century, and now in the late-nineteenth century the Paris Commune of 1871 revived them. 1877 was also the year in which "Reconstruction," the political and practical process of bringing the former Confederate states back into the Union, ended. The remaining federal troops who had been policing some of the more recalcitrant Southern states were pulled out, and the recently emancipated African American population was effectively abandoned. Its future was in theory secured by the Reconstruction Amendments, and by a number of civil rights laws passed between 1866 and 1875; in practice, of course, any kind of secure future was compromised by white Southern violence and a Supreme Court that eviscerated many of the newly-established rights.

It is worth stressing that the America in which Holmes composed *The Common Law* was a post-war world, dealing with the aftermath of what still remains the nation's most destructive conflict. The economic as much as the psychological repercussions persisted well into the twentieth century. But it was a world that had betrayed, in some respects, that war's legacy. During the presidency of former Union General Ulysses S. Grant, America appeared to have become a world of corruption and "machine politics," most publicly exemplified by the "Tweed Ring" in New York through which Democratic boss William M. Tweed bribed and bullied his way to power. And with slavery apparently no longer an issue, most white abolitionists moved on to business concerns or to new reform movements. Abolition's place in the reform imperative was now filled by the desire to control the capital that the war had accumulated, regulate the market, and thereby assure the uplift of the working masses recently returned from war.

The *National Republican*, founded to promote the policies of the Republican Party in 1860, was typical of conservative opposition to such "communistic ideas" that it believed were gaining ground in the United States at this time, advanced "by the workmen employed in mines and factories and by the railroads." The paper argued that these ideas were "poison," which "was introduced into our social system by European laborers." It outlined a world in which the impulse toward social equity had been replaced by one that sought instead "the regulation of morals." It may be no surprise, therefore, that Holmes cast so cynical an eye on that subject.[68]

"Man," Holmes famously argued, "is like a strawberry plant, the shoots he throws out take root and become independent centres. And one illustration of the tendency is the transformation of means into ends. A man begins a pursuit as a means of keeping alive—he ends by following it at the cost of his life. A miser is an example—but so is the man who makes righteousness his end. Morality is simply another means of living but the saints make it an end in itself."[69] In this respect, Holmes had some early experience. But as he accumulated more experience he became even more cynical about the cyclical nature of the moral perspective. As he wrote when in his eighties:

> It is amusing to see what used to strike me with the abolitionists before our war as an eternally recurring phenomenon. The abolitionists had a stock phrase that a man was either a knave or a fool who did not act as they (the abolitionists) *knew* to be right. So Calvin thought of the Catholics and the Catholics of Calvin. So I don't doubt do the more convinced prohibitionists think of their opponents today. When you know that you know persecution comes easy. It is as well that some of us don't know that we know anything.[70]

In this respect the consistency in Holmes' personal philosophy is striking; but surprisingly it strikes many scholars as cold and calculating, when it was quite the opposite.

Half a lifetime before, Holmes had tried to rationalize his thoughts in *The Common Law*. This work, so far from "a coldly passionate expression of intuitions," was his attempt to construct an intellectual, objective framework that located the law within the philosophical and scientific structures of the times, driven, to some extent, by disappointment in the post-war world in which it was conceived. By the time he came to compose *The Common Law*, the pattern of modern America was crystalizing around age-old conflicts between labor and capital, poverty and wealth, sickness and health, order and chaos. All, like the law, were susceptible of more robust analysis, as Holmes saw it, "in the interests of science," but the result was not, perhaps, entirely commensurate with "the preservation of one's ideals."[71]

By his fortieth year, for Holmes, everything had changed since the Civil War, and yet nothing had changed at all. In a sense, indeed, *The Common Law* emerged out of a professional ambition that was driven by a personal animus toward a society that had sacrificed so many of its sons and yet abandoned, in the end, the cause that had cost them their lives. It was hardly surprising that he looked for certainties in his professional world; or that, in his personal one, he was so consistently scathing of those men and women whom he had previously looked up to, whose reform imperative he had followed to war, whose ideals he had almost died for.

NOTES

1   Oliver Wendell Holmes, Jr., *The Common Law* (1881. Reprint. London: Macmillan and Company, 1882) 1.

2   Holmes to Harold J. Laski, November 22, 1917, in Mark DeWolfe Howe (ed.), *Holmes-Laski Letters: The Correspondence of Mr Justice Holmes and Harold J. Laski*, 2 Vols. (Cambridge, MA: Harvard University Press, 1953) I, 112; Holmes to parents, May 16, 1864, in Mark DeWolfe Howe (ed.), *Touched with Fire: Civil War Letters and Diary of Oliver Wendell Holmes, Jr., 1861–1864* (Cambridge, MA: Harvard University Press, 1946) 121–122.

3   G. Edward White, *Justice Oliver Wendell Holmes: Law and the Inner Self* (New York and Oxford: Oxford University Press, 1993) 88–89.

4   Max Lerner (ed.), *The Mind and Faith of Justice Holmes: His Speeches, Essays, Letters, and Judicial Opinions* (1943. Reprint. New Brunswick, NJ: Transaction Publishers, 2010) xxiv–xxv.

5   Holmes' diary entries, July 5 and 6, 1866; Holmes to Baroness Moncheur, January 9, 1915, September 15, 1914, OWH Papers, HLS; Sheldon M. Novick, *Honorable Justice: The Life of Oliver Wendell Holmes* (New York: Dell Publishing, 1990) 108–110.

6   [Henry James], "A Most Extraordinary Case," *The Atlantic Monthly*, 21:126 (April 1868) 461–485, 466. See also Sheldon M. Novick, *Henry James: The Young Master* (1996. Reprint. New York: Random House, 2007) 98–99; and on James' reaction to Holmes, Leon Edel, *Henry James: The Untried Years, 1843–1870* (Philadelphia, PA: Lippincott, 1953) 232; and John Halperin, "Henry James's Civil War," *The Henry James Review*, 17:1 (1996) 22–29, 28.

7   A.E. Housman, *More Poems*, XVI, 1936; Amelia Holmes to Holmes, June 11, 1866; Holmes to Baroness Moncheur, January 9, 1866, OWH Papers, HLS; Abbott to Holmes, November n.d., 1863, in Robert Garth Scott (ed.), *Fallen Leaves: The Civil War Letters of Major Henry Livermore Abbott* (Kent, OH: The Kent State University Press, 1991) 232.

8   White, *Law and the Inner Self*, 78.

9   Oliver Wendell Holmes, *Collected Legal Papers* (New York: Harcourt, Brace and Howe, 1920), Preface.

10 Holmes, "Autobiographical Sketch," in Frederick C. Fiechter, Jr., "The Preparation of an Aristocrat," *New England Quarterly*, 6:1 (March 1933) 3–28, 4–5; Holmes to Laski, May 18, 1919, in Howe, *Holmes-Laski Letters*, I, 205; see also Mark DeWolfe Howe, "Oliver Wendell Holmes at Harvard Law School," *Harvard Law Review*, 70:3 (January 1957) 401–421, esp. 401–402.

11 John T. Morse, *Life and Letters of Oliver Wendell Holmes*, 2 Vols. (London: Sampson Low, Marston and Company, 1896), I, 69.

12 Louis Menand, *The Metaphysical Club* (2001. Reprint. London: Harper Collins, 2002) 69; White, *Law and the Inner Self*, 10, 88–89.

13 Howe, "Holmes at Harvard Law School," 402–403.

14 Holmes to W.H. Brownell, May 9 and October 31, 1865, quoted in Howe, "Holmes at Harvard Law School," 411, 415, 417; Holmes to Morris Cohen, April 12, 1915, in Felix S. Cohen (ed.), "Holmes-Cohen Correspondence," *Journal of the History of Ideas*, 9:1 (January 1948) 3–52, 8; see also Holmes, "The Profession of the Law" (1886), in Oliver Wendell Holmes, *Speeches* (Boston: Little, Brown, and Company, 1896) 22.

15 William James to Thomas Ward, December 16, 1868, in Ralph Barton Perry, *The Thought and Character of William James*, 2 Vols. (London: Oxford University Press, 1935) I, 290; White, *Law and the Inner Self*, 91.

16 Holmes, "The Profession of the Law," 24.

17 Theophilus Parsons, *The Law of Contracts*, Third Edition, 2 Vols. (Boston: Little, Brown and Company, 1857) I, 3.

18 Howe, "Holmes at Harvard Law School," 404; Liva Baker, *The Justice from Beacon Hill: The Life and Times of Oliver Wendell Holmes* (New York: Harper Collins, 1991) 167–168; Bowen, *Yankee from Olympus*, 204, 215; Holmes, "The Use of Law Schools," in Holmes, *Speeches*, 34; Henry James, *Notes of a Son and Brother* (London: Macmillan and Co., 1914) 324; Holmes, *op. cit.*, 35, 29.

19 Timothy Walker, *Introduction to American Law*, Second Edition (Cincinnati, OH: Derby, Bradley and Co., 1846) 19, 18.

20 John Quincy Adams, *Argument . . . Before the Supreme Court of the United States in the Case of the United States, Appellants, vs. Cinque, and Others, Africans, Captured in the Schooner* Amistad . . . (New York: S.W. Benedict, 1841) 89.

21 Heather Cox Richardson, *The Greatest Nation of the Earth: Republican Economic Policies during the Civil War* (Cambridge, MA: Harvard University Press, 1997) 5; Leonard P. Curry, *Blueprint for Modern America: Nonmilitary Legislation of the First Civil War Congress* (Nashville, TN: Vanderbilt University Press, 1968) 8.

22 Novick, *Honorable Justice*, 97; Liva Baker, *The Justice from Beacon Hill: The Life and Times of Oliver Wendell Holmes* (New York: Harper Collins, 1991) 203.

23 Grant Gilmore, *The Ages of American Law* (New Haven, CT: Yale University Press, 1977) 41–42, 65–66.

24 Bruce Ackerman, *We, The People*, Vol. 1, *Foundations* (1991. Reprint. Cambridge, MA: Harvard University Press, 1993) 42–43; Gilmore, *Ages of American Law*, 63; Lerner (ed.), *The Mind and Faith of Justice Holmes*, xxv; Novick, *Honorable Justice*, 97.

25 James Bryce, *The American Commonwealth*, New Edition, 2 Vols. (New York: The Macmillan Company, 1922) I, 385; Novick, *Honorable Justice*, 97; Holmes, "The Use of Law Schools," in Holmes, *Speeches*, 40–41.

26 Holmes to Morris Cohen, April 12, 1915, "Holmes-Cohen Correspondence," 8; Novick, *Honorable Justice*, 160.

27 White, *Law and the Inner Self*, 88.

28 Bowen, *Yankee from Olympus*, 208; C.A. Bartol, *The Remission by Blood: A Tribute to Our Soldiers and the Sword* (Boston: Walker, Wise and Co., 1862); C.A. Bartol, *The Purchase by Blood: A Tribute to Brig-Gen. Charles Russell Lowell, Jr.* (Boston: John Wilson and Son, 1864) 3, 6.

29 Holmes, "The Use of Law Schools," 29; Bowen, *Yankee from Olympus*, 206; Oliver Wendell Holmes, Jr., "The Profession of the Law" (1886), in Oliver Wendell Holmes, *Speeches* (Boston: Little, Brown, and Company, 1896) 23–24.

30 New York *Daily Tribune*, July 24, 1865, quoted in Hamilton Vaughan Ball, "Harvard's Commemoration Day July 21, 1865," *The New England Quarterly*, 15:2 (June 1942) 256–279, 262.

31 Novick, *Honorable Justice*, 101–102; Mrs. William Wetmore Story quoted in Ball, "Harvard's Commemoration Day," 277; Richard Marius (ed.), *The Colombia Book of Civil War Poetry* (New York: Columbia University Press, 1994) 372; see also Edmund Wilson, *Patriotic Gore: Studies in the Literature of the American Civil War* (1962. Reprint. London: The Hogarth Press, 1987) 474–476.

32 Holmes, "George Otis Shattuck," in Mark DeWolfe Howe (ed.), *Oliver Wendell Holmes: Occasional Speeches* (Cambridge, MA: The Belknap Press of Harvard University Press, 1962) 92–96, 92.

33 Holmes, "George Otis Shattuck," ibid., 94; Novick, *Honorable Justice*, 119.

34 James quoted in Perry, *The Thought and Character of William James*, I, 504.

35 Holmes to Morris Cohen, February 5, 1919, "Holmes-Cohen Correspondence," 14–15; Perry, *The Thought and Character of William James*, I, 474–175, 504.

36 Holmes to William James, December 15, 1867, in Perry, *The Thought and Character of William James*, 505.

37 Holmes to William James, December 15, 1867, April 19, 1868, in Perry, *The Thought and Character of William James*, I, 505, 509–510.

38 James to Holmes, January 3, 1868; James to Thomas Ward, December 16, 1868, both in Perry, *The Thought and Character of William James*, I, 507–508, 289–290.

39 James to Henry James, October 2, 1869, in Perry, *The Thought and Character of William James*, I, 307.

40 Perry, *The Thought and Character of William James*, I, 519; Novick, *Honorable Justice*, 120–121.

41 See the extract from letter in Novick, *Honorable Justice*, 118; and on this generally 103, 133–134, 136–138; White, *Law and the Inner Self*, 89.

42 William to Henry James, July 5, 1876, in Perry, *The Thought and Character of William James*, I, 371; see also White, *Law and the Inner Self*, 89; and Albert W. Alschuler, *Law without Values: The Life, Work, and Legacy of Justice Holmes* (Chicago and London: University of Chicago Press, 2000) 15.

43 James to Holmes, January 3, 1868, in Perry, *The Thought and Character of William James*, I, 508.

44 Holmes to Laski, July 1, 1927, in Mark DeWolfe Howe (ed.), *Holmes-Laski Letters: The Correspondence of Mr Justice Holmes and Harold J. Laski*, 2 Vols. (Cambridge, MA: Harvard University Press, 1953) II, 958.

45 James to Holmes, January 3, 1868, in Perry, *The Thought and Character of William James*, I, 508.

46 Louis Menand, *The Metaphysical Club* (New York: Flamingo, 2002) 201; Gilmore, *Ages of American Law*, 50–51; Henry Adams, *The Education of Henry Adams*, ed. Ernest Samuels (Boston: Houghton Mifflin Company, 1973) 26.

47 Herman Melville, *Redburn: His First Voyage* (1849. Reprint. London: Penguin Books, 1986) 224; Wilson, *Patriotic Gore*, 745.

48 Holmes to Morris Cohen, February 5, 1919, "Holmes-Cohen Correspondence," 14–15.

49 Novick, *Honorable Justice*, 116; Charles E. Rosenberg, *No Other Gods: On Science and American Social Thought* (Baltimore, MD and London: The Johns Hopkins University Press, 1976) 2–3.

50 Jackson Lears, *No Place of Grace: Antimodernism and the Transformation of American Culture, 1880–1920* (New York: Pantheon Books, 1981) 50; Menand, *Metaphysical Club*, 217–219; on this subject see also Barbara Sicherman, "The Paradox of Prudence: Mental Health in the Gilded Age," *The Journal of American History*, 62:4 (March 1976) 890–912; and Tom Lutz, *American Nervousness, 1903: An Anecdotal History* (New York: Cornell University Press, 1991); Holmes to Laski, July 1, 1927, in Howe, *Holmes-Laski Letters*, II, 958.

51 Holmes to Emerson, April 16, 1876, quoted in Howe, "Holmes at Harvard Law School," 417.

52 Holmes to William James, December 15, 1867, in Perry, *The Thought and Character of William James*, 505.

53 Baker, *Justice from Beacon Hill*, 211; Gray quoted in White, *Law and the Inner Self*, 110; Holmes to Frederick Pollock, December 9, 1878, in Mark DeWolfe Howe (ed.), *Holmes-Pollock Letters: The Correspondence of Mr. Justice Holmes and Sir Frederick Pollock, 1874–1932*, Second Edition: Two Volumes in One (Cambridge, MA: The Belknap Press of Harvard University Press, 1961) I, 10–11.

54 Holmes to James Bryce, August 17, 1879, quoted in White, *Law and the Inner Self*, 129–130.

55 Holmes, *The Common Law*, 79–80.

56 Holmes, *Common Law*, 51.

57 Oliver Wendell Holmes, *Elsie Venner: A Romance of Destiny* (New York: Grosset and Dunlap, 1861) 167–168.

58 Holmes, *Elsie Venner*, 168.

59 Holmes to Frederick Pollock, August 30, 1929, in Howe, *Holmes-Pollock Letters*, II, 252; Menand, *Metaphysical Club*, 217.

60 Holmes, *Common Law*, 1.

61 Holmes, *Common Law*, 2–3, 35, 54; Menand, *Metaphysical Club*, 342–343; Novick, *Honorable Justice*, 149–150.

62 Holmes, *Common Law*, 3, 37.

63 Holmes, *Common Law*, 37, 26–27; Gilmore, *Ages of American Law*, 54; Novick, *Honorable Justice*, 158–159.

64 White, *Law and the Inner Self*, 129; Alschuler, *Law without Values*, 84–95.

65 Holmes, *Common Law*, 1–2, 35.

66 Holmes, *Common Law*, 36.

67 Frederick Jackson Turner, "The Significance of History" (1891), in Frederick Jackson Turner, *The Early Writings of Frederick Jackson Turner . . . with an Introduction by Fulmer Mood* (Madison, WI: The University of Wisconsin Press, 1938) 52.

68 Michael C.C. Adams, *Living Hell: The Dark Side of the Civil War* (Baltimore, MD: Johns Hopkins University Press, 2014) 181; *National Republican*, July 21, 1877; Nell Irvin Painter, *Standing at Armageddon: The United States, 1877–1919* (1987. Reprint. New York and London: W.W. Norton and Company, 1989) 1, 14–24.

69 Holmes to Morris Cohen, September 6, 1920, in "Holmes-Cohen Correspondence," 23–24.

70 Holmes to Pollock, August 30, 1929, in Howe, *Holmes-Pollock Letters*, II, 252–253.

71 Novick, *Honorable Justice*, 160; Holmes to William James, December 15, 1867, in Perry, *The Thought and Character of William James*, 505.

CHAPTER 4

A SOLDIER'S FAITH

"From the beginning, to us, children of the North, life has seemed a place hung about by dark mists, out of which comes the pale shine of dragon's scales and the cry of fighting men, and the sound of swords."
(Oliver Wendell Holmes, Jr., "Memorial Day Address, May 30, 1895.")[1]

In the years leading up to the publication of *The Common Law*, Holmes positioned himself, but in many ways had also been positioned by his peers, in the vanguard of the modernization not just of the legal profession but of the nation. Over the two decades since taking up the study of the law he had been student, scholar, working lawyer, editor, and, briefly, tutor in constitutional law and then University Lecturer in Jurisprudence at Harvard. Charles William Eliot, Harvard's president, saw Holmes as an ally in his plan to radically reform the college. Not surprisingly, Holmes saw himself, and was seen by others, as part of the forward march of progress in matters professional as much as philosophical.[2]

Yet in the immediate aftermath of the publication of *The Common Law*, Holmes experienced the emotional deflation common to all authors when a manuscript is finally done and dusted but the world, oddly, remains oblivious. He sent a copy to his friend, the English barrister Sir Frederick Pollock whom he had first met on a visit to England in 1874. Pollock had published his own legal study, *Principles of Contract*, only a few years before, and the appearance of the first American edition—a "hideous American reprint" as Holmes described it—of this coincided with the publication of *The Common Law*. "I have failed in all correspondence and have abandoned pleasure as well as a good deal of sleep for a year," Holmes wrote, "to accomplish a result which I now send you by mail." He was justifiably proud of a book that had cost so much effort, written in the small hours after the working day was over, as he described his punishing schedule. A touch of self-pity crept in here. "You are happy in being able to afford time to philosophy," Holmes lectured his admittedly more financially-secure friend, whereas "I have to make my living by my profession." But the self-pity swiftly reshaped itself into a more typical refrain. "I sometimes think," Holmes observed, "that there is a certain advantage in difficulties, and that one sails better with the wind on the quarter than when it is directly astern."[3]

As a man who had sailed since his youth, Holmes knew full well that control of a vessel is better sustained with the wind "on the quarter," but initially it seemed as if he had charted his course into a silent sea. *The Common Law* was published in early March, 1881; by May, only two reviews had appeared. Holmes had prompted Pollock for a positive reaction. "I hope you will read my book," he urged. "It cost me many hours of sleep and the only reward which I have promised myself is that a few men will say well done." He purported to worry that people might not "realize that the work is at least a serious one," although he can hardly have honestly believed that some might mistake it for anything else. Pollock took the hint, and delivered; indeed he delivered not just a glowing review in the *Saturday Review*, but discussed *The Common Law* in his new introduction to the third edition of *Principles of Contract*.[4]

The Common Law, Pollock wrote, offered "a searching and analytical criticism of several of the leading notions of English law; not," he stressed, "an antiquarian discussion first and a theoretical discussion afterwards but a continuous study in the joint light of policy and history." It will, he concluded, "be a most valuable—we should almost say indispensable—companion to the scientific study of legal history." And Pollock's praise was echoed by others, not least those who were in a position to advance Holmes' career, both back in Harvard and beyond.[5]

Harvard got to Holmes first. In the fall of 1881, Charles Eliot offered Holmes a permanent position, a professorship, on the law school faculty. Holmes accepted, on the understanding that he might focus his teaching on jurisprudence, or at least be allowed to concentrate on "such investigations as are embodied in my book on the Common Law," that his salary might go up as soon as possible, and that "if a judgeship should be offered me I should not wish to feel bound in honor not to consider it." In short, Holmes was every university administrator's worst nightmare: he wanted to teach what he liked, be paid as much as the institution could stand, and if a better offer came along, he wanted to be in a position to take it.[6]

In fact the money proved to be the main issue, and it was only after some considerable effort on the part of Harvard faculty that sufficient funds to endow Holmes' professorship were secured. In light of said efforts, it was more than usually galling to all concerned, but not to Holmes, of course, that only months later a better offer did come along; and Holmes, having just begun his teaching duties, promptly took it. By the end of 1882, and following the resignation of Justice Otis Lord, Holmes had been offered, and instantly accepted, the position of Associate Justice on the Supreme Judicial Court of Massachusetts.

The rapidity of his nomination, acceptance, and confirmation was not, however, of Holmes' making; he was given only hours in which to reach his decision. Nevertheless, his colleagues were aggrieved, both at the decision itself and the fact that they learned of it second-hand, through the news- papers, indeed, rather than from Holmes himself. It seemed to some that Holmes was, as William James had described him, "cold-blooded," egotistic, and conceited, careless of the feelings of others, and devoted solely to his own advancement. But this was a man who had already put his life on the line for others. Compared to that, possibly Holmes felt that leaving some faculty colleagues in the lurch at the start of an academic year really did not compare.[7]

He never said so, of course. What he did say was sometimes contradictory, but fully in line with how he saw legal rulings: he made his decision, and having made it, looked for reasons to support it. That he felt he needed to justify himself at all is evidence that he remained aware, for the rest of his life, that his actions in 1882 were perceived as unduly precipitate by some, fully understandable by others, but not necessarily his finest hour by anyone: except, of course, those closest to him. Perhaps fortunately, he did not offer his academic colleagues the explanation for his actions at the time that he later came up with.

"The place for a man who is complete in all his powers," Holmes advised the New York Bar Association in 1899, "is in the fight." That year Holmes had been made Chief Justice of the Massachusetts Court, to his father's delight. "To *think* of it,—my little boy a Judge," Dr. Holmes exulted, "and able to send me to jail if I don't behave myself." Yet perhaps even Dr. Holmes might have smarted at his son's assertion that the "professor, the man of let- ters, gives up on half of life that his protected talent may grow and flower in peace." He reiterated the point later to his legal colleague Felix Frankfurter: "academic life is but half life," he observed, "it is withdrawal from the fight in order to utter smart things that cost you nothing except the thinking of them from a cloister." By contrast, he believed, business "in the world is unhappy, often seems mean, and always challenges your power to idealize the brute fact—but it hardens the fibre and I think is more likely to make a man of one who turns it to success."[8]

Leaving aside the high probability that Holmes might not have found the academic and business worlds as far apart as all that had he been better able to compare them, the implication was clear: he had chosen what he believed was the more manly course of action. Whether this was related to his actions in the Civil War and his belief that, in selecting not to reenlist in 1864, he had somehow betrayed "the soldier's faith" may be more of a moot point. Indeed the biographical significance accorded the process of Holmes' elevation to a judgeship in 1882, his achievement of an ambition shared by many lawyers, has possibly lent the subject an importance that it may not have had to Holmes at the time. And after all that fuss, Holmes' twenty years on the Supreme Judicial Court of Massachusetts is often summarily dismissed, or at least swiftly dealt with as little more than a staging post before he ascended to the Supreme Court. If those years are recognized as significant, indeed, it is sometimes for all the wrong reasons.[9]

"If Holmes's tenure on the Massachusetts Court from 1882 to 1902 is one of the least-known periods of his life," the journalist Max Lerner once argued, "it was also one of the most important," not for what Holmes was doing, *per se*, but for the bigger picture of what was happening across the nation. As Lerner described it, "these were years of industrial development, political turmoil, cultural crudeness . . . during which business enterprise crystallized into a structure of corporate monopoly." It was the era that witnessed the rise of the "robber barons," the "consolidation of capitalist power," and the dominance of "materialist values." This was, and remains, of course, a fairly traditional popular summation of the sins of the "Gilded Age." It is factually accurate in most respects, if somewhat elitist in its charge of "cultural crudeness" and rather naïve in its assumption that materialist values were the invention of the latter part of the nineteenth-century and had not also underpinned earlier eras, most notably with regard to slavery.[10]

With Holmes as its focus, however, this representation of the "Gilded Age" too readily becomes little more than a carefully constructed backdrop, a scholarly stage setting for the drama of the Supreme Court Justice who would take arms against this particular sea of national troubles and seek to end them. But, with a view to the drama about to unfold, in directing the gaze to the clichéd characters of corporate power it not only obscures the wider cultural context within which Holmes was operating but misrepresents Holmes' particular role in the processes of modernization in the United States in the last decades of the nineteenth century and the first decades of the twentieth. For Holmes as much as for his nation, modernization and maturation consisted in a combination of continuity and change. To understand Holmes in this period one has to follow the lines of his argument in *The Common Law*; one has to consider what he was, and what his contemporaries thought he was before one can assess what he became.

★★★

Despite Harvard's unhappiness with his decision to leave academia behind in 1882, for Holmes it clearly was the right move. "Since my appointment

I have been sitting in banc and writing opinions all the time," he advised Pollock after only a few months in his new role. "Next month I hold equity alone and the next (May) sit in divorce causes. I enjoy the work so far extremely." The seriousness of his profession did not prevent Holmes from, at times, sounding rather like a child in a toy shop. But there was more to his sense of accomplishment than the work alone. Describing to Pollock the process of detinue (recovery of property) in Massachusetts, Holmes admitted that "it rather pleases me to remember that one of the most learned and best books on the subject was written by my grandfather." Familial as much as personal pride factored in to his satisfaction with his judgeship, but mainly it was the work itself that enthused him, "far more than I dreamed beforehand," as he told Pollock. "The experience is most varied—very different from that one gets at the bar—and I am satisfied most valuable for an all round view of the law," he declared.[11]

As was evident, Holmes still looked to the law to satisfy his philosophical interests, and to this end he still maintained a fairly robust reading regime. For a man who, critics claim, was so detached from human sympathies, Holmes was unusually engaged by and interested in "human nature" in all its infinite variety as he encountered it as a judge, which is not to say that he was necessarily sympathetic to all of it. Perhaps inevitably, Holmes sought to test out his arguments in *The Common Law* on actual cases, and did so, sometimes to the detriment of the defendant concerned. In *The Common Law*, Holmes had argued against subjective, moral assessments of motive in favor of objective, external standards of behavior, "independent of the degree of evil in the particular person's motives or intentions." His was, in effect, essentially a consequentialist perspective. The law, he argued, should also "take no account of incapacities, unless the weakness is so marked as to fall into well-known exceptions, such as infancy or madness."[12]

Early in his judgeship, a case arose that tested this: *Commonwealth v. Pierce* (1884). The defendant, Franklin Pierce, was a doctor whose treatment had caused the death of his patient, Ms. Bemis. The question Holmes posed in this case was "whether an actual good intent and the expectation of good results are an absolute justification of acts, however foolhardy they may be if judged by an external standard." And the answer he and the court arrived at was that the road to hell, or at least to guilt, is paved with good intentions. Although clearly innocent of malicious intent, and unaware that his treatment would result in death, the doctor was found guilty of manslaughter. For Holmes this was a success; as he had observed to Pollock whilst deliberations on the case were ongoing, if "my opinion goes through it will do much to confirm some theories of my book."[13]

Hindsight tends to dismiss Holmes' work on the Massachusetts Court at that time, as indeed Holmes once did, as "trifling and transitory," involving no more than "the trivial, violent constants of human life," comprising "adultery, greed, the private warfare of commerce, fights between neighbors and within families, wills, rapes [and] murders." Yet for Holmes, at least initially, all this was far from trivial. It was the stuff of life, and law. And it allowed him some opportunity to test out his ideas. It certainly kept him and his fellow judges busy but, as he pointed out to Pollock, for him this was "more interesting than if we had less to do." At the grand old age of forty-three, Holmes mused on his life. "I don't mind growing older," he commented, "for I think that I have found life as vivid as most people and have had my share so far of action and passion. If a man gets a year's life out of a year," he philosophized, "he can ask no more."[14]

Yet Holmes did ask for more, from both his professional and his personal life. And perhaps inevitably, his initial excitement at being a judge paled after several years of dealing with the same human drama, albeit with a different cast each time. Only five years after enthusing about his new role, he complained to Pollock that he felt constrained by his circumstances. "I wax impatient sometimes to think how much time it takes to do a little fragment of what one would like to do and dreams of. Life," he decided, was "like an artichoke: each day, week, month, year, gives you one little bit which you nibble off—but precious little compared with what you throw away."[15]

In hindsight, some of his pronouncements at this time, especially as regards old age and lost opportunities, seem rather overblown. But Holmes was a man who felt acutely the sense of time slipping away. Perhaps for that reason, he sought out the company of those who seemed to have rather more of it to spare. His social and cultural circle at this time rather resembled those his father had been involved in in his younger days, a mix of individuals torn between the legal and the literary, the philosophical and the political life, except that the age demographic was slightly different.

In fact Holmes was elected to the Saturday Club, where his father, then in his seventies, still dominated, but he preferred to surround himself with youth. "It will be many years before you have occasion to know the happiness and encouragement that comes to an old man from the sympathy of the young," Holmes later lectured Frankfurter. "That, perhaps more than anything else, makes one feel as if one had not lived in vain, and counteracts the eternal gravitation toward melancholy and doubt."[16] Youth was a more suitable audience, perhaps, for a man still bubbling with ideas in his forties and fifties—and well beyond—but possibly also a more receptive one for some of those ideas than his older legal colleagues were proving to be.

Holmes had always been a man located between two worlds. In his own youth, these had been encapsulated in Boston itself, poised socially, demographically, and geographically between its colonial past and its burgeoning commercial future. By the 1880s and 1890s, Holmes' world had grown.

His professional circle had extended to the state, but his personal circle was national in scope. And to some of the young men with whom he socialized, Holmes himself represented the living link between past and future, between the "highly cultivated, homogeneous world" of antebellum Boston and the more unsettling heterogeneous world of the latter part of the nineteenth century.[17] As a survivor of the Civil War, he served, too, as a contemporary medieval knight in an age when martial valor and values had gone out of fashion. Both were, arguably, roles that Holmes relished, but they were also ones in which he was encouraged by his peers and their progeny alike.

★★★

By the time that Holmes became a judge, the memory of the Civil War had become something of a national obsession. In that year *Century Magazine* began publishing a popular "Battles and Leaders" series, which offered the Civil War generation, North and South, the opportunity to tell their side of the story of a specific battle, engagement, or campaign, or simply share their memories of the war generally. Since the 1870s, the Union Veterans' organization, the Grand Army of the Republic (GAR), had become a potent social and political force. From relatively modest beginnings in 1866 by 1890 it had some 400,000 members, organized in over 7,000 posts across the nation. Its leaders held public office throughout the North. In an atmosphere so receptive to and encouraging of Civil War recollections, it was perhaps inevitable that a pillar of the establishment such as Holmes would, at some point, be invited to speak publicly about the war. Holmes was too firmly located in the legal world to risk becoming distracted, as his father had been, by extrajudicial pursuits. However, following the pattern set by Dr. Holmes his son did become a feature on the national lecture circuit, beginning in 1884 with what became possibly his most famous and certainly his most quoted speech: a Memorial Day Address delivered to the John Sedgwick GAR Post No. 4 at Keene, New Hampshire.

Memorial Day, Holmes announced on that occasion, was not just a "day sacred to memories of love and grief and heroic youth," but one on which "we pause to become conscious of our national life and to rejoice in it, to recall what our country has done for each of us, and to ask ourselves what we can do for our country in return." Although John F. Kennedy would rally the nation with a similar sentiment in his inaugural in 1961, Holmes was speaking in the context of ongoing sectional division. Indeed, whether it was entirely realistic to expect both North and South to "join in perfect accord" over this interpretation was a dubious proposition. But Holmes ploughed on, treating his audience to some of his higher thoughts on philosophy, law, and science, the search for "the hidden laws of creation that are graven upon the tablets of the rock," or for "the history of civilization that is woven in the tissue of our jurisprudence." He spoke not as a judge, of course, but as a veteran, and to that end he established his own Civil War credentials by detailing, and in parts exaggerating, his experiences during the war, and invoked "the armies of the dead" who had fallen in the cause of Union.[18]

But it was the living to whom Holmes was speaking, and he soon got to the heart of what the veterans gathered before him surely wanted to hear; that war is pain and sacrifice, but that the sacrifice is not in vain, that out of it is woven "the closest tie which is possible between men—a tie which suffering has made indissoluble for better, or worse." And he assured his audience that, through its suffering, it was special, "set apart by its experience."

> Through our great good fortune, in our youth our hearts were touched with fire. It was given to us to learn at the outset that life is a profound and passionate thing. While we are permitted to scorn nothing but indifference, and do not pretend to undervalue the worldly rewards of ambition, we have seen with our own eyes, beyond and above the gold fields, the snowy heights of honor, and it is for us to bear the report to those who come after us. But, above all, we have learned that whether a man accepts from Fortune her spade, and will look downward and dig, or from Aspiration her axe and cord, and will scale the ice, the one and only success which it is his to command is to bring to his work a mighty heart.[19]

This was the first of Holmes' many public invocations of a martial, heroic ideal. In 1895, he returned to the theme of Memorial Day in another major speech, this time at Harvard. And in the many speeches he delivered in the 1880s and 1890s he further developed the martial themes, often tying them to the law. But it would be a mistake to take these speeches entirely at face value, as a simple expression of Holmes' own sentiments. In fact they were very much products of both Holmes' Civil War and the culture of the second half of the nineteenth century.

In his 1895 Harvard Address, "The Soldier's Faith," Holmes drew a clear distinction between commerce and conflict, and bemoaned the fact that "war is out of fashion" in a world whose "aspirations" were those of wealth.

> The society for which many philanthropists, labor reformers, and men of fashion unite in longing is one in which they may be comfortable and may shine without much trouble or any danger. The unfortunately growing hatred of the poor for the rich seems to me to rest on the belief that money is the main thing (a belief in which the poor have been encouraged by the rich), more than on any other grievance . . . I have heard the question asked whether our war was worth fighting, after all. There are many, poor and rich, who think that love of country is an old wife's tale, to be replaced by interest in a labor union, or, under the name of cosmopolitanism, by a rootless search for a place where the most enjoyment may be had at the least cost.

Many scholars have found this speech disturbing because it elevated suffering in the service of strength, while praising struggle almost as an end in itself. At the same time he attacked the "whole literature of sympathy" that "points out in story and in verse how hard it is to be wounded in the battle of life, how terrible, how unjust it is that any one should fail." Holmes seemed almost to be equating himself with a medieval knight, or even with Beowulf in his declaration that "to us, children of the North, life has seemed a place hung about by dark mists, out of which come the pale shine of dragon's scales, and the cry of fighting men, and the sound of swords." It was almost surreal, made more so by his inducement to his young audience to "pray not for comfort, but for combat; to keep the soldier's faith against the doubts of civil life."[20]

It is worth contrasting Holmes' speech with what his former close friend and comrade in the Twentieth Massachusetts Pen Hallowell said on the same subject the following year. Holmes argued that "those who stood against us held just as sacred convictions that were the opposite of ours," and thus claimed that "we respected them as every man with a heart must respect those who give all for their belief."[21]

Hallowell, speaking in 1896 at Memorial Hall in Harvard, took a rather different tack, rejecting Holmes' implicit endorsement of the "Lost Cause" theory of the Confederacy and his former comrade's failure to recognize that slavery was the "cornerstone" of the Confederate cause (as Confederate Vice President Alexander Stephens had correctly asserted in 1861). Although "it is pleasant to dwell upon the virtues of our old friends, the enemy," Hallowell acknowledged, "yet there should be neither mental nor moral confusion as to the real meaning of this Memorial Day and this Memorial Hall." He warned against "the sentimental sophistry that since there were heroism and fidelity to conviction on both sides, we may commemorate those virtues of both armies as American, and thereby try to forget there were ever two armies or two causes."

> Fidelity to conviction is praiseworthy; but the conviction is sometimes very far from praiseworthy. Slavery and polygamy were convictions. Such monuments as Memorial Hall commemorate the valor and heroism that maintained certain principles,—justice, order, and liberty. To ignore the irreconcilable distinction between the cause of the North and that of the South is to degrade the war to the level of a mere fratricidal strife for the display of military prowess and strength.[22]

We do not know if Hallowell intended his address as a response to or even a criticism of what his former brother-in-arms had said. Nevertheless the difference between their respective positions was striking. And modern readers may share some of the contemporary dismay at the emphasis Holmes placed on "military prowess and strength," his delight at the idea of "dangerous sport," his belief that, if "once in a while in our rough riding a neck is broken," it should not be regarded "as a waste, but as a price well paid for the breeding of a race fit for headship and command." Holmes affected surprise that the speech was interpreted by some as "a jingo document!" It "seems to some of the godly," he fumed, "as if I were preaching a doctrine of blood!"[23]

That, of course, is exactly how it seemed to some. The New York *Evening Post*, for example, attacked Holmes' speech as "sentimental jingoism," designed "to glorify war and the war spirit." Holmes, the paper charged, had "abused the holiday occasion." It was especially irked that Holmes, "reared in a community which, as no other in the world, has exemplified what we may call the conscience of wealth" should hold all its benefits, "hospitals, kindergartens, colleges, libraries, museums, and pleasure grounds," as so much "dross," and should instead idealize "the commonplace act of dying and risk of death." The following day the paper continued its attack. It was outraged that "a Judge of the Massachusetts Supreme Court" should deliver "an address to young men in favor of war—that is, of killing people and destroying their property—on the ground that if you put it off too long, your character runs down and you get too fond of money."[24]

Holmes' speech, the *Evening Post* argued, was "part and parcel of the great movement against peace and law, as the two canker worms of modern society, which is spreading rapidly all over our nation," and concluded, dripping sarcasm, by thanking Holmes for his "manly warnings to a generation rapidly sinking into wealth, quiet nights, and regular meals."[25] The *Evening Post* had a point. Holmes did seem to be harking back a full three decades, to Harvard's Commemoration Day in 1865, echoing James Russell Lowell's invocation of the idea of a "new imperial race" having emerged from the Civil War. And in a sense he was. His Memorial Day Address in 1895 really was a voice from the past, a romanticized past, in many respects, although there was little romance in the resonance it had in 1895.

Of course Holmes was not really talking about the Civil War in this speech. He was addressing the main concerns of an age struggling with economic inequalities and labor unrest, an age that seemed to be lurching between boom and bust with depressing regularity. Only two years before Holmes spoke, the nation suffered yet another financial meltdown. As with that in 1873, rapid but not robust railroad investment was part of the problem, but not the entire story. The economic crisis that began in 1893 blighted the following five years. It had been preceded, the previous year, by yet another violent strike, similar to the railroad strike of 1877 that pitted federal troops against workers. This time it was at Homestead, Pennsylvania, the site of Andrew Carnegie's most modern and most famous steel plant.

"No well-wisher of his country's peace and prosperity can view the present relations of capital and labor, or more correctly, of employer and employed, without serious alarm," the Populist activist Conrad Reno observed that year. "Scarcely a week passes that some widespread strike or lockout does not endanger the public peace and order." As a consequence, Reno argued, America was presenting to the world the invidious "spectacle ... of two private armed forces holding a bloody carnage, in the midst of a great nation, calling itself civilized, but which has not devised any peaceful means of settling such labor disputes."[26] And more strikes followed, notably the Pullman Strike of 1894, which yet again brought transport across the nation to a halt. Over the course of the next few years, banks and businesses alike ceased trading, unemployment reached almost 50 percent in some regions, farms failed, and workers marched on Washington to raise awareness of their plight.

It was against this backdrop of high unemployment, economic instability, and class tension that Holmes delivered his second Memorial Day Address, although the pressure had been building ever since he delivered his first one. Only two years after Holmes' 1884 Memorial Day Speech, events in Chicago had highlighted some of the divisions then developing within American society. The explosion of a bomb and resultant riot that killed eight policemen and several civilians during a labor rally in Haymarket Square in Chicago in May of 1886 was supposedly the work of anarchists, and reinforced the growing fear that socialist subversives were working to undermine American republicanism. Partly this was related to concerns over immigration, but in part, too, it achieved its momentum from a more diffuse sense of unease as the nation moved further from its agrarian roots toward an urban, commercial, and industrial way of life.

Contemporary literature, the "literature of sympathy" that Holmes so summarily dismissed, had much to say about this developing urban trend, little of it positive. By the time Holmes spoke at Harvard in 1895, the reading public had already been introduced to Stephen Crane's Maggie Johnson, in *Maggie: A Girl of the Streets* (1893), a novel set in New York's Bowery district within which the young heroine is driven by poverty into prostitution, and to William Dean Howell's Silas Lapham, in *The Rise of Silas Lapham* (1885), a novel that tracked the hero's rise only to highlight his inevitable downfall. Utopian and dystopian literature, too, whilst not new to the late-nineteenth century, enjoyed something of a resurgence in those decades, driven by the social and scientific questions of the day, questions that Holmes had struggled with since his adolescent years in Boston and had tried to resolve in his intensive debates with William James.

One of the most famous of these was, in fact, written by another lawyer from Boston. Set in a futuristic, socialist, utopian version of that city, Edward Bellamy's best-seller, *Looking Backward: 2000–1887* (1888), spawned a veritable copy-cat cottage industry of literary utopianism; over 160 utopian works were published between 1888 and 1900 alone, and Bellamy's original novel even inspired the founding of a magazine, *The Nationalist*, which enjoyed a wide readership in its day. Between them, these publications set out a rather different blueprint for modern America, but no less powerful in many ways for being a literary rather than a legislative construction.[27]

Although many of these works were far from lightweight, and several dealt directly with subjects, such as Social and Reform Darwinism, that Holmes had long wrestled with, either with his father or the Metaphysical Club, he had little time for such fictional fantasies, as he saw them. He considered Bellamy, for example, to be "a pretentious imbecile." But not all of the literary contemplations of America's present problems and potential future were fictional, and not all could be so easily dismissed,[28] because this was also the era of the Social Gospel movement, whose founder, Protestant minister Josiah Strong, believed the ills infecting the nation were caused by Catholics, Mormons, Immigrants, labor unions, socialism, urbanization, and wealth.[29]And in case anyone was left in any doubt about the combined results of these national seven deadly sins, five years later photojournalist and social commentator Jacob Riis showed America *How the Other Half Lives* (1890), a graphic and grim representation of the slums and immigrant ghettoes of the nation's major cities.

Holmes disapproved of these journalists and social critics, known as "muckrakers," who were in fact doing no more than reflecting and responding to a growing level of both public and political concern that the nation's rapid economic growth was immoral and dangerous. Conditions at plants such as Homestead were harsh, far harsher than they had been for free workers in similar industries before the Civil War, and certainly more impersonal.

Nevertheless, in Massachusetts, and despite the passage in 1887 of the Employers' Liability Act, cases of industrial accident were on the increase, and Holmes had the opportunity to deal with several of these. Many related to the railroads, rather than to factory work, and they revealed that, with Holmes policing the potential application of the Employers' Liability Act, workers were only slightly more likely to receive compensation than they had been before the act came into force. That personal responsibility trumped employer liability seemed to be Holmes' default position, even when that responsibility was compromised by the nature of the task that had caused the injury. It was a hard line. But Holmes stuck to it.[30]

Individual injury was, of course, only one element of the challenges posed by the industrial world. On the national level, competition, not compensation, was the main focus of the concern expressed by social and economic reformers. This was because plants like Homestead represented component parts of much bigger operations than had been the norm in the Antebellum Era. Most, like Carnegie's, were vertically integrated, centrally controlled, destructive of competition, and extremely profitable. Since the Civil War, indeed, various business methods had been adopted that resulted in the creation of monopolies: pools, trusts, corporations, and holding companies all played a role, many of these underwritten by what was defined at the time as a rather inchoate but powerful "community of interest," by which was largely meant class interest, exemplified by the main financiers and industrialists of the era. Opposition to the process of consolidation and to the perceived restrictive practices that resulted was not new, but it was becoming more of a political concern.

"It had been natural enough," as historian Robert Wiebe pointed out, "to account for business success and failure in terms of individual virtue and vice," but "quite another matter to permit the corporations ill-gotten profits because the Supreme Court adjudged them 'persons' within the meaning of the Fourteenth Amendment."[31] Most of the industrial and financial magnates of the day, including John D. Rockefeller, Andrew W. Mellon, and J.P. Morgan (whose bank bailed the federal government out when the nation's gold reserves became dangerously depleted), attracted criticism for their restrictive business methods which benefitted the few at the expense of the many.

Popular publications and muckraking journalists encouraged both public and political opposition to big business, by exposing their monopolistic practices and their disregard for the public. These included political economist Henry George's *Progress and Poverty* (1879) and Henry Demarest Lloyd's *Wealth against Commonwealth* (1894). The latter, an attack on the Standard Oil Company, was one of "the most powerful polemics ever launched against monopoly in America." And by the turn of the twentieth century, all the political parties had antitrust planks as part of their platforms, six states had introduced antitrust clauses into their constitutions, and many more had passed antitrust legislation in one form or another.[32]

In this context it was not surprising that Holmes' future colleague on the Supreme Court, Justice Henry Billings Brown, advised Yale Law School's 1895 graduates that "the reconciliation of this strife between capital and labor" would be "the great social problem which will confront you as you enter upon the stage of professional life."[33] By this time two major federal laws, the Interstate Commerce Act (1887) which created the Interstate Commerce Commission (1887) and the Sherman Antitrust Act (1890) to regulate big business, had been passed. Both were introduced with a view to curbing the unrestrained growth of corporate power and creating a federally-enforced level playing field upon which healthy competition could flourish.

In fact the Sherman Act was limited in its applicability only to interstate commerce, and almost immediately was challenged in the so-called "Sugar Trust Case," *United States v. E.C. Knight Co.* (1895). And the Interstate Commerce Commission (ICC) had most of its teeth removed two years later, in *ICC v. Alabama Railway Company* (1897), a case that revolved around the right to charge variable rates for transport over short and long distances.

Dissenting, Holmes' future colleague on the Supreme Court, John Marshall Harlan, observed that the ruling rendered the ICC "a useless body for all practical purposes," and defeated "many of the important objects designed to be accomplished by the various enactments of Congress relating to interstate commerce." The ICC, he argued, "has been shorn, by judicial interpretation, of authority to do anything of an effective character." The issues raised by both cases would prove major sources of contention for Holmes once he ascended to the Supreme Court. And he was, and remained, suspicious of the notion that "the Sherman Act and smashing great fortunes are roads to an ideal." This, he once commented, "seems to me open to debate," if not in fact "a humbug based on economic ignorance and incompetence." Yet he was hardly oblivious to the ongoing economic conditions that had prompted the passage of these acts.[34]

"It is plain from the slightest consideration of practical affairs, or the most superficial reading of industrial history," he once observed, "that free competition means combination, and that the organization of the world, now going on so fast, means an ever increasing might and scope of combination." In 1893, during a lull in court proceedings, he even went so far as to seek the opinions of one of Boston's labor leaders, probably Frank Foster, president of the Typographers' Union, with a view to assessing both sides of the capital-labor divide. He tried to be objective. He struggled. "I see that you and your people have *aims*," he reported telling Foster, but I don't see that you have *ideals*." He recommended that they read Rudyard Kipling, whose "war songs" have "lifted up our hearts and made it easier to be valiant." Foster's response to this suggestion is, unfortunately, unrecorded.[35]

In effect, even as Holmes reflected on his Civil War past, the financial, social, and political framework for his years on the Supreme Court was being erected around him. There were, however, "comparatively few occasions when Holmes as a Massachusetts judge confronted the kinds of issues that were to play so important a part in the growth of his visibility as a Supreme Court Justice." But on those few occasions, it was evident which way his thoughts were tending. His most famous state court opinion, a dissent, occurred in *Vegelahn v. Guntner* (1896), a case that revolved around the question of whether it was lawful for labor to organize, to strike, and to picket. While the court concluded that picketing was unlawful, Holmes was not so sure. Holmes, in dissent, argued that there was a discrepancy in the law's treatment of the relationship between employer and employee and that between corporations. "Combination on the one side is patent and powerful," Holmes argued, but "[c]ombination on the other side is the necessary and desirable counterpart, if the battle is to be carried out in a fair and equal way." In a modification of what he had argued in *The Common Law*, Holmes considered motive here. And he concluded that so long as no malice was intended, union activity and picketing could be lawful.[36]

Holmes' dissent, as White stresses, was "in fact a statement of economic theory in the arena of labor relations," a critique of "the policy that combinations of labor were not justifiable even though combinations of capital were." This was an idea that he had earlier developed, although not fully, in an earlier article, "Privilege, Malice, and Intent" (1894). In working through his ideas, revisiting and, to an extent, revising his theories as expounded in *The Common Law*, of course, Holmes could not see into the future. Yet in seeking to educate himself on the economic questions of the day through an extensive reading regime that included Hobbes' *Leviathan*, Hegel, and Marx, and in his dissents while on the Massachusetts Court, Holmes was preparing himself to slot into that framework. Indeed, this period of Holmes' life, his final years on the Massachusetts Court, is generally identified as the one during which he clarified some of his more contradictory philosophical and professional ideas. In the context of the "continual exposure to the real world" that his work on the Massachusetts Court had afforded him, it is possible that he began to consider, in a consistent way, the implications of pragmatism as the most useful philosophical tool through which to approach the law.[37]

Certainly Holmes was prompted in this period to reconsider some of his earlier debates with the Metaphysical Club, the members of which increasingly came to adopt a practical, predictive approach to philosophy. The year of Holmes' *Vegelahn v. Guntner* dissent was the same year in which William James published, and sent to Holmes, his defense of religious faith, *The Will to Believe* (1896). As far as its theoretical framework was concerned, James sounded, in places, quite similar to Holmes. The "free-est competition of the various faiths with one another," James proposed, "and their openest application to life by their several champions, are the most favorable conditions under which the survival of the fittest can proceed . . . Religious fermentation is always a symptom of the intellectual vigor of a society, and it is only when they forget that they are hypotheses and put on rationalistic and authoritative pretensions, that our faiths do harm."[38]

James might have been talking about unions, or the law. And especially in regard to his discussion of determinism, he sounded very Holmesian indeed. "For, after all," he asked, "is there not something rather absurd in our ordinary notion of external things being good or bad in themselves?"

> Can murders and treacheries, considered as mere outward happenings . . . be bad without any one to feel their badness? And could paradise properly be good in the absence of a sentient principle by which the goodness was perceived? Outward goods and evils seem practically indistinguishable except in so far as they result in getting moral judgments made about them.[39]

But James was talking about religion, and it was in this respect that Holmes reacted against *The Will to Believe*, and emphasized the philosophical divide that had opened up between the former friends.

Although Holmes pronounced himself fully in sympathy with James' "justification of the idealizing impulse," he was less sure in himself about the implications. "I long ago made up my mind that all one needed was a belief in the significance of the universe," Holmes wrote James, but "more lately it has come to seem to me that even that may be ambiguous." James' later writings on pragmatism engaged him more, but even here he also was skeptical of James' perspective. "For a good many years I have had a formula for truth," Holmes observed, but he was not convinced that this could be described as pragmatism, *per se*.[40]

> I have been in the habit of saying that all I mean by truth is what I can't help thinking. The assumption of the validity of the thinking process seems to mean no more than that: I am up against it I have gone as far as I can go just as when I like a glass of beer. But I have learned to surmise that my can't helps are not necessarily cosmic can't helps that the universe may not be subject to my limitations; and philosophy generally seems to me to sin through arrogance . . . It seems to me that the only promising activity is to make my universe coherent and liveable, not to babble about the universe.[41]

In the end, Holmes admitted that James' world was "convex" while his own was "concave." Whether it was Holmes' years as a judge that had confirmed this for him, or whether one can locate in the Civil War the origins of Holmes' moral skepticism, is unclear. "The war was a great moral experience," Holmes admitted, but the "first five or ten years of one's profession was another, and perhaps a greater one."[42]

Undoubtedly Holmes saw life as a battle, the law as the rules of engagement, but the fact of his having been a soldier may not have informed this perspective to the degree sometimes assumed. What can be argued is that the Civil War proved to be a significant stepping-stone in his eventual appointment to the Supreme Court. Indeed, the Civil War proved to be both a personal and cultural catalyst not just for Holmes, but for a more widespread shift in social perspective in the last years of the nineteenth century. Holmes, largely through his 1895 Address, came to symbolize this shift, structured around the role of the solder, sacrifice, and struggle in the national psyche.

★★★

In the immediate aftermath of the Civil War it was perhaps inevitable that martial rhetoric of the kind Holmes delivered in 1895 went out of fashion. This change was partially tied to the emergence of a modern, commercial perspective that emphasized the economic benefits of peace, aligned with the rise of a scientific, progressive pattern of social development. This paralleled Holmes' analysis in *The Common Law*. Societies, as reflected in the laws that governed and guided them, moved through a three-stage process, from chaotic savagery "through barbarism to civilization."[43] For individual Americans, of course, the purely practical problem of reintegrating so many veterans, many of them wounded, physically and psychologically, back into society also played its part. It was unsurprising that there was little cultural appetite for conflict in the face of its corporeal consequences in the 1870s. But the body politic, like the individual one, has remarkable powers of recuperation.

By the 1880s and 1890s, as the resurgence of interest in the war revealed, Americans had reinvigorated the martial ideal and proved as susceptible, in cultural terms, to romantic notions of medieval chivalry as Holmes had been in his youth. In part this was a political development, not in a partisan sense, but in a purely practical one. Every elected Republican president since 1868 had been a Civil War officer, and the war proved to be a powerful weapon in holding off any attempts by a younger generation to take power. The 1896 election illustrates this. Voters were offered the choice between the thirty-six-year-old Democrat William Jennings Bryan and the Republican former Union Army major, William McKinley, whose campaign was supported by several of his former comrades: Oliver Otis Howard, who had lost an arm in the Peninsula Campaign, and Dan Sickles, who had lost a leg at Gettysburg. The point about service to the nation could hardly have been made more explicit. But in case it required reinforcement, Republican propagandists juxtaposed the image of McKinley holding a rifle in his Civil War uniform with that of Bryan waving a rattle in his cradle. Bryan's defeat may, in the end, have been unrelated to his youth. But the public, propagandist message was clear: the Civil War generation represented a safer pair of hands in such troubled times, and could be trusted to fight for the nation in 1896 as it had in 1861.

Yet Civil War veteran or not, McKinley's election might not have been so assured had the political landscape not been underpinned by broader cultural concerns prompted by the social and economic crises of the period. Since wealth appeared, to the reformers and socialists Holmes scorned as much as to Holmes himself, to have rendered the nation morally lax, the "martial ideal emerged as an antidote to overcivilization," a means of coping with, but also comprehending, the challenges offered by the industrial and commercial society driven and epitomized by men such as Carnegie, Rockefeller, and Morgan, the "robber barons" of Populist nightmare. In this context, a very different kind of literature emerged, focused not on the city slums but on the nation's wide open spaces of the West. Exemplified by the work of, among others, Holmes' friend Owen Wister, the West was the natural home of Anglo-Saxon self-reliance. Free from the contamination and class conflict of the cities, the frontier symbolized the "spirit of adventure, courage, and self-sufficiency" that defined the nation.[44]

But there were other frontiers. This may have been the age of machines as much as "machine politics," an age of westward expansion and exploration, but it was not one confined to the United States. This was also the "age of the explorer hero ... whose endeavours were chronicled in newspapers, lecture theatres, and best-selling books," in America as much as in Europe, and in language that echoed Holmes' own.[45]

In 1871, only a few years after Holmes left Harvard Law School, James Gordon Bennett, Jr., editor of the *New York Herald*, dispatched one of the paper's correspondents, Henry Morton Stanley, to the African continent in search of Scottish missionary and explorer David Livingstone. Stanley's famous discovery of Livingstone ("Dr. Livingstone, I presume?") was seen as an American national achievement. The *New York Herald*, unsurprisingly, took much of the credit for what it termed "the first bold adventure in the cause of humanity, civilization and science." And it sought to make patriotic as well as professional capital out of the story, which was, it argued, "distinctively the work of the American press, whose aspirations and ambitions have grown with the majesty of the land, and whose enterprise had been molded on the national character." Stanley's discovery of Livingstone was, according to the paper, "the emblem of the modern Christian crusade . . . the accomplishment, as well as the foreshadowing of the work of peaceful civilization in the future." In celebrating "the dynamism of a nation just beginning to flex its muscles as a world economic force," historian Edward Berenson has noted, the *New York Herald* represented Stanley as one of the "mythic heroes whose courage and manly abilities provided models for contemporary men."[46]

It might seem, at first glance, that there was more than a degree of irony at work here, given that so many of the contemporary men in question had, like Holmes, only some five years earlier been engaged in a civil conflict that had surely tested their manly abilities to the full; in its reference to "peaceful civilization," the *Herald* acknowledged as much. But this was precisely the point. "Until April 1865 the war still cast its heavy shadows over the nation," Mark DeWolfe Howe observed, but to assume that with Appomattox came absolution, either for Holmes or for America, would be a very great mistake. The language of heroism as that became dominant in the United States in the latter part of the nineteenth century was very much an outgrowth of that conflict. It represented the rhetorical, verbal afterglow of the war's visceral realities that resonated with those, like Holmes, who had fought, but even more with those, like Wister, who had not. In the context of what historian Robert Wiebe identified as the "search for order" in post-war America, the emergence of a society structured around "urban-industrial life," this may be unsurprising. As the individual vanished into the urban

crowd, individualism acquired increased resonance via the romanticized figure of the heroic adventurer.[47]

And Holmes increasingly presented himself in that guise. Only two years
after his Memorial Day Address at Harvard, in a speech at Brown University,
he described his early adventures on "the ocean of the Law." He recalled
that there "were few charts and lights," only "a thick fog of details." How
many of his youthful audience would have recognized Harvard Law School
in Holmes' description of the "black and frozen night, in which were no
flowers, no spring, no easy joys" of his early education may be wondered at.
Some may have concluded that Holmes, by then in his mid-fifties, was ram-
bling when he observed that "in the crush of that ice any craft might sink."
They may have been further confused at his injunction that they become
adventurers and "start for the pole," especially since most of them had no
intention of moving much beyond a courtroom.[48]

In some respects, of course, Holmes was doing little more on these occasions than echoing Walker's textbook from his student days. "Let no man
enter the profession as a sinecure," Walker had warned. "Genius, without
toil, may, to some extent, distinguish a man elsewhere; but here he must
labor, or he cannot succeed." But in his language Holmes revealed a much
broader ambition. The law, he initially hoped, and later effectively proved,
offered him the opportunity for heroism that the Civil War had not; or,
rather, he could replay that aspect of his life and his character in an environment where the risks were not so much physical as professional and philosophical.[49] In 1864, at least as he later recalled the experience, Holmes had
taken up arms yet again. But now the dragon to be slain was not slavery, but
ignorance: his own. And in this narrative he could with confidence locate
himself at its center, not just because he was simultaneously author and
actor, but because this particular story was one of intellectual success, not
individual slaughter. But it was a story whose context was still conflict: the
internal conflict of one individual seeking his way in the world, but also the
more recent conflict that he had experienced.

Holmes' biographers do recognize this impulse in him. However, there is
a tendency to interpret his habit of discussing the law in terms more appropriate to a battlefield or an Arctic expeditionary venture as a straightforward
reflection either of survivor's guilt or survivor's cynicism, a war-wrought
imperative "to see battle as a metaphor for life" that Holmes sustained
throughout his life.[50] It may have been both, but it was also a reflection
of the age that Holmes lived in: a rather more complex reaction to the
nineteenth-century's persistent fascination with scientific exploration as
much as with philosophical explanation.

Arctic exploration clearly held a fascination for Holmes. He enthused
over Norwegian scientist Fridtjof Nansen's *Farthest North*, published in the

same year (1897) that Holmes spoke to students at Brown. "I have been carried away both by the narrative itself and the reflections to which it gives rise," he enthused. "What a divine thing is adequate vitality—to be gay in the face of death and, almost worse, *ennui*—to be capable, though a complex and civilized man, to lark like a boy and to rejoice over a bellyful of blubber." In referencing ice-bound vessels, Holmes may also have had in mind the American Arctic explorer, U.S. Navy Lieutenant Robert E. Peary, who had been awarded the Cullum Medal by the American Geographical Society that year.[51]

Peary, whose ambition matched Holmes' own, had proved as adept at using "his scientific credentials" to promote his reputation as "the able, tough commander on whom all hopes for national success rested" as Holmes was in using his military credentials to promote his own reputation within the legal world. Just as Peary presented himself as the "rugged and primitive conqueror of an impossible climate," so Holmes, in drafting Arctic imagery into service as metaphor for intellectual study, sought to bolster his own image as a conqueror of the equally "impossible climate" that was Harvard Law School in 1864. In the process, he also located the law itself as culturally relevant in the context of a world faced by sweeping religious, intellectual, class, and material changes that had begun in the Antebellum Era but that became acute in the latter part of the nineteenth century: a world that needed heroes.[52]

In this respect, so far from unusual in his approach to the law as to life, Holmes was very much a man of his times. His Civil War experiences certainly lent veracity to the martial metaphors he deployed with increasing frequency throughout his career, in everything from speeches, private letters, and even notes to his fellow judges. But we run the risk of misrepresenting Holmes if we do not understand that late-nineteenth century American society was particularly receptive to precisely the kind of rhetoric that he provided. The language of heroism, as that was increasingly spoken across America in that period, came to be epitomized by Holmes, certainly, but it did not originate with him.

Holmes was clearly impressed by the exploits of individual explorers such as Peary, Nansen, and perhaps especially Robert Falcon Scott (of the Antarctic), whose exploits, Theodore Roosevelt concluded, were the epitome "of quiet, simple, and utterly disinterested heroism."[53] In the years before the Civil War, years of abolitionist agitation and social upheaval, Emerson had, somewhat tongue in cheek, critiqued the abolitionists as men with beards. But the later nineteenth and early twentieth centuries, by contrast, were in many respects the era of men with moustaches, men who were mapping and measuring the world and in the process demonstrating the kind of stoic endurance and self-reliance in the face of death that Holmes ultimately failed to find in himself during the Civil War. And yet, as was evident in the many speeches he delivered while serving on the Supreme Judicial Court of Massachusetts, Holmes held on to the belief that success in the life struggle was not simply to be had in fighting or on distant frontiers; in the legal universe, there remained new worlds to conquer beneath his feet.

★★★

In some respects, the new worlds in question were not what Holmes might have anticipated. Toward the end of his tenure as a judge in Massachusetts, he began to experience what may have been one of the most extreme mid-life crises—and in his case it almost merited the mid-life label—ever recorded. Not that he intended it to be recorded, of course, but the lady in question, Baroness Castletown of Upper Ossory, the Hon. Emily Ursula Clare St. Leger, kept his letters: always a risk. Holmes had first met her in 1889, on one of his fairly regular visits to Europe that he normally, but not always, took with his family. In 1889 as in the summer of 1896, however, when he met Clare again, Holmes had traveled alone. Fanny had been ill again, and was still too unwell to accompany Holmes abroad.[54]

It had been a difficult decade. Part of the reason for Fanny's illness was the debilitating domestic regime she had experienced whilst Holmes served on the court; to her had fallen the responsibility of running the home and nursing Dr. Holmes when he became older and physically less robust. And many of those closest to Holmes died in this decade: Holmes' brother in 1884, his mother four years later, and his father in 1894. Frank Palfrey, the former Lieutenant Colonel of the Twentieth Massachusetts, had also died in 1889, severing yet another of the living links Holmes had with the Civil War. And it was notable that Holmes believed that it was the war that had killed him. "At last the bullet which struck him at Antietam has done its work," Holmes observed in his obituary; "he fell in battle, although the end was delayed."[55]

This is not to say that Holmes, in establishing a relationship, albeit that it was mainly, possibly exclusively, an epistolary one, with another woman was acting under stress, out of loneliness in the absence of his wife, and wholly out of character. Throughout his life he was, by all accounts, a furious flirt. But whereas his previous forays into flirting had been of the usual type, control without commitment, his feelings for Clare Castletown went far beyond flirting. He was in love. But he had not lost all sense. "My life is my wife and my work," he once told Clare, "but as you see that does not prevent a romantic feeling which it would cut me to the heart to have you repudiate."[56] This was unfortunate, because Clare, although initially as infatuated as Holmes, eventually seems to have regarded the entire affair as a mild distraction rather than an emotional watershed. She was, in any case, as good at flirting as he was. And as a member of the British aristocracy she had a lot more spare time to devote to it. Although he may have been unaware of it, Holmes had never, in fact, been the only string to her beaux.

Holmes and Clare Castletown maintained, indeed intensified, their correspondence well into the twentieth century. She was clearly an important figure in his life, such that her death in 1927 left, as he told Harold Laski, "a great gap in my horizon." But even love, in the end, could not distract Holmes from the law for long.[57] In 1897, the same year that he was waxing lyrical to the lovely Clare about his feelings, and urging Brown's students to "strike for the pole," Holmes retraced some of his own steps on the legal frontier in a speech he delivered at Boston University, and later published in the *Harvard Law Review*, "The Path of the Law." In this Holmes built on his earlier "Privilege, Malice, and Intent" (1894) article and further modified his position on objective standards that he had set out in *The Common Law*. And in some respects, "The Path of the Law" did reflect the experience that eleven years of service on the court had had on Holmes' perspective on judicial decision making, but largely it simply clarified ideas that Holmes perhaps felt he had not expressed with sufficient force before. Most notably, in "The Path of the Law" Holmes provided his strongest statement yet of the differences, but also the symbiosis between "morality and law."[58]

"The law," Holmes asserted, "is the witness and external deposit of our moral life. Its history is the history of the moral development of the race. The practice of it, in spite of popular jests, tends to make good citizens and good men." At the same time, Holmes stressed, if "you want to know the law and nothing else, you must look at it as a bad man, who cares only for the material consequences which such knowledge enables him to predict, not as a good one, who finds his reasons for conduct, whether inside the law or outside of it, in the vaguer sanctions of conscience."

> The law is full of phraseology drawn from morals, and by the mere force of language continually invites us to pass from one domain to the other without perceiving it, as we are sure to do unless we have the boundary constantly before our minds. The law talks about rights, and duties, and malice, and intent, and negligence, and so forth, and nothing is easier, or, I may say, more common in legal reasoning, than to take these words in their moral sense, at some stage of the argument, and so to drop into fallacy.[59]

Almost as important as the confusions that evolved from morality, in Holmes' interpretation, were those that revolved around meaning. "We talk about a contract as a meeting of the minds of the parties," he explained, "and thence it is inferred in various cases that there is no contract because their minds have not met." Ultimately, he concluded, "the making of a contract depends not on the agreement of two minds in one intention, but on the agreement of two external signs,—not on the parties having *meant* the same thing but on their having *said* the same thing."[60]

In an extrajudicial sense, of course, the disjuncture that Holmes had identified between saying and meaning was perhaps not so readily rationalized, as the response to his 1895 Memorial Day Address had revealed to him. And despite the sometimes negative reception of his sentiments, Holmes maintained his advocacy of the martial ideal, rarely failing, when the occasion called for it and usually even if it did not, to establish his own credentials as a combat veteran.

"When I hear people talk about civil life as needing and teaching a courage equal to war," he once observed, "I feel very sure that I am listening to a noncombatant who never has known what it is to expect a bullet in his bowels in thirty seconds or to sail an ironclad over a mine." His anticipated audience was a naval one, hence the ironclads. And he often tried to have it both ways: to deny the jingoism he had been accused of in 1895, before sounding, four years later, just about as jingoistic as it was possible to be.

> People dwell on the sorrows of war. I know what they are. I saw my share of them when I was young with the Army of the Potomac. I shudder at them. I abhor the jingo spirit. I would do all that might be done honorably to avoid them. But the horrors of war after all are bodily suffering, the loss of property, and the loss of life. There are spiritual losses that are a thousand times worse. It is worse to be a coward than to lose an arm. It is better to be killed than to have a flabby soul.[61]

Holmes persisted, both in his extrajudicial speeches and in his professional ones, to offer his audience a sometimes confusing combination of the martial and the metaphysical. The relationship between these aspects of Holmes' personality, however, was a complex one, susceptible of confusion as Theodore Roosevelt found to his cost when he finally appointed Holmes to the Supreme Court in 1902.

Despite his ambition, and his growing professional reputation, appointment to the Supreme Court was not a given for Holmes. He may have wanted it. He could not be sure of ever getting it. Although, again, hindsight advises that Holmes would go on to serve three decades as an Associate Justice on the Supreme Court, the likely vacancy that arose at the turn of the twentieth century did so because Horace Gray, one of the Associate Justices, was seventy-three, and McKinley was considering a replacement. At sixty, Holmes was not the most obvious choice; and in fact another candidate, Alfred Hemenway, was already waiting in the wings for Justice Gray to resign. When McKinley was assassinated in September, 1901, and Gray suffered a stroke only a few months later, suddenly all bets were off. Former

Vice-President Roosevelt was in the White House, and he had ideas of his own. He was also susceptible to the ideas of leading Massachusetts statesman and close friend, both to Roosevelt and to Holmes, Henry Cabot Lodge. But even friends in high places might not have secured Holmes the appointment had it not been for the remarkable resonance between his public pronouncements and those of the new president.

Roosevelt had not fought in the Civil War but nevertheless already enjoyed a reputation as a man of action accrued, largely, from his famous charge up San Juan Hill in Cuba during the Spanish-American War of 1898. He famously advocated the "strenuous life," an approach he had set out in a speech in Chicago in 1899, a speech very close in sentiment to Holmes' own public and professional pronouncements. "I wish to preach," Roosevelt declared, "not the doctrine of ignoble ease, but the doctrine of the strenuous life, the life of toil and effort, of labor and strife; to preach that highest form of success which comes, not to the man who desires mere easy peace, but to the man who does not shrink from danger, from hardship, or from bitter toil, and who out of these wins the splendid ultimate triumph."

> A life of ignoble ease, a life of that peace which springs merely from lack either of desire or of power to strive after great things, is as little worthy of a nation as of an individual . . . We do not admire the man of timid peace. We admire the man who embodies victorious effort . . . If in 1861 the men who loved the Union had believed that peace was the end of all things, and war and strife the worst of all things, and had acted up to their belief, we would have saved hundreds of thousands of lives, we would have saved hundreds of millions of dollars . . . We could have avoided all this suffering simply by shrinking from strife. And if we had thus avoided it, we would have shown that we were weaklings, and that we were unfit to stand among the great nations of the earth.[62]

It was perhaps no surprise that, even before they ever met, Roosevelt believed that in Holmes, by then the Chief Justice of the Supreme Judicial Court of Massachusetts, he had identified a man of a mind with himself. But Roosevelt found out very quickly that, in Holmes' case, what was said was not always a reliable indication of what was meant.

Possibly the president should have read some of Holmes' professional and public pronouncements more carefully, since these were often contradictory in exposition. The philosophy of the man was in almost everything he wrote and said. But it was not a fixed philosophy. It was one born in Brahmin Boston, challenged, and in some respects changed, by the Civil War. But by the end of Holmes' tenure on the Massachusetts Court it was still evolving. By that point it appeared fully in tune with what historian Jackson Lears terms "antimodern militarism," the complex mixture of "medieval and martial ideals" that promised the retention of tradition and the possibility of positive regeneration even in the midst of apparently destructive social and economic transformation.[63] And Roosevelt believed above all in transformation, in particular the idea of regeneration in the cities as much as on the frontier, as encapsulated in his own book glorifying *Ranch Life and the Hunting Trail* (1888).

As the first of the three "Progressive" presidents (William Howard Taft and Woodrow Wilson were the other two), Roosevelt advocated a form of conservative progressivism that sought moral uplift through material reform. In theory, progressivism overall was, like Holmes' concept of the competing forces at play in the capital/labor relationship, effectively a political and social perspective aimed at balancing the competing claims of consumer and capitalist alike. It worked for change through legislation designed to secure, for example, reasonable working conditions, fair wages and minimum wages, a ban on child labor, federal control of taxes, and a curb on the perceived negative power of consolidation, or business trusts. In practice it was a rather uneasy and sometimes contradictory program—and never a legislatively or politically coherent one—that merged the ideal of individualism (the strenuous life) with the idea of increased state intervention (social welfare); and it set the agenda for the next few decades. Having been assured that Holmes shared his political proclivities, Roosevelt had no hesitation in nominating the Massachusetts Chief Justice to the Supreme Court. Holmes, he believed, would support his reform agenda.

In the main, the press concurred. And the popular reaction to Holmes' appointment was generally positive. Some of it was positively gushing. Most newspapers still introduced Holmes to the reading public as the son of a more famous father, but from their enthusiasm for the appointment it was clear that Holmes had already made his own, independent mark as "Soldier, Scholar, Legal Writer, and Scientist," as the *New York Times* headline summed it up. "His opinions are almost always brief," the *Times* commented, approvingly. "He does not hesitate to make a precedent when he has none to follow, and labor men have had occasion more than once to praise him for his decisions in cases involving their interests." Other papers followed suit. "Lucidity, powerful logic, flashing insight piercing to the heart of complicated questions," were just some of Holmes' many attributes that the press identified. And not only was Holmes the editor of Kent's *Commentaries* and the *American Law Review*, a lecturer and author of *The Common Law*, professor at Harvard and Chief Justice; on top of, or perhaps despite, all that he had the common touch.[64]

"Judge Holmes knows men as well as letters," one paper commented. "It will never be necessary to urge him . . . to go out among his fellow-men and discover what they are thinking about." This conclusion had nothing to do with Holmes' more recent behavior, far less his apparent support of labor, however, and everything to do with the Civil War. The war "could not but quicken his sympathies and broaden his views," the editorial opined, "through intimate contact with his kind." This, it concluded, was "certainly not a bad thing for a judge who has to pass upon great controversies involving the bosoms, as well as the business, of the citizens of a republic." What some of these controversies might be was made clearer on the front page of the *Richmond Times*. Alongside the announcement of Holmes' appointment to the Supreme Court the paper carried a report of the armed clash between strikers and federal deputies that had recently occurred at a Pennsylvanian coal mine. "Deputies and Strikers Join in a Lively Night Battle," the headline proclaimed. "It is Believed That No One Was Hurt."[65]

★★★

Despite the press praise, Holmes was generally disappointed in reactions to his appointment to the Supreme Court. "The president's choice of me has been received in a way that I think I may regard as a triumph," he told Lady Georgina Pollock, but he admitted that "at first by perversity of temperament I was very blue." As a result, even the praise irked him as "hopelessly devoid of personal discrimination or courage. They are so favorable," he complained, "that they make my nomination a popular success but they have the flabbiness of American ignorance." As far as his judicial record went, Holmes also knew full well that a one-dimensional representation was being offered the public, and he was truly dismayed that a fuller appreciation of his efforts was not evidenced in the papers. "It makes one sick when he has broken his heart in trying to make every word living and real," he moaned, "to see a lot of duffers . . . taking with the sanctity of print in a way that at once discloses to the knowing eye that literally they don't know anything about it . . . damn the lot of them," he concluded, somewhat uncharitably. It may have been just as well for Holmes' future career that the press remained ignorant of this "confidential ebullition of spleen."[66]

Although possibly an unusual assessment of a man of Holmes' age and reputation, it is entirely feasible that he was nervous about the move to Washington. That, combined with a contrary nature and a tendency to view opponents as ignorant, if not downright imbeciles, made him grumpy when he ought to have been glad. But it also made him somewhat unreliable, at least for Roosevelt's purposes. Because Holmes was hardly, in 1902, a finished product in his own mind, even though that is sometimes how he has been portrayed. "At sixty-one," as one of his earliest biographers noted, "he left Boston for Washington and national life. By that time, his character and aims were set. The machine was formed and fashioned; it had only to function." This was not at all how Holmes saw it.[67]

Looking back on his time as a judge in Massachusetts, Holmes had tried to sum up what he described as "the twenty happiest years of my life" by offering a summation of his evolving perspective on the law. "I have tried to see the law as an organic whole," he explained, and "I have also tried to see it as a reaction between tradition on the one side and the changing desires and needs of a community on the other. I have studied tradition in order that I might understand how it came to be what it is, and to estimate its worth with regard to our present needs." He had, too, as he told the Middlesex Bar Association, "considered the social and economic postulates on which we frame the conception of our needs," and arrived at the conclusion that he had posited in "The Path of the Law," that "certainty is an illusion."[68]

What Holmes had not done, however, was stop searching. For him, certainty implied that "a man is satisfied with himself . . . that he has ceased to struggle and therefore has ceased to achieve."[69] And Holmes had no intention of letting that happen. Following the pattern he had adopted in *The Common Law*, Holmes looked backward in the process of plotting his forward course. He was, he admitted, excited at having "the chance to do one's share in shaping the laws of the whole country," and rationalized any apprehension by comparing the moment before leaving for Washington to "the hush that one used to feel when awaiting the beginning of a battle." Yet again, he looked back to the Civil War, to the Battle of Glendale when his cousin had died, to that moment before the charge. And he invoked his own interpretation of the soldier's faith:

> The forces of one's soul rally and gather to a point. One looks down the lines and catches the eye of friends—he waves his sword—it may be the last time for him or them—but the advance is about to begin. The troops are deployed. They will follow their leader. We will not falter, we will not fail. We will reach the earthworks if we live, and if we fall we will leave our spirit in those who follow, and they will not turn back. All is ready. Bugler, blow the charge.[70]

Holmes was perhaps destined, by his own character as much as by the wider culture, to keep returning to the Civil War. But one might wonder, as he prepared to assume the mantle of Associate Justice of the Supreme Court, who he thought the enemy was this time.

Notes

1 Oliver Wendell Holmes, Jr., "Memorial Day Address, May 30 1895," in Mark DeWolfe Howe (ed.), *Oliver Wendell Holmes: Occasional Speeches* (Cambridge, MA: The Belknap Press of Harvard University Press, 1962) 78.

2 Liva Baker, *The Justice from Beacon Hill: The Life and Times of Oliver Wendell Holmes* (New York: Harper Collins, 1991) 205–206.

3 Holmes to Sir Frederick Pollock, March 5, April 10, 1881, in Mark DeWolfe Howe (ed.), *Holmes-Pollock Letters: The Correspondence of Mr. Justice Holmes and Sir Frederick Pollock, 1874–1932*, Second Edition: Two Volumes in One (Cambridge, MA: The Belknap Press of Harvard University Press, 1961) I, 16–17.

4   Holmes to Pollock, April 10, July 5, 1881, in Howe, *Holmes-Pollock Letters*, I, 17–18; see also 18, notes 1 and 2.

5   51, *Saturday Review* (London) 758 (June 11, 1881); G. Edward White, *Justice Oliver Wendell Holmes: Law and the Inner Self* (New York and Oxford: Oxford University Press, 1993) 188–189.

6   Holmes to Eliot, November 1, 1881, quoted in White, *Law and the Inner Self*, 198–199.

7   White, *Law and the Inner Self*, 202–204; James to Henry James, October 2, 1869, in Ralph Barton Perry, *The Thought and Character of William James*, 2 Vols. (New York: Oxford University Press, 1935) I, 307.

8   Holmes' 1899 speech quoted in Catherine Drinker Bowen, *Yankee from Olympus: Justice Holmes and His Family* (Boston: Little, Brown and Company, 1944) 295; Dr. Holmes quoted in John T. Morse, *Life and Letters of Oliver Wendell Holmes*, 2 Vols. (London: Sampson Low, Marston and Company, 1896) I, 322; Holmes to Felix Frankfurter, July 15, 1913, in Robert M. Mennel and Christine L. Compston, *Holmes and Frankfurter: Their Correspondence, 1912–1934* (Hanover: University of New Hampshire, 1996) 12.

9   White, *Law and the Inner Self*, 205–206. For example, Novick's section of his biography that covers Holme's tenure on the Supreme Judicial Court of Massachusetts is entitled "An Obscure Judge." Sheldon M. Novick, *Honorable Justice: The Life of Oliver Wendell Holmes* (New York: Dell Publishing, 1990) 161; and Baker, similarly, described Holmes' early period on the court as "The Fallow Years." Baker, *Justice from Beacon Hill*, 273.

10   Max Lerner (ed.), *The Mind and Faith of Justice Holmes: His Speeches, Essays, Letters, and Judicial Opinions* (1943. Reprint. New Brunswick, NJ: Transaction Publishers, 2010) xxvii.

11   Holmes to Pollock, March 25, August 27, 1883, in Howe, *Holmes-Pollock Letters*, I, 20–21, 22.

12   Oliver Wendell Holmes, Jr., *The Common Law* (1881. Reprint. London: Macmillan and Company, 1882) 50; White, *Law and the Inner Self*, 258–259.

13   White, *Law and the Inner Self*, 259–260; Holmes to Pollock, November 2, 1884, in Howe, *Holmes-Pollock Letters*, I, 26.

14   White, *Law and the Inner Self*, 291; Holmes to Pollock, August 27, 1883, March 9, 1884, in Howe, *Holmes-Pollock Letters*, I, 22, 24; Novick, *Honorable Justice*, 171.

15   Holmes to Pollock, January 17, 1887, in Howe, *Holmes-Pollock Letters*, 1, 29.

16   Holmes to Frankfurter, March 8, 1912, in Mennel and Compston, *Holmes and Frankfurter*, 6.

17   Louis Menand, *The Metaphysical Club* (2001. Reprint. London: Harper Collins, 2002) 69.

18   Oliver Wendell Holmes, Jr., "Memorial Day Address, May 30, 1884," in Mark DeWolfe Howe (ed.), *Oliver Wendell Holmes: Occasional Speeches* (Cambridge, MA: The Belknap Press of Harvard University Press, 1962) 6–7, 13.

19   Holmes, "Memorial Day Address, 1884," 15.

20   Holmes, "Memorial Day Address, 1895," 73–74, 78, 80–81.

21   Holmes, "Memorial Day Address, 1884," 80.

22   N.P. Hallowell, *An Address by . . . Delivered on Memorial Day, May 30, 1896 at a Meeting Called by the Graduating Class of Harvard University* (Boston: Little, Brown, and Company, 1896) 6–8.

23   Holmes, "Memorial Day Address, 1895," 73; Holmes to Pollock, December 27, 1895, *Holmes-Pollock Letters*, I, 66.

24   Anon., "Sentimental Jingoism," New York *Evening Post*, December 16, 1895; Anon., "Force as a Moral Instrument," New York *Evening Post*, December 17, 1895.

25   "Force as a Moral Instrument," New York *Evening Post*, December 17, 1895.

26   Reno quoted in Howard Gillman, *The Constitution Besieged: The Rise and Demise of Lochner Era Police Powers* (1993. Reprint. Durham, NC: Duke University Press, 2004) 116.

27   Kenneth M. Roemer, *The Obsolete Necessity: America in Utopian Writings, 1888–1900* (Kent, OH: The Kent State University Press, 1976) 2–3.

28   Novick, *Honorable Justice*, 217.

29   Josiah Strong, *Our Country: Its Possible Future and Its Present Crisis* (New York: The American Home Mission Society, 1885) 40–41.

30   White, *Law and the Inner Self*, 266–268.

31 Robert H. Wiebe, *The Search for Order, 1877–1920* (1967. Reprint. New York: Hill and Wang, 1989) 133–134.

32 Harold U. Faulkner, *The Decline of Laissez Faire, 1897–1917* (New York: Holt, Rinehart and Wilson, 1951) 177.

33 Brown quoted in Gillman, *The Constitution Besieged*, 102.

34 *ICC v. Alabama Midland Railway Company*, 168 U.S. 176 (1897); Holmes to Frankfurter, April 8, 1913, Mennel and Compston, *Holmes and Frankfurter*, 8; Holmes to Pollock, April 23, 1910, January 20, 1893, *Holmes-Pollock Letters*, I, 163, 44.

35 Holmes quoted in White, *Law and the Inner Self*, 287; Holmes, "Rudyard Kipling: Remarks at a Tavern Club Dinner, April 24, 1895," *Occasional Speeches*, 71–72; Novick, *Honorable Justice*, 198–199.

36 White, *Law and the Inner Self*, 288.

37 White, *Law and the Inner Self*, 280, 286–289, 294; Novick, *Honorable Justice*, 196–199.

38 William James, *The Will to Believe and Other Essays in Popular Philosophy* (1896. Reprint. New York and London: Longmans Green and Company, 1897) xii–xiii.

39 James, *Will to Believe*, 167.

40 Holmes to William James, May 24, 1896, March 24, 1907, Perry, *The Thought and Character of William James*, II, 458–459.

41 Holmes to William James, March 24, 1907, Perry, *The Thought and Character of William James*, II, 459–460.

42 Holmes to William James, April 1, 1907, Perry, *The Thought and Character of William James*, II, 462; Holmes, "A Provisional Adieu: Remarks at a Tavern Club Dinner," November 14, 1902, *Occasional Speeches*, 152.

43 Jackson Lears, *No Place of Grace: Antimodernism and the Transformation of American Culture, 1880–1920* (New York: Pantheon Books, 1981) 100–101.

44 Lears, *No Place of Grace*, 101; Owen Wister, "The Evolution of the Cow-Puncher," *Harper's Magazine*, 91 (September 1895) 602–617, 603–604.

45 Baker, *Justice from Beacon Hill*, 159; Max Jones, *The Last Great Quest: Captain Scott's Antarctic Sacrifice* (New York and Oxford: Oxford University Press, 2003) 1; see also Felix Driver, *Geography Militant: Cultures of Exploration and Empire* (New York and Oxford: Oxford University Press, 2001); and Beau Riffenburgh, *The Myth of the Explorer: The Press, Sensationalism, and Geographical Discovery* (New York and Oxford: Oxford University Press, 1994).

46 *New York Herald*, December 23, 1871, July 2, 1872; the latter issue was almost entirely devoted to Stanley's meeting with Livingstone; see Edward Berenson, *Heroes of Empire: Five Charismatic Men and the Conquest of Africa* (Berkeley and Los Angeles: University of California Press, 2011) 41–42, 48.

47 Mark DeWolfe Howe, "Oliver Wendell Holmes at Harvard Law School," *Harvard Law Review*, 70:3 (January 1957) 416; Wiebe, *Search for Order*, xiv.

48 Holmes, "Commencement Address at Brown University, 17 June 1897," in Howe (ed.), *Occasional Speeches*, 97–98; see also White, *Law and the Inner Self*, 90.

49 Timothy Walker, *Introduction to American Law*, 2nd Edn. (Cincinnati, OH: Derby, Bradley and Co., 1846) 19.

50 Baker, *Justice from Beacon Hill*, 159; White, *Law and the Inner Self*, 89–91.

51 Holmes to Lady Pollock, April 11, 1897, *Holmes-Pollock Letters*, I, 73.

52 Kelly Lankford, "Arctic Explorer Robert E. Peary's Other Quest: Money, Science, and the Year 1897," *American Nineteenth Century History* 9:1 (March 2008) 37–60, 42, 54–55. For contemporary representations of exploration, see, e.g., Frederick Schwatka, "Wintering in the Arctic," *Science*, 3:66 (May 9, 1884) 566–571; and on exploration's wider cultural impact, "Opening of the East Wing of the American Museum of Natural History," *Science*, 4:102 (December 11, 1886) 849–853.

53 Baker, *Justice from Beacon Hill*, 155–156; Roosevelt quoted in Jones, *Last Great Quest*, 1.

54 White, *Law and the Inner Self*, 230–235.

55 Novick, *Honorable Justice*, 193.

56 Holmes quoted in White, *Law and the Inner Self*, 233.

57 Holmes to Laski, April 29, 1927, in Mark DeWolfe Howe (ed.), *Holmes-Laski Letters: The Correspondence of Mr Justice Holmes and Harold J. Laski*, 2 Vols. (Cambridge, MA: Harvard University Press, 1953) II, 938.

58 Oliver Wendell Holmes, Jr., "The Path of the Law," *Harvard Law Review*, 10:8 (March 25, 1897) 457–478, 459.

59 Holmes, "Path of the Law," 459–460.

60 Holmes, "Path of the Law," 464.

61 Holmes, "Speech Prepared for Delivery at a Banquet, October 14, 1899," *Occasional Speeches*, 110.

62 Theodore Roosevelt, "The Strenuous Life," in Roosevelt, *The Strenuous Life: Essays and Addresses* (New York: Cosimo, 2006) 1–3.

63 Lears, *No Place of Grace*, 102.

64 *New York Times*, August 12, 1902; see also *Richmond Dispatch*, August 15, 1902; *The Progressive Farmer*, October 28, 1902.

65 *The Progressive Farmer*, October 28, 1902; *Richmond Times*, August 12, 1902.

66 Holmes to Lady Pollock, September 6, 1902; Holmes to Pollock, [September] 23, 1902, *Holmes-Pollock Letters*, 105, 106.

67 Bowen, *Yankee from Olympus*, xii.

68 Holmes, "Twenty Years in Retrospect: Speech at a Banquet of the Middlesex Bar Association, December 3, 1902," *Occasional Speeches*, 154, 155–156.

69 Holmes, "Despondency and Hope: Remarks at a Dinner of the Chicago Bar Association, October 21, 1902," *Occasional Speeches*, 147.

70 Holmes, "Twenty Years," 157.

CHAPTER 5

THE STRENUOUS LIFE

"Our moral horizon moves with us as we move, and never do we draw nearer to the far-off line where the black waves and the azure meet."
(William James, "The Dilemma of Determinism," 1896)[1]

As the press reaction to his appointment revealed, Holmes' reputation preceded him to the Supreme Court, but it was in many ways a contradictory one, comprising conservative and radical aspects in almost equal measure. In its public form, it was grounded in the Civil War, and had largely been constructed, as many papers made clear, through his father's writing about his search for his son on the battlefield on Antietam. To readers unfamiliar with Roosevelt's new appointee, the papers offered short extracts from "My Hunt after the Captain," and a brief summary of the occasions when Holmes had been wounded as a means of establishing his war veteran status.

At the same time, for many commentators, Holmes was a new man for new times. Civil War veteran he may have been, but the war was long over, and with it, at least according to the New York *Evening Post*, "the old questions which were so long the most important thing have been fully disposed of." Most of these questions had, the paper observed, revolved around "the slavery controversy." What exercised the courts now, the *Post* noted, were "the rights of capital and labor under the novel conditions bred of modern tendencies toward the consolidation of wealth and the organization of labor." With his record of support for union activity and the rights of labor generally, the paper proposed that in Holmes the man and the hour had met.[2]

Holmes' professional reputation, therefore, like his public one, suggested that Roosevelt was correct in assuming that he had selected a safe pair of hands to serve on the Supreme Court. But this assumption was possibly too glib. The image of Holmes as the great defender of labor was, at best, a simplification of a more mixed record. Holmes was perfectly prepared to level the field upon which the conflict between capital and labor would take place. He was not prepared, however, to extend a helping hand should labor falter, either through industrial accident or, arguably, capital design. His ruling in *Lynch v. Boston and Albany Railroad Co.* (1893), for example, had placed liability for an employee death that resulted from being run over by a train shunted from its track upon the deceased, who "was not relieved from the necessity of keeping watch for himself" and was therefore "not free from negligence in failing to do so." The deceased in question was obviously past caring but Holmes' ruling rather defied both common sense and sympathy.[3]

If Holmes on the eve of his ascension to the Supreme Court was not quite all he seemed to some, no more was the political and legal landscape quite as changed as it seemed to others. As the *Evening Post* pointed out, not all of the issues related to the "slavery controversy" had actually been resolved. Or, rather, they had been resolved in such a way as to store up trouble for the future by "a court with a large majority of Republicans affirming the principle of state rights, annulling the Civil Rights Act, and sustaining the Southern states in adopting Constitutions which practically disenfranchise the blacks, though on their faces so fair that no ground for Federal interference can be found." One cannot be certain whether Holmes took this hint. From the internal evidence of his letters, he undoubtedly read the editorial, but pounced instead on the throw-way comment that on the Massachusetts Court he had evinced a tendency to be "brilliant rather than sound."[4]

Yet in the context of a nation still struggling, as the twentieth century dawned, with many of the constitutional, social, and racial issues raised by the Civil War Holmes became a living embodiment of the uneasy relationship between the forces of federal power and states' rights, political argument, and military power. He understood that "all law ultimately rested on the power of the courts to summon the armed force of the state." The power of the written word is not always enough. But even when it is, it is a form of substitute. "Deep-seated preferences cannot be argued about," Holmes once observed, and "when differences are sufficiently far reaching, we try to kill the other man rather than let him have his way. But that is perfectly consistent with admitting that, so far as it appears, his grounds are just as good as ours."[5]

Holmes was always aware that he lived in a nation defined by war. The colonists in the eighteenth century were no more able than the unionists in the nineteenth to secure the nation by waving either *Common Sense* or the Constitution in the faces of the British and Confederate governments, respectively. Argument gave way to arms in both cases; and in the latter case, there was potentially even more at stake. If the American Revolution established a nation, the Civil War raised the question of what kind of nation it wanted to be. And some of the answers to that question came, rightly or wrongly, to inhere in Holmes himself. As a former soldier and a Supreme Court Justice, Holmes stood, as arguably he had always stood, between two worlds; in constitutional terms, however, he has almost come to be seen as the bridge between them.

★★★

Holmes did not, of course, leap straight into constitutional controversy on his arrival in Washington in December 1902. Auspiciously, however, he arrived in the city in the immediate aftermath of the Anthracite Coal Strike. This was only the most recent in a long-running series of strikes in that industry that arose out of the clash between the United Mine Workers (UMW) and the Morgan-Hill-Vanderbilt-Pennsylvania group, effectively a mining and transportation monopoly that controlled the distribution, and therefore price, of anthracite coal, the nation's main source of heat. The strike had therefore risked leaving many Americans shivering over the winter had it not been resolved, as it was in the fall of 1902.

The coal strike offered a stark reminder of exactly what had fueled the so-called Gilded Age, literally driven the age of steam, and underpinned the nation's move toward a modern, managerial, and industrial culture in the late-nineteenth and early-twentieth centuries. As historian Andrew Arnold has emphasized, "coal helped to shift the nation from more stable, customary, and place-based loyalties to a faster paced, more dynamic, modern society." By 1904 coal constituted "over 60 percent of the total tonnage of the Pennsylvania Railroad," and by 1920 America's railroads consumed some 28 percent of the nation's bituminous coal. The coal itself, however, was still wrenched from the ground under conditions that were far from modern, and indeed not susceptible to the organizational structures imposed on other industries of the era, notably steel and the railroads. The coal industry, Arnold stresses, was in many respects "a counterstory to the technological triumph of the railroads and large-scale manufacturing," but it was not alone in telling a darker tale about the costs involved in the rise of corporate capitalism.[6]

The month before Holmes arrived to take up his post had also seen the start of the publication of a series of articles, later published as a book, in *McClure's Magazine* attacking monopoly, but specifically John D. Rockefeller and Standard Oil. In *The History of the Standard Oil Company*, Ida M. Tarbell effectively revised and updated Henry Demarest Lloyd's *Wealth against Commonwealth* (1894), demonstrating the high price that industrial and corporate leaders were prepared to pay—or, rather, were prepared to let the American people pay—for economic growth and national power. Her book was enormously popular and influential.

Based on first-hand testimony and conversations with many leading oil-men—who may have assumed that, as a woman Tarbell would not dig too deep or, quite possibly, that she intended a positive account of their

business—the exposé that resulted painted a picture of control and corruption achieved through secrecy, and driven by an unholy trinity of oil,
railroad, and money men that, quite literally, railroaded the individual refin-
eries into submission. And some of the men involved would have been very
familiar to Holmes, since they included the former general in charge of the
Army of the Potomac, George B. McClellan, who had gone into the railroad business after the war. Although Holmes later patronizingly dismissed
this work as a "young woman's tale," in fact Tarbell's charges were hard to
refute. Her work was rigorously researched. It could be since, as she noted,
"almost constantly since its organization in 1870 the Standard Oil Company
has been under investigation," by Congress and individual states alike, "on
the suspicion that it was receiving rebates from the railroads and was practic-
ing methods in restraint of free trade." The amount of paperwork, therefore,
was considerable: a sign of how big the problem was, how resistant it would
prove to any effective resolution.[7]

Standard Oil found itself under investigation yet again during Holmes'
first year on the Supreme Court, when Congress, driven by Theodore Roosevelt's determination to deal with the perceived evils of "big business,"
passed the Expediting Act (1903). This gave preference to any suit brought
under either the Interstate Commerce or the Sherman Antitrust Acts. It also
created a new Department of Commerce and Labor along with a Bureau of
Corporations charged with making "diligent investigation into the organization, conduct and management of corporations."[8] Before this act was passed,
however, and even before Holmes arrived in Washington, Roosevelt had
already identified another, possibly more likely target for what was known as
"trust-busting," the forcible dissolution of large, uncompetitive commercial
combinations. In this case, the combination in question was a relatively new
railroad trust, the Northern Securities Company.

The case against this new trust was rumbling along in the background
as Holmes settled in to his new life in Washington. Doubtless he was aware
of it, but other matters had his attention at the time. "It is a devil of a job to
transport all one's belongings . . . when one is over sixty," Holmes later confided to his friend the diplomat Lewis Einstein, whose career, indeed, began
as Holmes joined the Supreme Court. Both men were starting out on a new
life, and Einstein probably appreciated Holmes' perspective, which was that
any move is often "vitalizing; you get rid of dead matter, and the circula-
tion is improved." For Holmes, too, there was an additional factor: a sense
of finally establishing his own position. "I feel that I am settled for good in
a place which is mine," he reported. "The Boston house never ceased to be
my father's."[9]

Indeed, any apprehension Holmes had felt about the move swiftly gave
way to enthusiasm, and soon he was again telling Frederick Pollock that

he was "more absorbed, interested and impressed than ever I had dreamed I might be. The work of the past seems a finished book," he observed, "and a new and solemn volume opens. The variety and novelty to me of the questions, the remote spaces from which they come, the amount of work they require," he reported, "all help the effect." He had not yet been in post a month, but was already fully engaged with his share of cases and fully up to speed in dealing with them. Indeed, so speedy was Holmes in dealing with his docket that the then Chief Justice, Melville Fuller, had to slow him down some to prevent his fellow justices feeling aggrieved at the apparent hyper-efficiency of their new colleague.[10]

Not that Holmes' colleagues were declining into their dotage and progressing cases slowly. Holmes' fellow justices in 1902 were, in the main, older than Holmes, certainly, but not by much. They were, however, a relatively conservative collection of individuals only a handful of whom had shared Holmes' life experiences. One who had was John Marshall Harlan, whose dissent in *ICC v. Alabama Railway Company* (1897) had critiqued the Court's apparent support for "big business," but whose most famous dissent had been in a case the previous year: *Plessy v. Ferguson* (1896). Harlan, who had been born into a slave-holding family in Kentucky, but whose father had emancipated his slaves, fought for the Union during the Civil War and for equal rights after it. His was the sole dissenting voice in a ruling—arguably the most notorious in Supreme Court history—that effectively sanctioned Southern racial segregation. One can only imagine the impact that Harlan and Holmes, dissenting voices both, could have had, had they pulled together after 1902. But on the Supreme Court, Holmes was still a man apart.

With the exception of Fuller, whose friendship Holmes may have deliberately cultivated since he was Chief Justice, Edward D. White, who succeeded Fuller as Chief Justice in 1910, and later Louis D. Brandeis, who joined the Court in 1916, Holmes did not establish any close friendships among his colleagues. Although he claimed that, on the Supreme Court, "[t]houghts of self are almost forgotten and it is just a concentrated effort to do one's part as a wheel in a tremendous machine," it is unlikely that Holmes ever saw himself as part of that machine. His habitual tendency to see himself as alone and act accordingly did not alter on the Supreme Court; if anything it intensified, to the point where he once compared his colleagues to "a cloud of biting mosquitoes." This may have made it easier for him to adopt a contrary stance when he felt the occasion called for it, as it did in the case of *Northern Securities Co. v. U.S.*[11]

Although *Northern Securities Co. v. U.S.* (1904) was one of "the 'great cases' of the early twentieth century," as far as Holmes is concerned it may now be remembered less for any surprises it threw up regarding his legal perspective and more for the fact that it was the moment when he clashed, openly, with Roosevelt's trust-busting reform agenda. It was unfortunate in some respects, since up to that point the Holmes and the Roosevelts had been on very good terms socially. But all that was about to change, and only a year after the president had appointed Holmes to the Court.

Northern Securities had arisen out of the attempt by railroad entrepreneur James J. Hill, the president of the Great Northern Railroad, and the banker J.P. Morgan to pull the shares in two parallel and potentially competing companies, the Great Northern and the Northern Pacific, together under one holding corporation, the Northern Securities Company. The charge was that this "was an illegal combination in restraint of interstate commerce." And by a narrow majority of 5–4, the Court concurred that the holding company did constitute a deliberate attempt to curtail competition. By effectively forming a cartel that could monopolize rail transport in the Northwest it posed a threat to the free flow of goods across state lines, and was therefore in breach of the (very narrow) terms of the Sherman Act. It was not, however, as the 5–4 division makes clear, a straightforward case.[12]

"Great cases," Holmes famously announced, "like hard cases make bad law. For great cases are called great not by reason of their real importance in shaping the law of the future but because of some accident of immediate overwhelming interest which appeals to the feelings and distorts the judgment." In *Northern Securities*, Holmes asserted, size mattered. "I am quite clear," he stated, "that it is only in connection with monopolies that size could play any part." Neither the public, politicians, nor the Court would be as concerned, he argued, were the combination between, for example, two grocers. Worse, he added, the case had been brought under a "law which in my opinion would make eternal the *bellum omnium contra omnes* ["the war of all against all"] and disintegrate society so far as it could into individual atoms." Were that its intent, Holmes observed, then the Sherman Act was not designed "to regulate commerce" at all, but instead represented "an attempt to reconstruct society," an imperative that, he concluded, the Constitution had not afforded Congress.[13]

Roosevelt was, reportedly, furious with Holmes. According to Henry Adams, the president "went wild" about the dissent. But although, to his friend Ellen Curtis, who had written to him on the subject, Holmes admitted that there had "been elements of pain in the situation," he expressed his "confidence" in the president's "great heartedness," and opined that "I don't expect for a moment that after he has had time to cool down it will affect our relations." He rejected any rumors that his appointment to the Court had been for the express purpose of advancing Roosevelt's reforms. If "his seeming personal regard for us was based on the idea that he had a tool," Holmes concluded, "the sooner it is ended the better." And although at first it seemed as if Holmes was right, and that the *Northern Securities* dissent was only a blip in the relationship between himself and Roosevelt, many years later, he admitted to Pollock that it "broke up our incipient friendship." Roosevelt, he acknowledged, had regarded Holmes' dissent "as a political departure (or, I suspect, more truly, couldn't forgive anyone who stood in his way). We talked freely later," Holmes recalled, "but it was never the same after that."[14]

In hindsight, Holmes concluded that Roosevelt "was very likeable, a big figure, a rather ordinary intellect, with extraordinary gifts, a shrewd and I think pretty unscrupulous politician." At the time, Holmes was perhaps struggling with the gradually dawning realization that he was surrounded by shrewd and possibly unscrupulous politicians in Washington. Many of them, specifically the current incumbent of White House, were less admiring of Holmes' intellect in the abstract than the practical, political uses to which it might be put. In Holmes, Roosevelt had not got what he expected, even if what he had expected was entirely unrealistic. Writing to Henry Cabot Lodge two years later, he complained that from "his antecedents, Holmes should have been an ideal man on the bench," but in fact "he has been a bitter disappointment."[15]

Whether Roosevelt was right to be disappointed in Holmes is a moot point. Certainly Holmes had made no real secret of his belief that enforcing the Sherman Act was not likely to achieve the ends desired either by reformers or by Roosevelt. This would have come as no surprise to Roosevelt had he read Holmes more carefully. Holmes' view, which he had stated categorically in his 1895 Memorial Day Address, was that it was not the imbalance of but the attitude to wealth that was the issue: the "unfortunately growing hatred of the poor for the rich," rather than the rich themselves. And whilst Holmes charged the rich with encouraging the attitude that money was an end in itself, he did not regard that as reason enough to redistribute their gains, ill-gotten or otherwise. No more was he entirely out on a legal limb as far as his dissent in *Northern Securities* was concerned, as Frederick Pollock confirmed. "I entirely agree with your reasons," he reassured Holmes. The agreement to establish Northern Securities was, he judged, "probably in restraint of trade . . . but was not on the face of it a violation of the [Sherman] Act . . . A *quia timet* ["because he fears"; used in cases of imminent risk] injunction to restrain the doing of something which may possibly lead to the commission of an offense in the future," Pollock observed, wryly, "is a new kind of equity."[16]

Holmes' fellow Boston Brahmin, Henry Adams, saw the bigger picture with perhaps more clarity than either Holmes or Pollock at this point. In turn-of-the-century America, power, he observed, "seemed to have outgrown its servitude and to have asserted its freedom. The cylinder had exploded, and thrown great masses of stone and steam against the sky." In

New York the "citizens were crying, in every accent of anger and alarm, that the new forces must at any cost be brought under control. Prosperity never before imagined, power never yet wielded by man, speed never reached by anything but a meteor," he concluded, "had made the world irritable, nervous, querulous, unreasonable and afraid." And Adams understood that it was the Trusts that "stood for the larger part of the new power." They "were obnoxious because of their vigorous and unscrupulous energy. They were revolutionary, troubling all the old conventions and values . . . They tore society to pieces and trampled it under foot."[17]

Yet Adams also understood that the problem was "not so much to control the Trusts as to create the society that could manage the Trusts. The new American must be either the child of the new forces," he argued, "or a chance sport of nature." Adams rather saw himself as an outsider in this new society, an attitude that he appreciated was likely to annoy "the players in the game, as the attitude of the umpire is apt to infuriate the spectators." Since Adams was an historian and not a Supreme Court justice, the players in the game may not have cared either way. But in fact it was Holmes, not Adams, who behaved more like an umpire than a player. That was how he saw his role on the Supreme Court, at least in its early stages. That, arguably, was what lay behind his dissent in *Northern Securities*, and informed many of his later decisions and dissents. That, and possibly a personal predilection for the wealthy over the weak. Holmes' was often a contrary voice and sometimes a contradictory one that would bring him into sometimes serious conflict with his fellow justices whilst, at the same time, lay the groundwork for his reputation as a great liberal judge, the "Yankee from Olympus."[18]

★★★

Almost a decade after his *Northern Securities* dissent, Holmes had refined, but not really revised, his judicial philosophy expressed at the start of his Supreme Court service. Writing to the more radically reform-minded Felix Frankfurter in 1913, Holmes delineated the problem, as he saw it, with the thinking behind not just the Sherman Act but much of the legislation of the Progressive Era:

> Philosophers are apt to try to retain the dogmatic supremacy formerly accorded to theologians by assuming a mystic infinite value for morality as *point d'appui*. But if one looks at ethics as a system of popular generalizations of the conditions of social welfare expressed in terms of emotion, one is led to ask for statistics that so far as I know are wanting. It may be true . . . that there has been a change of emphasis . . . and that we now articulately recognize that social welfare is the basis of individual rights—a principle always acted on whether recognized or not—*e.g.*, eminent domain [compulsory purchase] and conscription. But if the emphasis has changed the question what social welfare is, and if we have agreed

on that, which we haven't, which means tend to accomplish it seems to me very much in the air.[19]

By the time Holmes wrote this, of course, he was already well known for several notable liberal opinions that had confirmed the principle of judicial restraint, the idea of law as umpire which he had first set out in *Northern Securities*. One of these would come to define an era in Supreme Court history: *Lochner v. New York* (1905). The case, but in particular Holmes' dissent, has "come to be regarded as a major turning point in American constitutional jurisprudence, and the *Lochner* decision itself as one of the most notorious moments in the history of the Court."[20] And it all began in a bakery.

Joseph Lochner, a baker from Utica, had been indicted under state legislation that sought to limit the hours a baker could work to ten a day, or sixty a week. The charge was that one of Lochner's employees had exceeded that limit. Lochner was fined, not once but twice, and the second time he appealed. By 1905 the case had reached the Supreme Court, which was asked to decide whether, under the "due process" clause of the Fourteenth Amendment, Lochner was at liberty to offer his employees contracted working hours in excess of those established under the New York statute. The Court found that Lochner's "general right to make a contract in relation to his business is part of the liberty protected by the Fourteenth Amendment," and that the New York labor statute was "not a legitimate exercise of the police power of the State, but an unreasonable, unnecessary and arbitrary interference with the right and liberty of the individual to contract in relation to labor, and, as such, it is in conflict with, and void under, the Federal Constitution."[21]

Holmes' famous dissent in this case was short, but perhaps not entirely to the point. In effect he accused his colleagues of imposing on the New York legislature a decision based on "an economic theory which a large part of the country does not entertain." He emphasized his belief that Supreme Court justices ought not "to embody their opinions in law," because "a constitution is not intended to embody a particular economic theory" but is instead designed to govern "people of fundamentally differing views." On the specifics of the case, Holmes pointed out that the much-vaunted notion of "liberty of contract" was already compromised by, for example, Sunday trading regulations, so to elevate it to a point where it was beyond contradiction made no sense whatsoever. The Fourteenth Amendment, he asserted, "does not enact Mr. Herbert Spencer's *Social Statics*," and any "reasonable man" might consider the New York statute "a proper measure on the score of health . . . a first instalment of a general regulation of the hours of work."[22]

This dissent transformed Holmes, "almost overnight," according to Max Lerner, into "the leader of liberal jurisprudence in America." And for those, like Lerner, inclined to locate Holmes in a liberal light, Holmes' last point was the cornerstone of the dissent, because in his invocation of Spencer, Holmes was referencing what was, by 1905, a familiar Progressive argument, one put cogently and with some force by Conrad Reno in his 1892 analysis of "The Wage Contract and Personal Liberty." Reno attacked Spencer's *laissez-faire* philosophy, "that the State has no moral right to interfere with the freedom of contract between employer and employed," on the grounds that it was predicated on the "analogy supposed to exist between human labor and commodities . . . Is this analogy correct?" Reno asked, "Is human labor a commodity?"[23]

Reno had no hesitation in saying no, it was not, and reminded his readers that those who had believed it was had been slaveholders, against whom a brutal Civil War had been fought precisely to establish the point that humans were not chattels. "Labor is much more than a commodity," Reno asserted, it "is the bone and sinew of the State, the very essence of its existence." But labor was operating at a disadvantage. "The doctrine of freedom of contract," as Reno pointed out, "will never place the honest and generous employer upon an equal footing with the dishonest and avaricious employer."[24] The odds favored Holmes' "bad man," in effect. The deck was always stacked on the side of the unscrupulous. Therefore, for Reno in 1892, as possibly for Holmes in 1905, labor deserved the full protection of the state.

This is not to suggest that Lochner, as an employer, was in any sense a "bad man." The New York statute that he challenged had not arisen out of some arbitrary desire to control working hours, but was intended to alleviate some of the state's worst working conditions. And the case against him was partly predicated on the findings of the New York Bureau of Statistics of Labor that bakers worked exceptionally long hours and in conditions hazardous to their own health. Within a constitutional construction that emphasized the "neutral state," and restricted governmental interference on behalf of any class or group to such occasions as would "advance public health, safety, or morality," the case against Lochner—or more precisely the case in favor of the law limiting the hours of bakers—had some traction. It was strengthened by the fact that the New York statute came under the remit of Labor rather than Public Health Regulations, so the Court could conveniently sidestep the health issue. And the majority decision revealed that the Court concurred in the view that the attempt to restrict bakers' working hours was not "consistent with a neutral state in promoting public health."[25]

For those less inclined to interpret Holmes' dissent as a disinterested defense of workers' rights, however, the crux of the issue lies not in the ideal of the "neutral state" but in the problem of the neutral justice. Holmes' dissent in *Northern Securities* was perhaps a clearer indication of his thinking than that in *Lochner*. Although Holmes seemed to echo Progressive, indeed Populist arguments in *Lochner*, he did not deploy these in the same way as men such as Reno. For Holmes, "talk about the world being slaves to the man who commands the necessaries of life" was simply "rot." As he saw it, if a man such as "Jim Hill (the great railroad man) does not follow the economically necessary course he comes to grief." In Holmes' view, even the "dishonest and avaricious employer" was susceptible to market forces, and the economy itself would restrain his greed, a perspective that seemed of a piece with the original intent behind the idea of "liberty of contract."[26]

In some respects, this seems to contradict the view of Holmes as inherently cynical in his outlook. He appeared to believe that market forces would ensure not that everything would turn out for the best in the best of all possible worlds, but that it would do so even in the worst ones. For Holmes, indeed, the energy and enterprise of men such as Hill were attributes to be admired, although the world of corporate consumption they were building had an inherent flaw. As he admitted:

> I regard a man like Hill as representing one of the greatest forms of human power, an immense mastery of economic details, an equal grasp of general principles, and ability and courage to put his conclusions into practice . . . Yet the intense external activity that calls for such powers does not especially delight me. Barring the intellectual flowering of the last fifty years, most of the great things have been done with a thinner population. If civilization keeps on, and we don't discover a new source of energy before the coal is exhausted, the population must thin out . . . If we are destined to drop from Jim Hill to Aeschylus there are compensations. This thought makes me less unhappy at my duty of enforcing laws that I believe to embody economic mistakes."[27]

The emphasis on duty in Holmes' outlook may lend weight to the charge that his apparent advocacy of judicial restraint in *Lochner* was no more than an actual "abdication of judicial responsibility." Certainly Holmes' dissent was of a different order entirely from that proposed by his colleagues. But it was of a piece with Holmes' judicial, and arguably his personal philosophy generally, as that had been expressed in earlier cases. On the Massachusetts Court, notably in *Vegelahn v. Guntner* (1896) he had sought to accord equal rights to labor and capital in his support of the right to strike. Life was a battle, in his view, but both sides should be armed. At the same time, he did not necessarily see it as the Court's role to be active in this respect, but rather as neutral. This was made evident in his first opinion for the Supreme Court, *Otis v. Parker* (1903), when he upheld the constitutionality of a California statute seeking to prevent potentially damaging speculation in mining stocks.[28]

In delivering the majority opinion in *Otis v. Parker*, Holmes made many of the same points that the majority made in *Lochner*: that "neither a state legislature nor a state constitution can interfere arbitrarily with private business transactions, and that the mere fact that an enactment purports to be for the protection of public safety, health, or morals, is not conclusive upon the courts." But then his particular angle on the issue became evident. "Considerable latitude," he argued, "must be allowed for differences of view . . . Otherwise, a constitution, instead of embodying only relatively fundamental rules of right . . . would become the partisan of a particular set of ethical or economic opinions, which by no means are held *semper ubique et ab omnibus* ["always and by everyone"]."[29]

Both *Otis* and *Lochner* were cases that centered on the interpretation and implementation of the Fourteenth Amendment's "due process" clause, and specifically on what the word "liberty" might mean in each case. Both the Fifth Amendment, which applies to the federal government, and the Fourteenth, which applies to the states, establish that the government may not deprive an American citizen of life, liberty, or property "without due process of law." On one level, due process is a procedural matter (*procedural due process*) concerned with the actual procedures through which a case reaches the courts. On another level, it is substantive (*substantive due process*), and is concerned with "whether the benefits and burdens created by the challenged law are sufficiently fair to pass constitutional muster."[30]

In *Otis*, Holmes, speaking for the majority, concluded that the California statute was not contrary to the precepts of the Fourteenth Amendment. In *Lochner*, he maintained this position, but was in conflict with the majority opinion of the Court, whom he believed had imposed its own economic perspective through substantive due process. In both cases, however, Holmes asserted his ultimate belief in the dominance of the majority opinion of the country, in the face of which the judge could only ever be "a passive, 'deferential' figure, notwithstanding his ultimate power as the sovereign interpreter of the Constitution."[31]

In several subsequent dissents, Holmes made this aspect of his thinking even clearer. Only a few years after *Lochner*, a case came before the Court, *Adair v. United States* (1908), that is often regarded as defining the "*Lochner* era" of the Supreme Court: the years when the Court effectively supported corporations at the expense of the citizen. *Adair* concerned the constitutionality of a regulatory statute, specifically the Erdman Act (1898), a federal law intended to facilitate arbitration in railroad disputes. Section 10 of the Erdman Act rendered it illegal to fire a railroad employee because he joined a labor union. The Court concluded that this was unconstitutional, thereby confirming the legality of what became known as "Yellow Dog" contracts, contracts that prevented the employee from joining a labor union.

The majority opinion, again, deployed the "liberty of contract" clause to declare the statute unenforceable. "It is not within the power of Congress," the Court asserted, "to make it a criminal offense against the United States . . . to discharge an employee simply because of his membership in a labor organization." It "is not within the functions of government," it ruled, "to compel any person in the course of his business, and against his will, either to employ, or be employed by, another. An employer has the same right to prescribe terms on which he will employ one to labor as an employee has to prescribe those on which he will sell his labor, and any legislation which disturbs this equality," the Court concluded, "is an arbitrary and unjustifiable interference with liberty of contract."[32]

For Holmes, the majority decision in *Adair* seemed to be a surprise. He had, as he stated, believed the statute to be constitutional, and "but for the decision of my brethren, I should have felt pretty clear about it." In fact he was pretty clear about it. He was clear that the ruling simply revealed that "the right to make contracts at will that has been derived from the word liberty in the amendments has been stretched to its extreme." Holmes admitted "that the question what and how much good labor unions do is one on which intelligent people may differ—I think that laboring men sometimes attribute to them advantages, as many attribute to combinations of capital disadvantages, that really are due to economic conditions of a far wider and deeper kind." Nevertheless, Holmes concluded, "I could not pronounce it unwarranted if Congress should decide that to foster a strong union was for the best interests not only of the men, but of the railroads and the country at large."[33]

Holmes reiterated the point many years later in *Coppage v. Kansas* (1915), a similar case revolving around the right to unionize, and this time his dissent spelled it out:

> In present conditions a workman not unnaturally may believe that only by belonging to a union can he secure a contract that shall be fair to him. If that belief, whether right or wrong, may be held by a reasonable man, it seems to me that it may be enforced by law in order to establish the equality of position between the parties in which liberty of contract begins. Whether in the long run it is wise for the workingmen to enact legislation of this sort is not my concern, but I am strongly of the opinion that there is nothing in the Constitution of the United States to prevent it, and that *Adair v. United States* . . . and *Lochner v. New York* . . . should be overruled.[34]

Holmes' perspective on the unions was, of course, relative. He seemed, on the surface, to be pro-union, his dissents a defense of workers' rights in the face of corporate power, but as White has pointed out, Holmes "was 'pro-union' only to the extent that his detachment contrasted with the decidedly anti-union views of his judicial colleagues." There can be no doubt that he approached the subject with a degree of skepticism. He "who administers constitutional law should multiply his scepticisms," Holmes asserted, "to avoid reading into vague words like 'liberty' his private convictions or prejudices of his class." With age came a certain skepticism about this perspective, however, perhaps an insight into his own motivations. "People for the most part believe what they want to," Holmes observed in 1927, since "their postulates are rooted in their total experience and life. Those of us who flatter ourselves that we have intellectual detachment," he suggested, "only get one story lower in our personality and in the end are trying to make the kind of world we should like."[35]

It is not, however, surprising that, for some, Holmes' apparent deference to statutes in cases such as *Otis* and *Lochner* seems an abnegation of responsibility rather than an attempt to sustain and impose an objective standard upon judicial review in cases challenging the constitutionality of legislative acts. And Holmes, in his personal correspondence as much as in his judicial decisions, certainly provided enough ammunition for both sides of the debate to make a case. He once confessed to Pollock that he was "so sceptical as to our knowledge about the goodness or badness of laws that I have no practical criterion except what the crowed wants," a statement that could be read as a philosophical meditation on interpretative mutability, an admission that Holmes simply saw himself as the corporeal vessel through which the common law flowed, or simply a more sophisticated way of denying any responsibility whatsoever for the lives of those affected by the legal rulings he issued.[36] Perhaps most pertinent in this respect was Holmes' lifelong tendency to locate himself, intellectually at least, apart from society, a position that lends itself equally to those who would praise and those who would damn him. But it was in some ways a contrived stance.

Although Holmes claimed never to "read the papers or otherwise feel the pulse of the machine," he was sufficiently in tune with the popular concerns of his times to critique them. "Under modern conditions," he observed to Pollock in the immediate aftermath of *Lochner*, "the crowd presents the inevitable to itself as the fiat of some great man, and hates him, but it is very silly." They had both been reading Brooks Adams' recently published essays on the "Nature of Law," and "Law Under Inequality," but Holmes was unconvinced by their arguments, as well he might have been since Adams' perspective on the subject was somewhat at odds with his own, both as presented in *The Common Law* and in the few years he had served on the Supreme Court.

"I can recommend the historical method as a means of mental training," Adams acknowledged, "but as a system of instruction in the modern law, I consider it insufficient." It got worse. "So far does the law lag behind business," according to Adams, "that the law has become an impediment, and one of the most important functions of counsel is to devise means of conducting necessary business operations, which the law either forbids or discourages." In his second essay, Adams honed in on the heart of the matter. "American civilization is based upon the theory of freedom of contract," he noted, but "freedom of contract is an effect of unrestrained economic competition, a social condition which favors men of a certain type." And the dominance of these "men of a certain type," the financiers and railroad magnates, had upset the national equilibrium. America was, for Adams in 1906, at a point of inevitable transition as far as the law was concerned. New laws were needed for the new economic landscape.[37]

As Holmes saw it, Adams was guilty of at least a degree of exaggeration, as he observed:

> Brooks at present is in a great stir and thinks a world crisis is at hand, for us among others, and that our Court may have a last word as to who shall be master in the great battle between the many and the few. I think this notion is exaggerated and half cracked . . . I merely speculate. My hobby is to consider the stream of products, to omit all talk about ownership and just to consider who eats the wheat, wears the clothes, uses the railroads, and lives in the houses. I think the crowd now has substantially all there is, that the luxuries of the few are a drop in the bucket, and that unless you make war on moderate comfort there is no general economic question. I agree however that there are great wastes in competition, due to advertisement, superfluous reduplication of establishments, etc. But those are the very things the trusts get rid of.[38]

And this was, on the whole, the position that Holmes maintained for the rest of his life. Over two decades later, he still asserted his belief that the idea of "robbery of labor by capital" was nothing but "a humbug." For him, "the real competitors are different kinds of labor. The capitalist by his power may turn a part into directions that you deem undesirable," but only did so "because he thinks a body of consumers will want the product and he is the best prophet we can get." "Some kind of despotism," he believed, "is at the bottom of the seeking for change. I don't care to boss my neighbors," he complained, "and to require them to want something different from what they do even when, as frequently, I think their wishes more or less suicidal." And he thought he knew what the root cause of the problem was: simple envy. "I don't disparage envy," he admitted, "but I don't accept it as legitimately my master." Live and let live, he seemed to be saying as he approached his ninth decade of life, by which time he described himself as "reduced to a nearly exhausted spectator." But in many ways, arguably, and perhaps especially on the Court, he had always seen himself, and came to be seen by others, as the outsider looking on, the "Great Dissenter."[39]

★★★

Holmes' eventual reputation as the "Great Dissenter," of course, bore little if any relation to the actual number of dissents he offered (173 out of a total of 873 opinions over the course of his Court career). Many of his colleagues dissented as frequently, and some more often. This aspect of his lasting reputation derived from the nature of the dissents, and the cases concerned. In those such as *Lochner, Coppage*, and, later, *Abrams v. United States* (1919), Holmes came across, to the public at least, not just as the champion of the common man but as a reformist voice on a Court still wedded to tradition. In the context of a nation shocked by the picture of political corruption presented by journalist Lincoln Steffens' *The Shame of the Cities* (1904) and horrified by the findings of Upton Sinclair's *The Jungle* (1906), an exposé of the appalling conditions in Chicago's meat-packing industry that has been credited with ensuring the passage of both the Pure Food and Drug Act and the Meat Inspection Act, any voice that spoke for the worker would have had resonance.

In some ways, indeed, Brooks Adams had not been as far off the mark as Holmes had charged. During Roosevelt's presidency, the Supreme Court was positioned, in many respects, between the "social and corporate" worlds of modernizing America, its judgments a sometimes awkward balancing act "between the rights of the individual and the rights of society."[40] Effectively it operated at the eye of the social, economic, and cultural storm sweeping across the nation and, as befits that location, has often been interpreted as a center of, if not calm, exactly, then certainly a judicial conservatism.

During the *Lochner* era, the Court, it was long assumed, sought to hinder progressive "social legislation intended to protect economically powerless people against the vicissitudes of industrialization and the depredations of big business." In this interpretation, only Holmes, and later his colleague and close friend Justice Brandeis, perceived the need to drag the Court into the modern age, and did so by challenging the "sincere, if unintelligent nostalgia for a *laissez-faire* world that no longer existed" expressed by their fellow justices. That contemporary views of the *Lochner* court have become rather more nuanced is in no small part because Holmes and his reputation have undergone extensive revision over the years. No longer viewed as a Progressive, Holmes is now regarded as the instigator of the theory of judicial restraint. But even that is not as straightforward a shift as it may seem,[41] because so much of Holmes' reputation, as that of the Court, rests not on the apparently radical dissents he offered but on the conservative ones: in other words, not on what he did do, but what he failed to do.

Over the course of Holmes' first decade on the Supreme Court, the issue of the Trusts, and regulatory legislation dealing with them, and the question of workers' rights to unionize in the face of the corporate machine were not the only ones to come before the Court. The perceived problem of consolidation diminished somewhat over that decade anyway, simply because there was little left to consolidate. The rise of new industries in the second decade of the twentieth century, including the car and film industries, produced new kinds of corporations in the form of General Motors and Paramount-Famous-Lasky, of course, but the nation was not marching in equal step toward the brave new business world. In many of the Southern states, still economically hampered by defeat in the Civil War even in the early twentieth century, agricultural workers, many of them African American, struggled under a system of debt peonage that, in material terms, left them little better off than under slavery, and simultaneously suffered from a political system that, on a state level, sought to restrict their voting rights. Several such cases came before the Supreme Court, carrying with them echoes of slavery, of a war fought to secure equal rights, and of a victory that had let many of them slip away.[42]

"In the first thirteen years of Holmes' tenure on the Court," White notes, "the sorts of persons whose civil rights tend to be infringed by majorities—racial and ethnic minorities, political radicals, and aliens—fared comparatively poorly before the Supreme Court, and Holmes," he charged, "contributed to their relatively ineffectual showing." And while it is true that the Court at that time, dominated as it was "by a generation for whom talk of civil war was not empty bluster," was understandably cautious in its wielding of federal authority through the Fourteenth Amendment, there was no imminent danger of the white South rising again, at least not in military formation. So Holmes' perceived personal retreat from Reconstruction in cases such as *Giles v. Harris* (1903) or *Bailey v. Alabama* (1911) demands, from Holmes' scholars at least, some explanation.[43]

Giles v. Harris (1903) concerned voter registration in Alabama brought by Jackson W. Giles on behalf of some 5,000 residents of Montgomery. It challenged the state's recently introduced and racially motivated restrictions on voting such that all residents who had registered to vote before 1903 (mostly white) would automatically continue to be registered, whilst all who had not (mostly black) would have to meet new registration requirements in the form of a citizenship test. In dismissing the case, Holmes spoke for the majority of the Court and effectively ruled that the Court was helpless in the face of racial discrimination at state level. He seemed to accept that the situation in Alabama was as described, "that the great mass of the white population intends to keep the blacks from voting," but noted that "something more than ordering the plaintiff's name to be inscribed upon the [voter] lists of 1902 will be needed" to defeat white racism. "If the conspiracy [to exclude blacks from the polls] and the intent [white supremacy] exist," Holmes averred, "a name on a piece of paper will not defeat them. Unless we are prepared to supervise the voting in that state by officers of the court," Holmes concluded, "it seems to us that all that the plaintiff could get from equity would be an empty form."[44]

Holmes was probably correct in this assumption. But in sidestepping the constitutionality of Alabama's citizenship test, and thereby failing to do for black voting rights what he had done for the unions—openly supporting these even if he believed that the result would be largely meaningless—he was sending, at best, a confusing message. He seemed to suggest that, as he stated, "individual relief from a great political wrong" was not the business of the Supreme Court but of "the legislative and political department of the government of the United States." This was not the view of the dissenting justices in this case, none of whom seemed to have any trouble with the concept of the Court having the jurisdiction, and accepting the responsibility of righting racial wrongs. Almost a decade later, in *Bailey v. Alabama* (1911), that is precisely what the majority of the Court sought to do. But in this case, and on very convoluted grounds, Holmes dissented.[45]

Bailey v. Alabama (1911) grew out of the restrictive labor contracts, but also the underlying racial restrictions relating to jury trial, that pertained in the state and indeed across much of the "Deep South" in the early twentieth century. The case had been funded, in part, by the nation's leading African American writer and spokesman, Booker T. Washington, keen to test the validity of the contract labor law. Bailey had secured a year's contract, carrying a monthly salary of $12.00, along with a $15.00 advance, from the Riverside Company in 1908. He ceased employment after a month, but failed to refund his advance, and under Alabama state law was held criminally liable. As such, he would be required to work without pay, effectively under a form of peonage, until he had repaid what he owed, or go to jail.

As historian Pete Daniel has noted, for years the federal Department of Justice had been concerned that peonage violated the Thirteenth Amendment and other federal laws. It was "a species of slavery, reeked of a Gothic past revived and embarrassingly misplaced in the Progressive era," but difficult to counter, let alone prosecute successfully in the context of all-white Southern juries. However, by the time the case reached the Supreme Court Bailey's briefs were as robust as they could be. The main one, provided by Montgomery attorney Fred Ball, argued that the "real object" of the Alabama law was "to enable the employer to keep the employee in involuntary servitude by the overhanging menace of prosecution," which the plaintiff could not counter because the law at the time prevented his testifying on his own behalf." And the Court agreed with Ball. Citing the Thirteenth Amendment, it noted that "[w]hilst its immediate concern was African slavery" it nevertheless represented "a charter of universal civil freedom for all persons of whatever race, color, or estate, under the flag." The words "involuntary servitude" have a larger meaning than slavery," it asserted, and critiqued the

Alabama law as an "instrument of compulsion peculiarly effective as against the poor and the ignorant, its most likely victims." By seeking to establish "control by coercion of the personal service of one man for the benefit of another," the Court concluded, the Alabama law was unconstitutional under the provisions of the Thirteenth Amendment. But Holmes disagreed.[46]

Holmes' dissent rested on his assertion that the "Thirteenth Amendment does not outlaw contracts for labor." He chose to ignore the fact that the form of debt peonage into which Bailey had fallen was neither labor nor a contract in the legal sense by suggesting that Alabama, by adding "to civil liability a criminal ability to fine . . . simply intensifies the legal motive for doing right; it does not," he asserted, "make the laborer a slave." In his dissent, Holmes had "been uncharacteristically formalistic" as well as "uncharacteristically solicitous of juries," but what he had also been was uncharacteristically complicated in his language, which may reveal more about his perspective in such cases than anything else.[47]

Holmes was undoubtedly not just skeptical but entirely cynical about civil rights. In 1909 he recounted a case in which an African American, charged with rape, "had asked for a *habeas corpus* and had taken an appeal to our Court on the ground that his trial was a tragic farce. Whereupon he was taken out of jail and lynched. The State to which punishment of the murder belongs will do nothing," Holmes reported, "but we had to take steps to deal with the contempt of our authority." And ultimately what Holmes had predicted in *Giles* was effectively proven in the aftermath of *Bailey*: peonage continued in the South until the Second World War. For "many agricultural workers less fortunate than Bailey," Daniel notes, "the federal weapons had proved impotent." In the end, as muckraking journalist and fundraiser for Bailey's case Ray Stannard Baker suggested, Bailey simply served, like Dred Scott before him, as "a sort of symbol in this new struggle for freedom."[48]

What sort of symbol Holmes represented in this struggle, however, is another matter entirely. But it is one that goes to the heart of, and in significant ways undermines, the Holmes legend. Holmes was open to the charge of what legal historian Paul Finkelman terms "judicial villainy" in the matter of civil rights and racial equality in early twentieth-century America because he was in tune with a Court fully prepared to sacrifice "its own substantive due process and Commerce Clause jurisprudence in order to support segregation." Holmes concurred, for example, in the opinion offered in *Berea College v. Kentucky* (1908), and failed to take a stand against a Kentucky statute that supported segregation at private colleges. And he need not have done. The Court need not have done, since, as Finkelman explains, the statute under consideration effectively constrained the college's economic imperative to admit paying students. The Court "might easily have struck down the Kentucky law at issue in *Berea College* as a violation of substantive due process, citing its earlier decision in *Lochner.*" But it failed to do this. And Holmes did not dissent. But his Civil War comrade Harlan did, and highlighted "the mischievous, not to say cruel, character of the statute in question," and emphasized "how inconsistent such legislation is with the great principle of the equality of citizens before the law."[49]

Harlan's language revealed his continuing commitment to the spirit of the Reconstruction Amendments, and offered a sharp contrast to Holmes in this respect. That Holmes chose not to adopt a similar stance to Harlan in 1908 makes his dissent in *Bailey v. Alabama* (1911) less of a surprise, but also a crucial clue to some of his subsequent opinions. Indeed, had *Bailey* been the end of the matter, then Holmes might well have remained as a diminutive negative counterpoint to such symbols of freedom as Dred Scott and Alonzo Bailey represented. And it might have been. Holmes was already thinking about leaving the Court at the end of 1912, and could have done so, leaving only his *Lochner* dissent as his lasting legacy to the liberal ideal, albeit one tainted by cases such as *Giles* and *Bailey.*

In 1910, and in "spite of feeling as keen an interest in life as ever," he admitted to his friend Pollock that as his seventieth birthday loomed "the shadows begin to lengthen. I am more lonely as my old friends die off. I reflect on the mistake that I have seen it to be in others to remain on the bench after seventy." He reiterated these gloomy thoughts to Canon Patrick Sheehan, whom he had first met in Ireland. "Sadness comes with age—or ought to, I suppose." But, perhaps because he was writing to a priest he felt prompted to confess that his "interest in life" remained "keen," and that he hoped to continue working, "[e]specially, candor compels me to admit, when I am led to think that my work is valued as I should like it to be." Vanity, he admitted, "is the only way to get any work out of me, and . . . my only significance is that which I have in common with the rest of things, that of being a part of it."[50]

Age was not perhaps the only thing wearying Holmes at this point, however, and his work was not, perhaps, as valued as he would have liked. 1910 may well have seemed like the end of an era to him. In August, William James had died. They had grown very far apart, but nevertheless his death, as Holmes admitted, "cuts a root for me that went far into the past." His former Civil War sergeant, Gustave Magnitzky, died in September. And following the death of Chief Justice Fuller in July, Edward White, and not Holmes, had been elevated to Chief Justice.[51]

Given Holmes' tendency to operate within what he understood to be the letter of the law and beyond political considerations, this was perhaps inevitable. *Northern Securities* had not been the only case in which Holmes' ruling had ruffled Republican feathers. In the year after *Lochner*, in *Lincoln v. United States*, Holmes, speaking for the majority, had declared unconstitutional the tariffs imposed on American offshore possessions, in this case the Philippines. Imposed during the Spanish-American War in 1898, the Court ruled that the right to levy duties "on goods brought from the United States ceased on the exchange of ratifications of the treaty of peace." The tariff issue had, as White notes, been "regarded as a litmus test of Holmes' political ideology" at the time of his appointment. But for Holmes, loyalty was one thing; the law was quite another.[52]

There was a certain inevitability about all this. Holmes' principled, apolitical, possibly overly philosophical perspective was the cornerstone of his personality, but it isolated him, politically but also personally. When, in 1909, he had the opportunity to ride in a procession of Civil War veterans, on the occasion of Roosevelt's successor in the White House, William Taft, reviewing a parade he recalled, as he often did, his boyhood wish to ride in a procession, as a survivor. But as he admitted to Canon Sheehan, he had "little thought what it was to be a survivor, then." Life, he later opined to the Canon, "is painting a picture not doing a sum," but as the second decade of the twentieth century began, Holmes may have been wondering what his own life actually added up to. "Oh my dear Canon you are lonely, but so am I," he commiserated. Although "I am in the world and surrounded by able men—none of those whom I meet has the same interests and emphasis that I do."[53]

Holmes nevertheless clearly liked the idea of life summed up as "painting a picture not doing a sum," since he repeated it in a speech he delivered on the fiftieth anniversary of the graduation of his Harvard class of 1861. "I own that I am apt to wonder whether I do not dream that I have lived," he admitted on that occasion, "and may not wake to find that all I thought done is still to be accomplished and that life is all ahead." There was not, as White notes, all that much evidence at that point that by the time of Holmes' eventual retirement from the Court some two decades later he "would be lionized by 'progressives' and 'liberals' as one of the greatest justices of all time." But war had framed Holmes' life and it was another war, supposedly the war to end all wars, which would provide the context for some of his most memorable rulings on the Court.[54]

★★★

Before that war broke out, however, and long before America's involvement in it, Holmes established, entirely unexpectedly given his comments to Canon Sheehan, new and very close friendships with men who did share his interests, who would influence his decisions on the Supreme Court, and who would define, and eventually defend, his lasting legal reputation. These included the British political theorist Harold Laski and American writer and political commentator Walter Lippmann; but the most important, as far as Holmes' legal legacy was concerned, were Felix Frankfurter and Louis D. Brandeis. Both Frankfurter and Brandeis were Jewish intellectuals, both progressives in their political outlook at a time in the United States when anti-Semitism was an unpleasantly potent force, and both destined to become, like Holmes, Associate Justices of the Supreme Court: Brandeis in 1916, during Holmes' tenure, and Frankfurter after it. As with so many of Holmes' closest friends, several of these relationships were largely initiated and to an extent sustained through letters, even that with Frankfurter whom Holmes could meet regularly.

In many ways, indeed, there was a "symbiotic relationship" between the establishment of Holmes' reputation as a great liberal justice and Frankfurter's own career before he was appointed, in 1939, to the Supreme Court by Franklin D. Roosevelt. It was through Frankfurter that Holmes met and came to be part of a new circle of young intellectuals, some of whom founded the journal *The New Republic* in 1914. This was a publication devoted to the consideration and analysis of American society from a broadly liberal, progressive perspective, and its founders saw in Holmes' judicial philosophy a political sensibility similar to their own. Whether they were entirely right to do so may be questioned. Whether, indeed, there was as much of a divide between concern for "the humanitarian dimensions of work in an industrial society" and Holmes' particular take on social Darwinism as has been suggested is itself debatable. Holmes, after all, had noted the "despotism" that lay "at the bottom of the seeking for change," one he claimed to have encountered early in his life in the form of the antebellum abolitionists. Possibly the idea of the survival of the fittest intellect was simply another manifestation of that despotism, because progressivism had its darker side, and if Holmes' eventual reputation was bathed in its light it was also, toward the end of his career, blighted by its shadow.[55]

Whether right or wrong in their assumption of a meeting of minds between themselves and Holmes, men like Frankfurter and Lippmann clearly admired, possibly hero-worshipped him. In an article "To Justice Holmes" that appeared in *The New Republic* in early 1916, Lippmann poetically described the political atmosphere of Washington as one permeated by the "odor of dead and dying cigars suspended in steam heat . . . a [t]hick, tepid, tired air . . . in which vision dies."[56] As an inveterate smoker of cigars, Holmes may have contributed his fair share to this fug, but that was not Lippmann's point. For him, Holmes was surrounded by quite a different air, and it was, perhaps unsurprisingly, a martial one.

As Lippmann described him, Holmes was the "soldier who can talk of Falstaff and eternity in one breath, and tease the universe with a quip," a man who "fought in the Civil War and was wounded," and could consequently look "at death lightly," and has "known what it is to live dangerously. A sage with the bearing of a cavalier," Holmes' very presence was "an incitement to high risks for the sake of enterprise and its memories. He wears wisdom

like a gorgeous plume," Lippmann gushed, "and likes to stick the sancti-
ties between the ribs." But Lippmann saved his most telling point for last,
assuming he saw it for what it was. Holmes was an inspiration to the young,
Lippmann asserted, because he "never fails to tell them what they want to
hear."[57]

Ultimately, however, Holmes' late-flowering reputation was not solely the
product of such effusive outpourings of admiration as appeared in *The New
Republic*. By his seventy-fifth year, Holmes was well on the way to a popular
acclaim that possibly he did not merit, at least not in all its elements, but it
was one predicated on his dissents and decisions on the Court through the
years of the First World War and into the "Roaring Twenties," years in which
the voice that people heard, possibly because it was the voice they wanted to
hear, was one that emphasized the importance of their voices, their rights, in
a world that Holmes knew well, a world divided and at war.

The catalyst for the emergence of Holmes' new civil libertarian persona
was the Espionage Act of 1917, devised to prevent any interference with or
impingement upon America's war effort. Several cases brought under the act
came before the Court in 1919, but perhaps the best known of these was
Schenck v. United States (1919). The defendant, Charles Schenck, Secretary of
the Socialist Party, was charged with distributing anti-war leaflets that had
intimated that conscription was a violation of the Thirteenth Amendment
and a conscript "little better than a convict. In impassioned language," as
Holmes summarized Schenck's leaflet, "it intimated that conscription was
despotism in its worst form and a monstrous wrong against humanity in the
interest of Wall Street's chosen few."[58]

For Holmes, it was a clear-cut case. The Espionage Act required that the
language and behavior under consideration should show "intent" to cause
harm and be of a "bad tendency" in that respect. Arguing that the "most
stringent protection of free speech would not protect a man in falsely shout-
ing fire in a theatre and causing a panic," Holmes had no difficulty in locating the literature that Schenck had been distributing, and the fact that he had
been distributing it, within the "intent" clause. As far as "bad tendency" was
concerned, however, he gave grounds for modification. He was in no doubt
that, in such a case, the First Amendment protection accorded free speech
was irrelevant. But the question, he asserted, was essentially "whether the
words used are used in such circumstances and are of such a nature as to create a clear and present danger that they will bring about the substantive evils
that Congress has a right to prevent . . . When a nation is at war," he stressed,
"many things that might be said in time of peace are such a hindrance to
its effort that their utterance will not be endured so long as men fight, and
no Court could regard them as protected by any constitutional right." And
Holmes held that line in two similar cases: *Frohwerk v. United States* (1919)

and *Debs v. United States* (1919), this last resulting in the conviction and imprisonment for ten years of socialist leader Eugene V. Debs for delivering an anti-war speech.[59]

There was a degree of duplicity in these opinions, however, not least in Holmes' suggestion, in *Debs*, that Debs might have been aware of the *Schenck* decision: hardly feasible since it had only been delivered weeks before. Perhaps more significantly, both the *Schenck* and *Debs'* opinions were not entirely what they seemed on the surface. On the one hand, they represented the efforts of the Supreme Court to balance individual freedom and community welfare; but on the other, they were grounded in an understanding of "danger" that had less to do with immediate physical risk and more with social, scientific, and—particularly in Debs' case—political definitions, not just of danger but of difference. The threat that Debs, as the Socialist Party of America's presidential candidate whose popular appeal was on the increase (his share of the popular vote in 1904 and 1908, just under 3 percent, had doubled by 1912 to just under 6 percent, almost a million votes), seemed to offer was mainly political. But it was also more broadly cultural in a nation becoming increasingly xenophobic in outlook, increasingly fearful that a way of life predicated on what were understood to be white, Anglo-Saxon, Protestant values was under threat.[60]

As far as Holmes' thinking was concerned, this contextual interpretation of danger was of a piece with his argument in *The Common Law*. Here he had proposed that "acts, taken apart from their surrounding circumstances, are indifferent to the law," and had used the example of a crooked finger and its proximity, or not, to a gun. In *Schenck*, he had similarly stressed that "the character of every act depends upon the circumstances in which it was done." This was a perspective reinforced in a subsequent case that came before the Court in the same year as *Schenck* and *Debs: Abrams v. United States* (1919). On the surface, there was little to differentiate this case from the others, and the majority verdict confirmed this. But in this case, Holmes, along with Brandeis, dissented.[61]

Abrams was a case that, again, involved the distribution, as in *Schenck*, of anti-war leaflets in New York. Several months did separate the cases. *Schenck*, *Frohwerk*, and *Debs*, along with a similar ruling for which Brandeis, not Holmes, wrote the opinion, *Sugarman v. United States*, had been decided in March. *Abrams* came before the Court in November. There was also a material difference in the form of anti-war protest under scrutiny in *Abrams*. The four cases heard in March had all involved attacks upon America's war effort; in *Abrams*, the leaflets critiqued President Woodrow Wilson's decision to send a task force to Russia to aid in the fight against communism. Jacob Abrams and his co-defendants, in short, were more pro-communist than anti-American, and the pamphlets specifically said that the authors were not opposed to the war with Germany. And Holmes accepted this. The leaflets, he argued, "in no way attack the form of government of the United States." But the *Abrams'* defense did not rest on this, but rather on the charge that the Espionage Act (1917) and the Sedition Act (1918) passed the following year constituted unconstitutional infringements of their First Amendment right to free speech.[62]

Whether or not, in dissenting from the Court majority in *Abrams*, Holmes had in mind Pollock's comment about *Northern Securities* having been a *quia timet* ["because he fears"] injunction, he certainly regarded the ruling in *Abrams* as one predicated on the possibility of a negative impact rather than on any proven impact, and clarified the "clear and present danger" test that he had established in *Schenck* accordingly. "It is only the present danger of immediate evil or an intent to bring it about that warrants Congress in setting a limit to the expression of opinion . . . Congress certainly cannot," he argued, "forbid all effort to change the mind of the country." Given Holmes' general predilection for nuancing judicial decisions, often his own, his dissent in *Abrams* may not have been as dramatic or decisive a shift in his perspective as is often claimed. Certainly the debate over First Amendment rights had intensified in the months between *Schenck* and *Abrams*. Most importantly, these months had seen the publication, in the *Harvard Law Review*, of an article discussing "Freedom of Speech in Wartime," by law professor Zechariah Chafee, Jr. "Never in the history of our country, since the Alien and Sedition Laws of 1798," Chafee asserted, "has the meaning of free speech been the subject of such sharp controversy as to-day."[63]

In his article, Chafee effectively prodded Holmes for some clarity on this issue. "Justice Holmes in his Espionage Act decisions had a magnificent opportunity to make articulate for us that major premise, under which judges ought to classify words as inside or outside the scope of the First Amendment. He, we hoped, would concentrate his great abilities on fixing the line. Instead," Chafee complained, "he has told us that certain plainly unlawful utterances are . . . unlawful." You cannot, as Chafee noted, "limit free speech to polite criticism," but some definition of when the impolite became not just the impolitic but potentially an incitement to insurgency remained unclear. Chafee had the solution. And in part he found it in a decision made by federal district judge Learned Hand in a case involving a New York postmaster's refusal to allow a radical, anti-war journal, *The Masses*, to pass through the mails, a refusal Hand rejected.[64]

"The normal test for the suppression of speech in a democratic government, Judge Hand insists," Chafee noted, "is neither the justice of its substance nor the decency and propriety of its temper, but the strong danger that it will cause injurious acts." And he saw a parallel here with Holmes' opinion in *Schenck*: that only in cases of "*clear and present danger*" can the

First Amendment be dispensed with, temporarily. Had the Court applied this standard in *Debs*, Chafee argued, it "is hard to see how he could have been held guilty." But Chafee wanted more. He proposed that it was further "regrettable that Justice Holmes did nothing to emphasize the social interest behind free speech, and show the need of balancing even in war time." All these points may have resonated with Holmes, but perhaps it was Chafee's final point that actually did. "Those who gave their lives for freedom," Chafee concluded, "would be the last to thank us for throwing aside so lightly the great traditions of our race."[65]

For a man who had seen close friends give their lives for freedom over half a century before there was, quite possibly, more than a desire for "intellectual cover" involved in the decision to respond to Chafee's argument, and compose the dissent that Holmes did in *Abrams*. That it was a critical dissent is certain. As legal scholar David Rabban has emphasized, it "actually developed the concept of clear and present danger from a theory of judicial deference to majority will," and thereby established "a protective standard of constitutional adjudication."[66] But ultimately, there was much more of Holmes than Chafee in the dissent itself. It began in logical, legal fashion, and made its points carefully. Resistance "to the United States," Holmes averred, "means some forcible act of opposition to some proceeding of the United States in pursuance of the war," and "no such intent was proved or existed in fact." The imposition of a twenty-year prison sentence, therefore, was inappropriate; it had "been imposed for the publishing of two leaflets that," Holmes asserted, "the defendants had as much right to publish as the Government has to publish the Constitution of the United States now vainly invoked by them." But then Holmes explained his new philosophy of freedom of expression—one that was dramatically different from what he had articulated just a few months before in *Schenck*:

> Persecution for the expression of opinions seems to me perfectly logical . . . But when men have realized that time has upset many fighting faiths, they may come to believe . . . that the ultimate good desired is better reached by free trade in ideas—that the best test of truth is the power of the thought to get itself accepted in the competition of the market, and that truth is the only ground upon which their wishes safely can be carried out. That at any rate is the theory of our Constitution. It is an experiment, as all life is an experiment. Every year if not every day we have to wager our salvation upon some prophecy based upon imperfect knowledge. While that experiment is part of our system I think that we should be eternally vigilant against attempts to check the expression of opinions that we loathe and believe to be fraught with death, unless they so imminently threaten immediate interference with the lawful and pressing purposes of the law that an immediate check is required to save the country.[67]

★★★

In many respects, and although it remains a point of sometimes still heated debate, Holmes' *Abrams* dissent effectively established, and his many subsequent dissents ensured, his position in the Progressive pantheon. In the longer term, too, it was the *Abrams* dissent, and not the Court's opinion, that influenced the development of constitutional doctrine in free speech cases. This was reinforced by a similar case a few years later, *Gitlow v. New York* (1925). Benjamin Gitlow had been convicted of criminal anarchy for publishing *A Left Wing Manifesto* in the summer of 1919. His appeal had been brought by the American Civil Liberties Union, founded in 1920 in the context of the "Red Scare," the reaction against the Russian Revolution abroad that had prompted the fear of communist insurgency at home, a fear encouraged by another spate of labor strikes across the nation after the First World War.

The dissent was a joint Holmes-Brandeis production, but essentially it reiterated many of Holmes' earlier arguments regarding the "scope that has been given to the word 'liberty'" in the Fourteenth Amendment, and reemphasized the point in *Abrams* that the conviction was unwarranted because there was no "clear and present danger" of Gitlow's manifesto resulting in the overthrow of the American government. "It is said that the manifesto was more than a theory, that it was an incitement," Holmes argued, but

> [e]very idea is an incitement. It offers itself for belief and if believed it is acted on unless some other belief outweighs it or some failure of energy stifles the movement at its birth. The only difference between the expression of an opinion and an incitement in the narrower sense is the speaker's enthusiasm for the result. Eloquence may set fire to reason. But whatever may be thought of the redundant discourse before us it had no chance of starting a present conflagration. If in the long run the beliefs expressed in proletarian dictatorship are destined to be accepted by the dominant forces of the community, the only meaning of free speech is that they should be given their chance and have their way.[68]

Here again, in his emphasis on the "competition of the market" that he had referenced in *Abrams*, Holmes' position was as much about abnegating responsibility as it was about advancing free speech in any real sense. Free expression, in the context of the Deep South in the early twentieth century, was hardly productive of freedom for all. And in the nation as a whole, the marketplace of ideas included a great many predicated on fear—of the immigrant, of socialism, of change. The ideas it was trading in, that Holmes, to some extent, was trading in, revolved not around freedom at all, but around fear.

Yet as Holmes often stressed in his discussion of these cases—and as some scholars confirm in their critiques—his views had not really changed. Truth, for Holmes, was not "progressive" truth, "part of a process in which public opinion could become more informed and enlightened," a perspective that Brandeis endorsed. Rather it was "the equivalent of majoritarian prejudice at any point in time." In *Abrams*, Rabban argues, Holmes simply "reapplied rather than abandoned his Social Darwinism . . . He still believed in the survival of the fittest, but he was now willing to let ideas battle each other rather than brute force."[69]

Holmes' analysis of how law emerged from a primitive and violent past in *The Common Law* notwithstanding, it is debatable whether he ever saw ideas and brute force as alternatives. He fully knew, as his generation fully knew, that one too often led to the other. And he was not William James, to think that there might be a moral equivalent of war. "I agree with your condemnation of armchair pacifists," he wrote Pollock many years later, "on the general ground that until the world has got farther along war not only is not absurd but is inevitable and rational." He added that "of course I would make great sacrifices to avoid one." But, like James, he was aware that the "military feelings are too deeply grounded to abdicate their place among our ideals" readily. Holmes, perhaps better than anyone, understood that there was "something highly paradoxical in the modern man's relation to war."[70]

It would be tempting to suggest that, if Holmes had not changed, the world around him had. The First World War, in particular, arguably "transformed many progressives into civil libertarians," but how much of a transformation did that actually involve? Not the least reason for the enthusiasm the young intellectuals like Lippmann had for Holmes was the resonance that they recognized between certain aspects of his thinking and their own; and not the least reason for Holmes' enthusiasm for them was that they were echoes from his past, although in some respects they were discomfiting ones.

Holmes had, after all, been raised in a world of ideas, the world of Brahmin Boston where intellect was currency, the battles were fought in books, and the field was won by the sharpest mind, or tongue. Yet all the talk in the world had not prevented a civil war, a war that, for some of his social circle at the time, had been a war simply to secure the Union and conserve the Constitution. For others, of course, for some of his peers, notably Pen Hallowell, it had been one for a greater cause, for equality before the law, and for social and economic equality that recognized no racial distinctions.

But after that war was won, many decades later on the Supreme Court, Holmes saw that the imperative toward equality had been rendered impotent by the combined lack of political but also public will. And the power of the public will was something Holmes fully appreciated, as his reaction to the publicity stirred up by the Sacco and Vanzetti case in 1927 revealed. This case involved two Italian immigrants and supposed communist anarchists, Nicola Sacco and Bartolomeo Vanzetti, who had been charged and found guilty of armed robbery and murder in Massachusetts. Their trial was popularly believed to have been unfair, and raised a public outcry, prompting Holmes to ask Laski, probably rhetorically, why there was "so much greater interest in red than black. A thousand-fold worse cases of negroes come up from time to time," Holmes observed, "but the world does not worry over them. It is not," he concluded, "a mere simple abstract love of justice that has moved people so much."[71]

And yet, in his final years on the Supreme Court, and in particular in his close friendship with the more liberal and reform-minded Brandeis, Holmes almost came full circle, back to the months before the Civil War when he was encouraged by the abolitionist Pen Hallowell to take up arms for a greater cause. The influence of Hallowell and of Brandeis bookended, in some respects, a career in which cynicism perhaps too often curtailed the better angels of Holmes' nature, but not entirely. That career also included some significant pro-civil rights opinions, mostly in its closing stages.

One of the most notable in this respect, although it was a dissent written by Brandeis in which Holmes concurred, was *Olmstead v. United States* (1928). In this case the Court had found that unauthorized wiretapping of a private phone had not breached the defendant's constitutional rights. Brandeis' dissent had argued that government should adhere to the rules it imposes:

> Decency, security, and liberty alike demand that government officials shall be subjected to the same rules of conduct that are commands to the citizen. In a government of laws, existence of the government will be imperiled if it fails to observe the law scrupulously. Our government is the potent, the omnipresent teacher. For good or for ill, it teaches the whole people by its example. Crime is contagious. If the government becomes a lawbreaker, it breeds contempt for law; it invites every man to become a law unto himself; it invites anarchy. To declare that in the administration of the criminal law the end justifies the means—to declare that the government may commit crimes in order to secure the conviction of a private criminal—would bring terrible retribution. Against that pernicious doctrine this court should resolutely set its face.[72]

Supporting Brandeis, Holmes opined that it was preferable "that some criminals should escape than that the government should play an ignoble part."[73] And his late-flowering sense that the Court might seek actively to secure citizens' rights extended even to the one subject with which he had, in the past, been reluctant to engage: racial equality.

In *Moore v. Dempsey* (1923), for example, Holmes was harsh in his critique of white mob violence against African Americans in Arkansas, and five years later, in *Nixon v. Herndon* (1927), he showed how far he had come from *Giles v. Harris* (1903) in his willingness to assert black voting rights. *Nixon v. Herndon* (1927) declared unconstitutional a Texas statute that sought to restrict the black vote via the imposition of a poll tax. Holmes was scathing in his opinion. "The important question," he noted, "is whether the statute can be sustained. But although we state it as a question the answer does not seem to us open to doubt . . . it seems to us hard to imagine a more direct and obvious infringement of the Fourteenth [Amendment]," he declared, and that Amendment "was passed, as we know, with a special intent to protect the blacks from discrimination against them . . . The statute of Texas," he noted, "assumes to forbid negroes to take part in a primary election . . . discriminating against them by the distinction of color alone. States may do a good deal of classifying that it is difficult to believe rational," Holmes concluded, "but there are limits."[74]

And yet, even as Holmes stood shoulder to shoulder with Brandeis and sought to establish a more progressive jurisprudential tradition through Supreme Court opinions on a raft of social welfare issues, from child labor to wages reform, from free speech to eugenics, his dissents retained more than a taint of cynicism. At the same time, there is evidence that he was increasingly receptive to the new progressive ideas that permeated the air around him at this stage in his life. In many ways, it might have been better, for all concerned and for his lasting reputation, had he been slightly less receptive, however, since some of these ideas led to the ruling that almost single-handedly undermined his reputation as the great liberal judge, the champion of civil liberties: *Buck v. Bell* (1927).[75]

Buck v. Bell (1927) challenged Virginia's Eugenical Sterilization Act (1924). The case centered on Carrie Buck, a white, unmarried woman with a young child, Vivian, who had been admitted to the Virginia Colony for Epileptics and Feebleminded in Lynchburg. Many states had also introduced eugenicist sterilization legislation in the early twentieth century, the first to do so being Indiana in 1907. But in 1922 Harry Laughlin, the superintendent of the Eugenics Record Office, began to agitate for a "model sterilization law" designed "to prevent the procreation of persons socially inadequate from defective inheritance," which led, in time, to *Buck v. Bell*. Eugenics at that time had solid scientific currency, up to a point, and merged with some aspects of progressive thinking insofar as it related to issues such as birth control and social improvement. So Holmes' opinion, when delivered, may not have seemed as chilling to his peers as it has to posterity.[76]

Holmes defined, indeed dismissed, Carrie Buck as "a feeble minded white woman . . . daughter of a feeble minded mother . . . and the mother of an illegitimate feeble minded child," and in upholding the decision to sterilize her without her consent felt moved to note that:

> We have seen more than once that the public welfare may call upon the best citizens for their lives. It would be strange if it could not call upon those who

already sap the strength of the State for these lesser sacrifices, often not felt to be such by those concerned, in order to prevent our being swamped with incompetence. It is better for all the world if, instead of waiting to execute degenerate offspring for crime or to let them starve for their imbecility, society can prevent those who are manifestly unfit from continuing their kind. The principle that sustains compulsory vaccination is broad enough to cover cutting the Fallopian tubes . . . Three generations of imbeciles are enough.[77]

The full tragedy of the Carrie Buck case was not revealed, of course, until years later. She had not been admitted to the asylum for being "feeble minded" at all, but because she had been raped, and was pregnant, and had been sent away to have her child. Yet Holmes, even with his quaintly antiquated views on women's rights, might have suspected that there was more to this case than met the eye, or reached the Court, except that on the subject of eugenics he was, as Baker noted, a "true believer." Only two years before *Buck v. Bell*, he had observed that whereas one "can change institutions by fiat," populations change "only by slow degrees . . . I listen with some skepticism to plans for fundamental amelioration," he observed. "I should expect more from systematic prevention of the survival of the unfit." Towards the end of his life, Holmes made no secret of his dismissal of "any scheme that begins with property instead of life," and unfortunately for Carrie Buck, by that point he was not alone.[78]

In some sad respects, *Buck v. Bell* brought Holmes' life full circle, back to Brahmin Boston and to dinner-table discussions with his father, the author of *Elsie Venner*, the famous medicalized novel that explored the question of hereditary tendencies and the moral implications of free will. Dr. Holmes' real focus, of course, had not been genetic but religious inheritance. But as his son had noted, there was with his father, "as with the rest of his generation a certain softness of attitude toward the interstitial miracle – the phenomenon without phenomenal antecedents – that I did not feel."[79]

Perhaps in compensation, Holmes had sought in philosophy and in the law the certainties that, even as a young man in Cambridge, he suspected were unreachable. He had tussled with William James over metaphysics and morals but, crucially, had parted company with James' insistence that it is only when we forget that our "faiths" are "hypotheses and put on rationalistic and authoritative pretensions," that they "do harm." Yet for much of his Supreme Court service, Holmes had heeded that warning. *Buck v. Bell*, by contrast, made him feel as if, for once, he "was getting near to the first principle of reform." At the same time, he recalled the antebellum abolitionists who believed, erroneously in his view, that "their antagonists must be either knaves or fools." But he sounded very like them when he reported the receipt of a letter telling him that he "was a monster and might expect the judgment of an outraged God" for *Buck. v. Bell.* "Cranks," he commented, absent any sense of irony, "as usual do not fail."[80]

By the year of *Buck v. Bell* Holmes was starting to feel his age mentally, if not yet physically. He had gone to Arlington on Memorial Day that year, as usual, but could muster only "some, not quite all the old emotion." He was still working hard, however, and he was still reading voraciously, but once he turned ninety, in 1931, he started to move and write more slowly. In the spring of 1929, his wife, Fanny, died after a fall that broke her hip, an often fatal break in older age and so it proved for her. After her death, as Holmes admitted to Pollock, he felt "time quietly taking down the building little by little." But he had already prepared, and provided the inscription for, the smaller construction that would serve as a lasting reminder of the larger structure: his own headstone. He summed his life up: "Oliver Wendell Holmes/Brevet Colonel & Captain, 20th Mass. Volunteer Infantry/Justice Supreme Court of United States/March 1841–."[81]

He had a further opportunity to sum his own life up on the occasion of the radio broadcast organized in celebration of his ninetieth birthday. "To express one's feelings as the end draws near is too intimate a task," he told his listeners, but he gave them a brief glimpse into his philosophy. To "live is to function," he told them. "That is all there is in living." But on the Supreme Court, Holmes could no longer really function effectively. In January of 1932, he finally resigned. It had always been his work that kept him going, and so it was perhaps inevitable that, once that ceased, his life might diminish. And yet, for the three brief years of his retirement he was not unhappy. "I have nothing to complain of," he observed. "I wonder if I am witnessing the approach of the end," he mused, "but the doctors talk as if I had a good prospect ahead . . . I still enjoy life and am very willing for it to keep on."[82]

Inevitably Holmes' life could not keep on for ever. In early 1935 a cold developed into pneumonia, and on March 6, Holmes died. He was buried, as he was entitled to be, as a war veteran, in Arlington, next to his wife, to the strains of "The Battle Hymn of the Republic."

Notes

1 William James, *The Will to Believe and Other Essays in Popular Philosophy* (1896. Reprint. New York and London: Longmans Green and Company, 1897) 169.
2 New York *Evening Post*, August 12, 1902.
3 G. Edward White, *Justice Oliver Wendell Holmes: Law and the Inner Self* (New York and Oxford: Oxford University Press, 1993) 267–268.
4 New York *Evening Post*, August 12, 1902; Holmes to Pollock, August 13, 1902, *Holmes-Pollock Letters*, I, 103. In the *Civil Rights Cases* (1883) the Court held the Civil Rights Act (1875) to be unconstitutional; Harlan dissented.
5 Sheldon M. Novick, *Honorable Justice: The Life of Oliver Wendell Holmes* (New York: Dell Publishing, 1990) 259; Holmes, "Natural Law," *Harvard Law Review* (1918), 40, quoted in Albert W.

Alschuler, *Law without Values: The Life, Work, and Legacy of Justice Holmes* (Chicago and London: University of Chicago Press, 2000) 193.

6   Andrew B. Arnold, *Fueling the Gilded Age: Railroads, Miners and Disorder in Pennsylvania Coal Country* (New York: New York University Press, 2014) vii–viii; Nell Irvin Painter, *Standing at Armageddon: The United States, 1877–1919* (1987. Reprint. New York and London: W.W. Norton and Company, 1989) 180.

7   Holmes to Pollock, August 10, 1908, *Holmes-Pollock Letters*, I, 141; Ida M. Tarbell, *The History of the Standard Oil Company*, Vols. I and II (New York: McClure, Phillips and Co., 1905) viii.

8   Harold U. Faulkner, *The Decline of Laissez Faire, 1897–1917* (New York: Holt, Rinehart and Winston, 1951) 163.

9   Holmes to Lewis Einstein, November 23, 1903, quoted in White, *Law and the Inner Self*, 310.

10 Holmes to Pollock, December 28, 1902, Mark DeWolfe Howe (ed.), *Holmes-Pollock Letters: The Correspondence of Mr. Justice Holmes and Sir Frederick Pollock, 1874–1932*, Second Edition: Two Volumes in One (Cambridge, MA: The Belknap Press of Harvard University Press, 1961) I, 109; White, *Law and the Inner Self*, 317.

11 White, *Law and the Inner Self*, 314–316; Holmes to John G. Palfrey, December 27, 1902 quoted in Novick, *Honorable Justice*, 248; Holmes to Felix Frankfurter, March 28, 1922, Robert M. Mennel and Christine L. Compston, *Holmes and Frankfurter: Their Correspondence, 1912–1934* (Hanover: University of New Hampshire, 1996) 150.

12 White, *Law and the Inner Self*, 330; *Northern Securities Company v. United States*, 193 U.S. 197 (1904).

13 *Northern Securities Company v. United States*, 193 U.S. 401, 411 (1904).

14 Adams quoted in White, *Law and the Inner Self*, 307; Holmes to Ellen Curtis, March 8, 1904, OWH Papers, HLS; Holmes to Pollock, February 9, 1921, *Holmes-Pollock Letters*, II, 63–64.

15 Holmes to Pollock, February 9, 1921, *Holmes-Pollock Letters*, II, 64; Roosevelt to Lodge, quoted in White, *Law and the Inner Self*, 307.

16 Holmes, "Memorial Day Address, 1895," *Occasional Speeches*, 73–74; Pollock to Holmes, May 11, 1904, *Holmes-Pollock Letters*, I, 117.

17 Henry Adams, *The Education of Henry Adams*, ed. Ernest Samuels (Boston: Houghton Mifflin Company, 1973) 499–500.

18 Adams, *Education*, 501.

19 Holmes to Felix Frankfurter, April 8, 1913, Mennel and Compston, *Holmes and Frankfurter*, 8.

20 White, *Law and the Inner Self*, 324.

21 *Lochner v. New York*, 198 U.S. 45 (1905).

22 *Lochner v. New York*, 198 U.S. 75 (1905).

23 Max Lerner (ed.), *The Mind and Faith of Justice Holmes: His Speeches, Essays, Letters, and Judicial Opinions* (1943. Reprint. New Brunswick, NJ: Transaction Publishers, 2010) 143; Conrad Reno, "The Wage Contract and Personal Liberty," *Popular Science Monthly*, 41 (September 1892) 646–647.

24 Reno, "The Wage Contract and Personal Liberty," 649.

25 Howard Gillman, *The Constitution Besieged: The Rise and Demise of Lochner Era Police Powers* (1993. Reprint. Durham, NC: Duke University Press, 2004) 125, 128.

26 Holmes to Pollock, May 25, 1906, *Holmes-Pollock Letters*, I, 123.

27 Holmes to Pollock, September 1, 1910, *Holmes-Pollock Letters*, I, 167.

28 Gillman, *The Constitution Besieged*, 131.

29 *Otis v. Parker*, 187 U.S. 606 (1903).

30 Michael J. Phillips, *The Lochner Court, Myth and Reality: Substantive Due Process from the 1890s to the 1930s* (Westport, CT: Praeger Publishers, 2001) 4.

31 White, *Law and the Inner Self*, 324.

32 *Adair v. United States*, 208 U.S. 161 (1908).

33 *Adair v. United States*, 208 U.S. 192 (1908).

34 *Coppage v. Kansas*, 236 U.S. 27 (1915).

35 White, *Law and the Inner Self*, 333; Holmes to Pollock, June 23, 1906, *Holmes-Pollock Letters*, 127; Holmes to Laski, June 16, 1927, Mark DeWolfe Howe (ed.), *Holmes-Laski Letters: The Correspondence of Mr Justice Holmes and Harold J. Laski*, 2 Vols. (Cambridge, MA: Harvard University Press, 1953) II, 955.

36 Holmes to Pollock, April 23, 1910, *Holmes-Pollock Letters*, I, 163.

37 Holmes to Pollock, May 25, 1906, *Holmes-Pollock Letters*, 124; Brooks Adams, "Nature of Law: Methods and Aim of Legal Education," and in "Law Under Inequality: Monopoly," in Melville M. Bigelow, Brooks Adams *et al.*, *Centralization and the Law* (Boston: Little, Brown, and Company, 1906) 40, 64–65.

38 Holmes to Pollock, May 25, 1906, *Holmes-Pollock Letters*, 124.

39 Holmes to Laski, May 12, 1927, *Holmes-Laski Letters*, II, 942.

40 Liva Baker, *The Justice from Beacon Hill: The Life and Times of Oliver Wendell Holmes* (New York: Harper Collins, 1991).

41 Phillips, *Lochner Court*, vii–viii, 23.

42 Faulkner, *Decline of Laissez Faire*, 161–163.

43 White, *Law and the Inner Self*, 333; Novick, *Honorable Justice*, 248.

44 *Giles v. Harris*, 189 U.S. 488 (1903).

45 *Giles v. Harris*, 189 U.S. 488 (1903).

46 Pete Daniel, "Up from Slavery and Down to Peonage: The Alonzo Bailey Case," *The Journal of American History*, 57:3 (December 1970) 654–670, 656, 665; *Bailey v. Alabama*, 219 U.S. 219 (1911).

47 *Bailey v. Alabama*, 219 U.S. 246 (1911); White, *Law and the Inner Self*, 337.

48 Holmes to Pollock, March 7, 1909, *Holmes-Pollock Letters*, I, 151; the case Holmes referred to was that of Edward Johnson, who had been lynched in Tennessee; the sheriff, John A. Shipp, was indicted for contempt; see *United States v. Shipp*, 214 U.S. 386 (1900) and *United States v. Shipp*, 203 U.S. 563 (1906); Baker quoted in Daniel, "Up from Slavery," 670.

49 Paul Finkelman, "Civil Rights in Historical Context: In Defense of Brown," *Harvard Law Review*, 118 (2005) 973, 979–980; *Berea College v. Kentucky*, 211 U.S. 45 (1908).

50 Holmes to Pollock, September 1, 1910, *Holmes-Pollock Letters*, I, 167; Holmes to Canon Patrick Augustus Sheehan, September 3, 1910, David H. Burton (ed.), *Holmes-Sheehan Correspondence: Letters of Justice Oliver Wendell Holmes, Jr. and Canon Patrick Augustus Sheehan* (New York: Fordham University Press, 1993) 52–53.

51 Holmes to Pollock, September 1, 1910, *Holmes-Pollock Letters*, I, 167.

52 *Lincoln v. United States*, 202 U.S. 484 (1906); Novick, *Honorable Justice*, 278; White, *Law and the Inner Self*, 300.

53 Holmes to Sheehan, September 13, 1909, March 1, 1911, *Holmes-Sheehan Correspondence*, 31, 58; White, *Law and the Inner Self*, 352.

54 Holmes, "The Class of '61: At the Fiftieth Anniversary of Graduation, June 28, 1911," in Mark DeWolfe Howe (ed.), *Oliver Wendell Holmes: Occasional Speeches* (Cambridge, MA: The Belknap Press of Harvard University Press, 1962) 161.

55 White, *Law and the Inner Self*, 357, 359; Holmes to Laski, May 12, 1927, *Holmes-Laski Letters*, II, 942.

56 [Walter Lippmann], "To Justice Holmes," *The New Republic*, March 11, 1916, 156.

57 Lippmann, "To Justice Holmes," 156.

58 *Schenck. v. United States*, 249 U.S. 47, 51 (1919).

59 *Schenck. v. United States*, 249 U.S. 52 (1919): *Debs v. United States*, 249 U.S. 211 (1919). Debs was pardoned by the president, Warren Harding, in 1921.

60 Mark Kessler, "Legal Discourse and Political Intolerance: The Ideology of Clear and Present Danger," *Law & Society Review*, 27, 3 (1993) 559–598, 563–564; on this see also Michael J. Heale, *American Anticommunism* (Baltimore, MD: Johns Hopkins University Press, 1990); John Higham, *Strangers in the Land: Patterns of American Nativism 1860–1925* (New York: Atheneum, 1963); and Samuel A. Stouffer, *Communism, Conformity and Civil Liberties* (Garden City, NY: Doubleday, 1955).

61 Holmes, *Common Law*, 2–3, 35, 54; *Schenck. v. United States*, 249 U.S. 52 (1919).

62 *Abrams v. United States*, 250 U.S. 616 (1919).

63 Pollock to Holmes, May 11, 1904, *Holmes-Pollock Letters*, I, 117; *Abrams v. United States*, 250 U.S. 616 (1919); Zecheriah Chafee, "Freedom of Speech in Wartime," *Harvard Law Review*, 32 (1919) 932.

64 Chafee, "Freedom of Speech," 961; David M. Rabban, *Free Speech in Its Forgotten Years* (New York and Cambridge: Cambridge University Press, 1997) 6–7.

65 Chafee, "Freedom of Speech," 967, 973.

66 Rabban, *Free Speech*, 7.

67 *Abrams v. United States*, 250 U.S. 616 (1919).

68 *Gitlow v. People of State of New York*, 268 U.S. 652 (1925).

69 Rabban, *Free Speech*, 349.

70 Holmes to Pollock, September 20, 1928, *Holmes-Pollock Letters*, II, 230; White, *Law and the Inner Self*, 409, 412–417, 435; Rabban, *Free Speech*, 3.

71 Holmes to Laski, August 24, 1927, *Holmes-Laski Letters*, II, 674.

72 *Olmstead v. United States*, 277 U.S. 438, 470, 485 (1928).

73 *Olmstead v. United States*, 277 U.S. 438, 470, 485 (1928).

74 *Moore v. Dempsey*, 261 U.S. 86 (1923); *Nixon v. Herndon*, 273 U.S. 536, 541 (1927).

75 White, *Law and the Inner Self*, 450.

76 Stephen Jay Gould, "Carrie Buck's Daughter," in *The Flamingo's Smile: Reflections in Natural History* (London: Penguin Books, 1985) 307–309; Gerald V. O'Brien, *Framing the Moron: The Social Construction of Feeble-Mindedness in the American Eugenic Era* (Manchester and New York: Manchester University Press, 2013) 121–123; White, *Law and the Inner Self*, 408.

77 *Buck v. Bell*, 274 U.S. 200 (1927).

78 Gould, "Carrie Buck's Daughter," 314; Baker, *Justice from Beacon Hill*, 600; Holmes to Laski, July 17, 1925, and October 23, 1926, in *Holmes-Laski Letters*, I, 761; II, 888.

79 Holmes to Morris Cohen, February 5, 1919, Felix S. Cohen (ed.), "Holmes-Cohen Correspondence," *Journal of the History of Ideas*, 9:1 (January 1948) 3–52, 14–15.

80 William James, *The Will to Believe and Other Essays in Popular Philosophy* (1896. Reprint. New York and London: Longmans Green and Company, 1897) xii–xiii; Holmes to Laski, May 12, July 23, 1927, *Holmes-Laski Letters*, II, 942, 964.

81 Holmes to Pollock, May 30, 1927, September 27, 1929, *Holmes-Pollock Letters*, II, 200, 254; White, *Law and the Inner Self*, 460.

82 White, *Law and the Inner Self*, 464.

CONCLUSION

Ensanguining the skies
How heavily it dies
Into the west away;
Past touch and sight and sound
Not further to be found,
How hopeless under ground
Falls the remorseful day.

(A.E. Housman, *More Poems*, XVI, 1936)

In assessing the evolution of the law as of a life it is a mistake, as Holmes observed in *The Common Law*, to "start with the man full grown." But it is a mistake that any historical assessment, of an individual or a nation, finds hard to avoid. In Holmes' case, the problem is particularly acute. "The mysteries of our lives and of ourselves resolve themselves very slowly with the progress of the years," Holmes' father had once observed. "Every decade lifts the curtain, which hides us from ourselves, a little further, and lets a new light upon what was dark and unintelligible." But what was a gradual process for Holmes becomes a finished project for the historian, and the danger of too readily reading backwards from the Supreme Court to antebellum Boston is acute; equally risky, however, is the danger of reading forwards, tracing a smooth trajectory that actually proceeded by fits and starts.[1]

The issue is further complicated by the fact that, with his appointment to the Supreme Court, Holmes crossed a line from the private to the public, not just in professional terms but in personal ones. Arguably his public persona, in its professional and personal elements, had originated in the pages of *The Atlantic Monthly* during the Civil War and been in a continuous process of development over the course of the twenty years he spent on the

Supreme Judicial Court of Massachusetts. But in 1902 it became, almost overnight, public property in a way that it had never been before. After that date, Holmes' biographers are no longer dealing with Holmes the individual, but with Holmes the public figure. And that is a very different prospect altogether. Few biographies, of course, are written about people no one has ever heard of, so the public dimension drives the interrogative process in most cases, but not, perhaps, to the degree it has done with Holmes.

In part, this may have been inevitable. More than most, America is a nation of laws, a nation created *de novo* through documentation, invoked through and politically predicated almost entirely upon the power of the written word. From the Mayflower Compact, through Thomas Paines' *Common Sense*, to the Declaration of Independence and the Constitution, those who founded the nation sought written confirmation both of its moral right to exist and of its political and practical existence. And these documents live in a popular, public way to a degree unmatched in other nations. Across the Atlantic, for example, most people in Britain have heard of *Magna Carta*, but few could quote even a single line from it. Which is not to say that every American has the Constitution memorized, but it remains a living document in a way few others can match. Indeed, so potent are its precepts that the constitutional language of the United States continues to have a contemporary cultural resonance in nations not even governed by it.

Within this broader cultural context, Supreme Court justices tend to have a higher public profile in the United States than comparable figures in other nations, as even a brief glance at publications on the subject will suggest. A close survey of the amount of material produced on Holmes alone confirms this. But this particular Supreme Court Justice's reputation carries more cultural baggage than most. In part this is simply because, as his leading modern biographer has noted, while Holmes was most active on the Supreme Court, "a group of early twentieth-century intellectuals began a process of canonizing his attitude toward constitutional adjudication."[2] But in part, too, it derives from the fact that Holmes' reputation resonated, and continues to resonate, beyond the legal world, and beyond the United States. His close links with British colleagues, his frequent trips across the Atlantic, all helped in this respect. Nevertheless, it remains notable that one of the locations of a fulsome obituary of Holmes was the London-based *Alpine Journal*, the publication of the Alpine Club, of which Holmes (and indeed several of his close friends, including former British Ambassador to the United States, James Bryce) was a member.

Composed by James Monroe Thorington, the president of the American Alpine Club, the obituary offered an insight into the somewhat simplified, but resonant reputation Holmes held beyond the legal world sphere. He brought to the Supreme Court, Thorington noted, "a mentality sparkling with wit and imbued with lofty sentiments" that placed "the rights of man as paramount to property rights, and not only championed the welfare of the people but fought to protect State rights against Federal encroachment." Although not a noted climber, Thornington summed Holmes up as "one of the last links with the Golden Age of mountaineering in the Alps."[3] And Holmes was also, in many respects, a link with a different kind of American Golden Age, an antebellum world that, in hindsight, seemed simpler and simultaneously more culturally sophisticated than America post-First World War.

By the time he reached the Supreme Court, Holmes' was very much a voice from a past that seemed conveniently shorn of slavery and its implications, productive of values that the modern era had too readily relinquished in its rush toward the brave new world of corporate power and commercial opportunity. And Holmes had long encouraged that interpretation of his own and his nation's past through his status as Union veteran, through his Memorial Day Addresses on the war that were never, when one drilled into them, really about the war at all, through a more diffuse martial language appropriate to and fully appreciated by a nation that felt itself besieged by the forces of industrialization, immigration, and urbanization, by increasing class conflict, and by persistent racial divisions that seemed only to worsen as the twentieth century began. Holmes was undoubtedly a difficult man, but he lived through very difficult times for America. To take just one obvious example, only four American presidents have been assassinated, and Holmes' life covered three of them: Abraham Lincoln (1865), James A. Garfield (1881), and William McKinley (1901). This was not a settled world; for him, it never had been.

Holmes' reputation by the early twentieth century, indeed, located him firmly between two worlds. On the one hand he was a Civil War veteran, whose judgments on the Court were, Roosevelt had hoped, likely to be those of the antebellum and Civil War eras combined, a time before the "Trusts," an age that prioritized the individual over the corporate, industrial machine. On the other, he was very much part of the world of the corporate machine, admired by men, like James Hill, who had helped to build it, and felt no compunction to compromise its progress, far less rescue anyone who fell victim to its vicissitudes. In both cases, his perspective could be, and has been, conveniently located in his Civil War experiences. And in part this may be an accurate assumption.

The Civil War, Holmes once told Harold Laski, had taught him "some great lessons," among which were "to be prepared for catastrophe to endure being bored and to know that however fine [a] fellow I thought myself in my usual routine there were other situations alongside and many more in which I was inferior to men that I might have looked down upon had experience not taught me to look up."[4] Holmes had selected the law as the closest approximation to "the strenuous life" that he could achieve, and rejected the groves of academe as a place where there was no opportunity for risk, no real engagement with the world. Yet the rarefied atmosphere of a courtroom was not all that different, and while he could, and did, read about the exploits of explorers, and the economic successes of men like Hill, he may have felt that others had chosen a more demanding path. His was the path of duty, a duty that may have derived from his upbringing and been defined through war, but duty was, for Holmes perhaps, a denial of self-determination in the end, a surrender of his life to forces he neither controlled nor fully comprehended.

Throughout his life, Max Lerner argued, "Holmes was ridden by two myths: that of the soldier and that of the gambler. Life was a campaign, requiring heroic and disciplined individual qualities. Life was a throw of the dice, but the stakes were worth the risks." His own "memory of the war made his approach to life that of the good soldier," Lerner asserted, "his philosophy was an aleatory philosophy—the gods playing at dice with human destinies; his theory of law was that it was merely 'the rules of the game.'" And within "this framework it was amazing how successful Holmes was in handling the problems of a complicated industrial world." For his critics, however, Holmes handled the problems not by confronting them but by retreating in the face of their human implications. Particularly in the context of the civil rights cases, Holmes' popular persona of Union war veteran did him no favors, at least as far as his long-term reputation was concerned. There was no overt assumption at the time that a man who had fought for the Union in the nineteenth century would necessarily fight for civil rights in the twentieth, but that assumption has been imposed after the fact by those who cannot comfortably reconcile Holmes' apparent abolitionist sentiments in 1861 with his almost complete retreat from the subject of civil rights when on the Supreme Court.[5]

The default position in many cases is to travel backwards in time to Brahmin Boston, and argue that Holmes, the product of an intellectual if not an economic elite, who perceived himself as an "aristocratic champion of honor and chivalry and duty," had no social, intellectual, or moral tools at his disposal to deal with the disturbing reality of race relations in the early twentieth century. An alternative approach reverses the time machine and whisks us forward to extract from the later twentieth century a clinical construction of war trauma and attribute it to Holmes. In both cases, what is being offered is not evidence but an excuse and not a wholly plausible one.[6]

One has to consider what it is that Holmes stands accused of at the bar of legal history. And that would seem to be, in essence, moral skepticism. He is often located at the forefront of the intellectual revolution of the late-nineteenth century that swept away moral realism or natural law and replaced it with a Social Darwinist perspective. "Holmes led this revolution," legal scholar Albert Alschuler argues, "partly because the disillusionment induced by his war experience fit neatly with the social Darwinism that he discovered 'in the air' and then embraced." That Holmes was not alone either in fomenting or effecting this revolution is acknowledged, but that almost makes matters worse, since it suggests that virtually an entire generation was so brutalized by its battlefield experiences as to be rendered helpless in the face of the very real racial, social, and economic inequalities of modernizing America. And clearly that was not the case.[7]

This is not to suggest that Holmes' war experiences left no lasting impact. But it may not have been the war itself but its aftermath that proved the decisive factor in the development of his moral skepticism, and that made him less accepting of idealism in any form when the ideals were not supported by concrete, concerted action. There is no reason to suppose that the disillusionment he expressed at the likely outcome of, for example, *Giles v. Harris* (1903) was not genuine, but it was, in a sense, a denial of responsibility. He was a Supreme Court Justice. What he said mattered. What he said was heard. In his famous dissents, in *Lochner*, and in *Abrams*, although his opinion did not carry the day in Court, it established a marker for the future, forwarded "an appeal to the brooding spirit of the law," as a dissent was once described. And there is no doubt that Holmes did not, in the main, do this when a civil rights case came before him. Yet the assumption that he ought to have done reveals more about the popular interpretation of the Civil War, perhaps, than it does about Holmes himself.[8]

In advancing the argument that so much of Holmes' moral and philosophical outlook derived from the Civil War, his supporters and detractors alike reveal a defensiveness about that war and its outcome that came to inhere in Holmes. As a young man at Harvard he had supported the abolitionists. As a Union soldier, he seemed to have rejected anti-slavery as a cause worth fighting for, in the context of a regiment whose Democratic politics tinged its reputation with opposition to emancipation as a war aim. And as a Supreme Court Justice, his martial bearing and rhetoric alike recalled, perhaps even more than his civil rights opinions, a war that had not achieved all it had promised. In that sense, Holmes came to serve as a living reminder of a past that had promised so much to a present fighting to live up to the sacrifices made by Holmes' generation.

The fact that modern scholarly assessments of Holmes tend toward the critical would not likely have troubled him. As he once observed, "bad statues are better than no statue. They are points of interest, and give you something to think about." And Holmes continues to be someone that gives the modern world something to think about. His reputation as soldier, scholar, and Supreme Court Justice has proved to be an enduring one, one that continues to resonate in contemporary America, a legal reputation to rival the literary one held by his father. Indeed, writing about Holmes' father, John Morse noted that, by the end of his life, "the Doctor had outlived his own generation," and stood alone in the world. And the same was true of his son. By 1935, Holmes had certainly outlived most of his generation. But in some senses he believed that he had already done so at the start of his life, not its end, when he emerged, not unscathed but alive from the battlefield.[9]

Although the majority of soldiers did not die in the Civil War, Holmes had lost many close friends along with the abolitionist ideals that had taken him to war in the first place. He could never return to the man he had been in 1861, nor retrieve that early enthusiasm for emancipation, even if toward the end of his life he appreciated more keenly the importance of civil rights along with civil liberties. And he knew by then what he had lost. "Do you know how beautiful the Potomac is?" he had once asked Laski. "We often drive up to the Chain Bridge some miles up, cross and come down on the other side or return on our steps. I wish I could go on to Ball's Bluff where over 65 years ago I climbed those banks but I doubt if I ever shall."[10]

NOTES

1 Oliver Wendell Holmes, Jr., *The Common Law* (1881. Reprint. London: Macmillan and Company, 1882) 2; John T. Morse, *Life and Letters of Oliver Wendell Holmes*, 2 Vols. (London: Sampson Low, Marston and Company, 1896), 1, 28–29.

2 G. Edward White, *Justice Oliver Wendell Holmes: Law and the Inner Self* (New York and Oxford: Oxford University Press, 1993) 280.

3 OWH Papers, HLS, "Diary Trip to Europe."

4 Holmes to Laski, December 15, 1926, *Holmes-Laski Letters*, II, 905.

5 Max Lerner, intro. to "The Scar Holmes Leaves," in *Ideas Are Weapons: The History and Uses of Ideas* (1939. Reprint. New Brunswick, NJ: Transaction Publishers, 1991) 56–57.

6 White, *Law and the Inner Self*, 342; Albert W. Alschuler, *Law without Values: The Life, Work, and Legacy of Justice Holmes* (Chicago and London: University of Chicago Press, 2000) 49–51, 185.

7 Alschuler, *Law without Values*, 185.

8 Catherine Drinker Bowen, *Yankee from Olympus: Justice Holmes and his Family* (Boston: Little, Brown and Company, 1944) 373, n.7.

9 Holmes, "A Provisional Adieu," *Occasional Speeches*, 151; John T. Morse, *Life and Letters of Oliver Wendell Holmes*, 2 Vols. (London: Sampson Low, Marston and Company, 1896) II, 92.

10 Holmes to Laski, June 1, 1927, *Holmes-Laski Letters*, II, 949.

PART **II**

DOCUMENTS

Oliver Wendell Holmes, Jr., "Autobiographical Sketch," 1861 (Harvard Class Album)

Holmes had already made the decision to leave Harvard and join up to fight in the Civil War when he composed this entry for the Harvard Class Album in 1861. Although it has been suggested that he composed it in military camp, it seems more likely that he wrote it at home in Boston while he was awaiting a commission. In this sketch, Holmes located himself very firmly within the history of his nation, his state, and above all the republican aristocracy that was Brahmin Boston, his membership of which derived from a combination of familial and educational tradition. It was this tradition, one that had revolved around religion but had evolved into a more secular sense of social and cultural duty, which took Holmes to war in 1861. He had, as his concluding comments made clear, decided to follow his maternal line's tradition—his grandfather had been a judge—by pursuing a career in the law once the war was over.

———————

I, Oliver Wendell Holmes, Jr., was born March 8, 1841, in Boston. My father was born in Cambridge, graduated at Harvard, studied medicine in Paris and returning to Boston practiced as a physician there a number of years. Giving this up, however, he has since supported himself by acting as a professor of the Medical School of Harvard College, by lecturing, and by writing a number of books. In 1840 he married Amelia Lee Jackson, daughter of Judge Jackson of Boston, where he has since resided. All my three names designate families from which I am descended. A long pedigree of

Olivers and Wendells may be found in the book called 'Memorials of the Dead in Boston. – King's Chapel Burying Ground,' pp. 144 and 234–5–6–7–8. Of my grandfather Abiel Holmes, an account may be found in the biographical dictionaries. (He was the author of the *Annals of America*, etc.) as also of my other grandfather Charles Jackson – (See, for instance, *Appleton's New American Cyclopaedia* where the account of Judge Jackson was written by my father.) I think it better thus to give a few satisfactory references than to write an account which is half so. Some of my ancestors have fought in the Revolution; among the great grandmothers of the family were Dorothy Quincy and Anne Bradstreet ('the tenth Muse'); and so on; but these things can be picked up from other sources I have indicated. My Grandfather A. Holmes was graduated from Yale in 1783 and in 1792 was 'gradu honorario donatur,' at Harvard. Various Wendells and Olivers will be found in the triennial, as also various Jacksons; including my grandfather. Our family has been in the habit of receiving a college education and I came of course in my turn, as my grandfathers, fathers, and uncles had been before me. I've always lived in Boston and went first to a woman's school there, then to Rev. T.R. Sullivan's, then to E.S. Dixwell's (Private Latin School) and thence to College. I never had any business but that of a student before coming to College; which I did with the majority of our class in July, entering without conditions. I was while in College, a member and editor of the Institute (had somewhat to do with our two private clubs), of the Hasty Pudding, the Porcellian, the ΦBK and the 'Christian Union;' not that I considered my life justified belonging to the latter, but because I wished to bear testimony in favor of a Religious society founded on liberal principles in distinction to the more 'orthodox' and sectarian platform of the 'Xtian Brethren.' I was editor in the Senior year of the Harvard Magazine (the chief piece I wrote in it being on 'Albert Durer.') I was author of an article on Plato which took the prize as the best article by an undergraduate (for the first year of its existence) in the 'University Quarterly.' The only College prize I have tried for was the Greek which was divided between one of the Juniors and me. When the war broke out I joined the '4th Battalion of Infantry' and went down to Fort Independence expecting when drilled to go south (as a private). While at the Fort and after we were ordered up I had to patch up a Class Poem as quickly and as well as I could under the circumstances, since I had been elected to that office before going (2nd term Senior). We stayed about a month at the Fort and then I came to Boston and on Classday (a week and a half ago) I delivered my poem side by side with my friend Hallowell who was orator and who had also been at the Fort. The tendencies of the family and of myself have a strong natural bent to literature, etc., at present I am trying for a commission in one of the Massachusetts Regiments, however, and hope to go south before very long. If I survive the war I expect to study law as my profession or at least for a starting point.

(in haste)

[*signed*]

O.W. Holmes, Jr.

July 2nd, 1861.

[*and then in pencil*]

(N.B. I may say I don't believe in gushing much in these College Biog's and think a dry statement much fitter. Also I am too busy now to say more if I would).

Source

Taken from Frederick C. Fiechter, Jr., "The Preparation of an Aristocrat," *New England Quarterly*, 6:1(March 1933) 3–28.

OLIVER WENDELL HOLMES' CIVIL WAR DIARY (BALL'S BLUFF)

Holmes edited his writings—his diary and his letters—from the front after the Civil War, so the impression the modern reader receives from what remains is very much the one that Holmes intended posterity to have. In this diary entry, Holmes was attempting to rationalize his experiences in his first proper military engagement, the first occasion on which he was wounded, and the first time that death in the war seemed a very real possibility to him. As was often the case with Holmes, the physical experience is heavily overlaid by philosophical musings on the meaning of it. For him, both in the Civil War and on the Supreme Court, the thought tended to overshadow the action, as this extract already makes clear.

No.2

There are a great many things, of course,—thoughts, occupations & events,—of which I wish I'd kept Memoranda during my past life—But I wish especially that after the military affairs—battles etc. in which I've been concerned I had noted many of those facts which so rapidly escape the memory in the mist which settles over a fought field.

Wound at Ball's Bluff

Not to speak of while the fight was actually going on, I have been struck with the intensity of the mind's action and its increased suggestiveness, after one has received a wound—

At Ball's Bluff, Tremlett's boy George told me, I was hit at 4½ P.M., *the heavy firing having begun about an hour before, by the watch*—I felt as if a horse had kicked me and went over—1st Serg^t Smith grabbed me and lugged me to the rear a little way & opened my shirt and ecce! the [the] two holes in my breasts and the bullet, which he gave me—George says he squeezed it from the right opening—Well—I remember the sickening feeling of water in my face—I was quite faint—and seeing poor Serg^t Merchant lying near—shot through the head and covered with blood—and then the thinking begun— (Meanwhile hardly able to speak—at least, coherently)—Shot through the lungs? Lets see—and I spit—Yes—already the blood was in my mouth. At once my thoughts jumped to "Children of the New Forest." (by Marryatt) which I was fond of reading as a little boy, and in which the father of one of the heroines is shot through the lungs by a robber—I remembered he died with terrible haemorrhages & great agony—What should I do? Just then I remembered and felt in my waist coast pocket—Yes there it was—a little bottle of laudanum which I had brought along—But I won't take it yet; no, see a doctor first—It may not be as bad as it looks—At any rate wait till the pain begins—

When I had got to the bottom of the Bluff the ferry boat, (the scow,) had just started with a load—but there was a small boat there—Then, still in this half conscious state, I heard somebody groan—Then I thought "Now wouldn't Sir Philip Sydney have that other feller put into the boat first?" But the question, as the form in which it occurred shows, came from a *mind* still bent on a becoming and consistent carrying out of its ideals of conduct—not from the unhesitating instinct of a still predominant and heroic *will*—I am not sure whether I propounded the question but I let myself be put aboard.

I have never been able to account for the fact that bullets struck in the bank of the island over our heads as we were crossing—Well; the next question was how to get me from the ferry to the hospital—this was solved by another early recollection—the "Armchair"—Two men crossed their hands in such a way that I could sit on 'em & put my arms around their necks—& so they carried me—The little house was filled so I was taken into the large building which served as a general hospital; and I remember the coup d'oeuil on which I closed my eyes with the same sickening which I had felt on seeing poor Merchant—Men lying round on the floor—the spectacle wasn't familiar then—a red blanket with an arm lying on it in a pool of blood—it seems as if instinct told me it was John Putnam's (then Capt. Comdg Co H)—and near the entrance a surgeon calmly grasping a man's finger and cutting it off—both standing—while the victim contemplated the operation with a very grievous mug . . .

Much more vivid is my memory of my thoughts and state of mind for though I have been light-headed my reason was working—even if through a cloud. Of course when I thought I was dying the reflection that the majority vote of the civilized world declared that with my opinions I was *en route* for Hell came up with painful distinctness—Perhaps the first impulse was tremulous—but then I said—by Jove, I die like a soldier anyhow—I was shot in my breast doing my duty up to the hub—afraid? No, I am proud—then I thought I couldn't be guilty of a deathbed recantation—father and I had talked of that and were agreed that it generally meant nothing but a cowardly giving way to fear—Besides, thought I, can I recant if I want to, has the approach of death changed my beliefs much? & to this I answered – No—Then came in my Philosophy—I am to take a leap in the dark—but now as ever I believe that whatever happens is best—for it is in accordance with a general law—and *good & universal* (or *general law*) are synonymous terms in the universe—(I can now add that our phrase *good* only means certain general truths seen through the heart & will instead of being merely contemplated intellectually—I doubt if the intellect accepts or recognizes that classification of good and bad).

Source

Mark DeWolfe Howe (ed.), *Touched with Fire: Civil War Letters and Diary of Oliver Wendell Holmes, Jr., 1861–1864* (Cambridge, MA: Harvard University Press, 1946) 23–33.

OLIVER WENDELL HOLMES TO FATHER: DECEMBER 10, 1862

As the Civil War progressed, the division between home-front and battlefront inevitably widened, since despite the close ties between them, the soldiers' experiences could only ever be imperfectly understood by non-combatants. The growing enthusiasm for emancipation at home was not always matched by those fighting, and dying to effect it in the field. Holmes was not unusual, at this stage in the war, in expressing some doubts about the likelihood of Union victory. But it is clear from this letter to his father that Holmes' early abolitionist enthusiasm was already being replaced by a sense of duty, a shift that may have owed something to the political make-up of his regiment as much as to any particular disillusionment with the war.

I never I believe have shown, as you seemed to hint, any wavering in my belief in the right of our cause—it is my disbelief in our success by arms in wh. I differ from you . . . I think in that matter I have better chances of judging than you—and I believe I represent the conviction of the army—& not the least of the most intelligent part of it—The success of wh. you spoke were to be anticipated as necessary if we entered into the struggle—But I see no farther progress—I don't think either of you realize the unity or the determination of the South. I think you are hopeful because (excuse me) you are ignorant. But if it is true that we represent civilization wh. is in its nature, as well as slavery, diffusive and aggressive, and if civ. & progress are the better things why they will conquer in the long run, we may be sure, and will stand a better chance in their proper province—peace—than in war, the brother of slavery—brother—it is slavery's parent, child and sustainer at once—At any rate dear Father don't, because I say these things imply or think that I am the meaner for saying them—I am, to be sure, heartily tired and half worn out body and mind by this life, but I believe I am as ready as ever to do my duty. But it is maddening to see men put in over us & motions forced by popular clamor when the army is only willing to trust its life & reputation to one man—.

SOURCE

Oliver Wendell Holmes, Jr. to Oliver Wendell Holmes, Sr., December 20, 1862, in Mark DeWolfe Howe (ed.), *Touched with Fire: Civil War Letters and Diary of Oliver Wendell Holmes, Jr., 1861–1864* (Cambridge, MA: Harvard University Press, 1946) 79–81.

OLIVER WENDELL HOLMES, JR., "AN ADDRESS DELIVERED FOR MEMORIAL DAY, MAY 30, 1884, AT KEENE, NH, BEFORE JOHN SEDGWICK POST NO. 4, GRAND ARMY OF THE REPUBLIC"

This Memorial Day Address was the first of two such speeches that really established Holmes' reputation as a spokesman for his class and genera-tion as far as the popular understanding of the Civil War was concerned by the later nineteenth century. Interest in the war was peaking by this point in the United States, and the Union veterans' organization, the Grand Army of the Republic (GAR), was a powerful political and social force in the nation. Given that he was addressing Civil War veterans on Memorial Day, it is not surprising that Holmes was seeking to establish his own military credentials in this speech, nor that he devoted so much of it to honoring the dead. The claim he staked in this address—that the Civil War generation was set apart by its experiences in the war—is frequently quoted uncritically, but it placed greater emphasis on the military experience than on any moral meaning that may have inspired it.

I have spoken of some of the men who were near to me among others very near and dear, not because their lives have become historic, but because their lives are the type of what every soldier has known and seen in his own company. In the great democracy of self-devotion private and general stand side by side. Unmarshalled save by their own deeds, the army of the dead sweep before us, "wearing their wounds like stars." It is not because the men I have mentioned were my friends that I have spoken of them, but, I repeat, because they are types. I speak of those whom I have seen. But you all have known such; you, too, remember!

It is not of the dead alone that we think on this day. There are those still living whose sex forbade them to offer their lives, but who gave instead their happiness. Which of us has not been lifted above himself by the sight of one of those lovely, lonely women, around whom the wand of sorrow has traced its excluding circle—set apart, even when surrounded by loving friends who would fain bring back joy to their lives? I think of one whom the poor of a great city know as their benefactress and friend. I think of one who has lived not less greatly in the midst of her children, to whom she has taught such lessons as may not be heard elsewhere from mortal lips. The story of these and her sisters we must pass in reverent silence . . .

Comrades, some of the associations of this day are not only triumphant, but joyful. Not all of those with whom we once stood shoulder to shoulder—not all of those whom we once loved and revered—are gone. On this day we still meet our companions in the freezing winter bivouacs and in those dreadful summer marches where every faculty of the soul seemed to depart one after another, leaving only a dumb animal power to set the teeth and to persist—a blind belief that somewhere and at last there was bread and water. On this day, at least, we still meet and rejoice in the closest tie which is possible between men—a tie which suffering has made indissoluble for better, for worse.

When we meet thus, when we do honor to the dead in terms that must sometimes embrace the living, we do not deceive ourselves. We attribute no special merit to a man for having served when all were serving. We know that, if the armies of our war did anything worth remembering, the credit belongs not mainly to the individuals who did it, but to average human nature. We also know very well that we cannot live in associations with the past alone, and we admit that, if we would be worthy of the past, we must find new fields for action or thought, and make for ourselves new careers.

But, nevertheless, the generation that carried on the war has been set apart by its experience. Through our great good fortune, in our youth our hearts were touched with fire. It was given to us to learn at the outset that life is a profound and passionate thing. While we are permitted to scorn nothing but indifference, and do not pretend to undervalue the worldly rewards of ambition, we have seen with our own eyes, beyond and above the gold fields, the snowy heights of honor, and it is for us to bear the report to those who come after us. But, above all, we have learned that whether a man accepts from Fortune her spade, and will look downward and dig, or from Aspiration her axe and cord, and will scale the ice, the one and only success which it is his to command is to bring to his work a mighty heart.

Such hearts—ah me, how many!—were stilled twenty years ago; and to us who remain behind is left this day of memories. Every year—in the full tide of spring, at the height of the symphony of flowers and love and life—there comes a pause, and through the silence we hear the lonely pipe of death. Year after year lovers wandering under the apple trees and through the clover and deep grass are surprised with sudden tears as they see black veiled figures stealing through the morning to a soldier's grave. Year after year the comrades of the dead follow, with public honor, procession and commemorative flags and funeral march—honor and grief from us who stand almost alone, and have seen the best and noblest of our generation pass away.

But grief is not the end of all. I seem to hear the funeral march become a paean. I see beyond the forest the moving banners of a hidden column. Our dead brothers still live for us, and bid us think of life, not death—of life to which in their youth they lent the passion and joy of the spring. As I listen, the great chorus of life and joy begins again, and amid the awful orchestra of seen and unseen powers and destinies of good and evil our trumpets sound once more a note of daring, hope, and will.

SOURCE

Oliver Wendell Holmes, Jr., "Memorial Day Address, May 30 1884," in Richard A. Posner (ed.), *The Essential Holmes: Selections from the Letters, Speeches, Judicial Opinions, and Other Writings of Oliver Wendell Holmes, Jr.* (1992. Reprint. Chicago and London: The University of Chicago Press, 1996) 80–87.

THE PURITAN: 250TH ANNIVERSARY OF THE FIRST CHURCH IN CAMBRIDGE, FEBRUARY 12, 1886

Following his Memorial Day Address in 1884, and in the context of his grow-ing legal reputation, Holmes became something of a feature on the lecture circuit on occasions such as this one, the anniversary of the establishment of the First Church in Cambridge, Massachusetts. In this address Holmes links the state's Puritan past to the Crusades, and attempts to establish a deep historical lineage for the national impulse toward democratic freedom in the United States. Holmes' tendency, which arguably he developed during the Civil War and which would become increasingly evident as he grew older, not just to see his own life as a battle but to locate the larger story of his state and his nation within a martial narrative, is very pronounced here.

———————

Six hundred years ago a knight went forth to fight for the cross in Palestine. He fought his battles, returned, died among his friends, and his effigy, cut in alabaster or cast in bronze, was set upon his tomb in the Temple or the Abbey. Already he was greater than he had been in life. While he lived, hundreds as good as he fell beneath the walls of Ascalon, or sank in the sands of the desert and were forgotten. But in his monument, the knight became the type of chivalry and the church militant. What was particular to him and individual had passed from sight, and the universal alone remained. Six hundred years have gone by, and his history, perhaps his very name, has been forgotten. His cause has ceased to move. The tumultuous tide in which he was an atom is still. And yet to-day he is greater than ever before. He is no longer a man, or even the type of a class of men, however great. He has become a symbol of the whole mysterious past,—of all the dead passion of his race. His monument is the emblem of tradition, the text of national honor, the torch of all high aspiration through all time.

Two hundred and fifty years ago a few devout men founded the First Church of Cambridge. While they lived, I doubt not, hundreds as good as they fell under Fairfax at Marston Moor, or under Cromwell at Naseby, or lived and died quietly in England and were forgotten. Yet if the only monuments of those founders were mythic bronzes, such as stand upon the Common and the Delta,—if they were only the lichened slates in yonder churchyard,—how much greater are they now than they were in life! Time, the purifier, has burned away what was particular to them and individual, and has left only the type of courage, constancy, devotion,—the august figure of the Puritan.

Time still burns. Perhaps the type of the Puritan must pass away, as that of the Crusader has done. But the founders of this parish are commemorated, not in bronze or alabaster, but in living monuments. One is Harvard College. The other is mightier still. These men and their fellows planted a congregational church, from which grew a democratic state. They planted something mightier even than institutions. Whether they knew it or not, they planted the democratic spirit in the heart of man. It is to them we owe the deepest cause we have to love our country,—that instinct, that spark that makes the American unable to meet his fellow man otherwise than simply as a man, eye to eye, hand to hand, and foot to foot, wrestling naked on the sand. When the citizens of Cambridge forget that they too tread a sacred soil, that Massachusetts also has its traditions, which grow more venerable and inspiring as they fade,—when Harvard College is no longer dedicated to truth, and America to democratic freedom,—then perhaps, but not till then, will the blood of the martyrs be swallowed in the sand, and the Puritan have lived in vain.

SOURCE

Oliver Wendell Holmes, Jr., "The Puritan" (1886), in Oliver Wendell Holmes, *Speeches* (Boston: Little, Brown, and Company, 1896) 19–21.

THE PROFESSION OF THE LAW: CONCLUSION OF A LECTURE DELIVERED TO UNDERGRADUATES OF HARVARD UNIVERSITY, FEBRUARY 17, 1886

In this speech to students at Harvard, Holmes looked back to his early years as a law student, and sought to persuade his audience—and perhaps also himself—that the law was a profession that could be heroic, in the sense that Holmes understood heroism. In some respects this was a traditional type of vocational address for lawyers of the time: an attempt to emphasize the ideals of justice that lay behind what was sometimes regarded as an entirely cynical profession. Holmes was also speaking at a time when the opportunities for the kinds of heroic conquests of uncharted wildernesses, mental and physical alike, that he had in mind were diminishing; both "surveys and railroads," he noted, "have set limits to our intellectual wildernesses." Only four years after Holmes delivered this address, the United States Census of 1890 revealed that the frontier had ceased to exist; the nation had, effectively, met in the middle. This prompted the historian Frederick Jackson Turner to develop his famous "Frontier Thesis" in 1893, which posited the alarmist suggestion that the democratic dynamism that underpinned the nation would diminish in the context of an increasingly closed national space. Holmes seems, in this address, to be moving toward a similar conclusion.

And now, perhaps, I ought to have done. But I know that some spirit of fire will feel that his main question has not been answered. He will ask. What is all this to my soul? You do not bid me sell my birthright for a mess of pottage; what have you said to show that I can reach my own spiritual possibilities through such a door as this? How can the laborious study of a dry and technical system, the greedy watch for clients and practice of shopkeepers' arts, the mannerless conflicts over often sordid interests, make out a life? Gentlemen, I admit at once that these questions are not futile, that they may prove unanswerable, that they have often seemed to me unanswerable. And yet I believe there is an answer. They are the same questions that meet you in any form of practical life. If a man has the soul of Sancho Panza, the world to him will be Sancho Panza's world; but if he has the soul of an idealist, he will make—I do not say find—his world ideal. Of course, the law is not the place for the artist or the poet. The law is the calling of thinkers. But to those who believe with me that not the least godlike of man's activities is the large survey of causes, that to know is not less than to feel, I say—and I say no longer with any doubt—that a man may live greatly in the law as well as elsewhere; that there as well as elsewhere his thought may find its unity in an infinite perspective; that there as well as elsewhere he may wreak himself upon life, may drink the bitter cup of heroism, may wear his heart out after the unattainable. All that life offers any man from which to start his thinking or his striving is a fact. And if this universe is one universe, if it is so far thinkable that you can pass in reason from one part of it to another, it does not matter very much what that fact is. For every fact leads to every other by the path of the air. Only men do not yet see how, always.

And your business as thinkers is to make plainer the way from some thing to the whole of things; to show the rational connection between your fact and the frame of the universe. If your subject is law, the roads are plain to anthropology, the science of man, to political economy, the theory of legislation, ethics, and thus by several paths to your final view of life. It would be equally true of any subject. The only difference is in the ease of seeing the way. To be master of any branch of knowledge, you must master those which lie next to it; and thus to know anything you must know all.

Perhaps I speak too much the language of intellectual ambition. I cannot but think that the scope for intellectual, as for physical adventure, is narrowing. I look for a future in which the ideal will be content and dignified acceptance of life, rather than aspiration and the passion for achievement. I see already that surveys and railroads have set limits to our intellectual wildernesses,—that the lion and the bison are disappearing from them, as from Africa and the no longer boundless West. But that undelightful day which I anticipate has not yet come. The human race has not changed, I imagine, so much between my generation and yours but that you still have the barbaric thirst for conquest, and there is still something left to conquer. There are fields still open for occupation in the law, and there are roads from them that will lead you where you will.

But do not think I am pointing you to flowery paths and beds of roses,— to a place where brilliant results attend your work, which shall be at once easy and new. No result is easy which is worth having. Your education begins when what is called your education is over,—when you no longer are stringing together the pregnant thoughts, the "jewels five words long," which great men have given their lives to cut from the raw material, but have begun yourselves to work upon the raw material for results which you do not see, cannot predict, and which may be long in coming,—when you take the fact which life offers you for your appointed task. No man has earned the right to intellectual ambition until he has learned to lay his course by a star which he has never seen,—to dig by the divining rod for springs which he may never reach. In saying this, I point to that which will make your study heroic. For I say to you in all sadness of conviction, that to think great thoughts you must be heroes as well as idealists. Only when you have worked alone,—when you have felt around you a black gulf of solitude more isolating than that which surrounds the dying man, and in hope and in despair have trusted to your own unshaken will,—then only will you have achieved. Thus only can you gain the secret isolated joy of the thinker, who knows that, a hundred years after he is dead and forgotten, men who never heard of him will be moving to the measure of his thought,—the subtle rapture of a postponed power, which the world knows not because it has no external trappings, but which to his prophetic vision is more real than that which commands an army. And if this joy should not be yours, still it is only thus that you can know that you have done what it lay in you to do,—can say that you have lived, and be ready for the end.

SOURCE

Oliver Wendell Holmes, Jr., "The Profession of the Law" (1886), in Oliver Wendell Holmes, *Speeches* (Boston: Little, Brown, and Company, 1896) 22–25.

OLIVER WENDELL HOLMES, JR., "AN ADDRESS DELIVERED ON MEMORIAL DAY, MAY 30, 1895, AT A MEETING CALLED BY THE GRADUATING CLASS OF HARVARD UNIVERSITY"

This speech, the second of Holmes' two famous Memorial Day Addresses, has come to be known as "The Soldier's Faith." In it, Holmes went even further than he had in 1884 in his emphasis on individual heroism and on life as essentially a battlefield. He drew a clear distinction between what he by then clearly regarded as an unrealistic idealism—the kind of idealism he had espoused when still a student at Harvard and supported abolition—and the more rigorous and, in his view, realistic requirements of commerce and conflict in the modern world. This speech really encapsulated Holmes' understanding of the life-struggle, one he approached, again, through his own Civil War experiences. Yet his harsh assertions that achievement and success came only through destruction and sometimes death, his injunction to his listeners "to keep the soldier's faith against the doubts of civil life," did not meet with universal approval at the time, and the speech was regarded by some as little more than a jingoistic paean to war.

I once heard a man say, "Where Vanderbilt sits, there is the head of the table. I teach my son to be rich." He said what many think. For although the generation born about 1840, and now governing the world, has fought two at least of the greatest wars in history, and has witnessed others, war is out of fashion, and the man who commands attention of his fellows is the man of wealth. Commerce is the great power. The aspirations of the world are those of commerce. Moralists and philosophers, following its lead, declare that war is wicked, foolish, and soon to disappear.

The society for which many philanthropists, labor reformers, and men of fashion unite in longing is one in which they may be comfortable and may shine without much trouble or any danger. The unfortunately growing hatred of the poor for the rich seems to me to rest on the belief that money is the main thing (a belief in which the poor have been encouraged by the rich), more than on any other grievance. Most of my hearers would rather that their daughters or their sisters should marry a son of one of the great rich families than a regular army officer, were he as beautiful, brave, and gifted as Sir William Napier. I have heard the question asked whether our war was worth fighting, after all. There are many, poor and rich, who think that love of country is an old wife's tale, to be replaced by interest in a labor union, or, under the name of cosmopolitanism, by a rootless self-seeking search for a place where the most enjoyment may be had at the least cost.

Meantime we have learned the doctrine that evil means pain, and the revolt against pain in all its forms has grown more and more marked. From societies for the prevention of cruelty to animals up to socialism, we express in numberless ways the notion that suffering is a wrong which can be and ought to be prevented, and a whole literature of sympathy has sprung into being which points out in story and in verse how hard it is to be wounded in the battle of life, how terrible, how unjust it is that any one should fail.

Even science has had its part in the tendencies which we observe. It has shaken established religion in the minds of very many. It has pursued analysis until at last this thrilling world of colors and passions and sounds has seemed fatally to resolve itself into one vast network of vibrations endlessly weaving an aimless web, and the rainbow flush of cathedral windows, which once to enraptured eyes appeared the very smile of God, fades slowly out into the pale irony of the void.

And yet from vast orchestras still comes the music of mighty symphonies. Our painters even now are spreading along the walls of our Library glowing symbols of mysteries still real, and the hardly silenced cannon of the East proclaim once more that combat and pain still are the portion of man. For my own part, I believe that the struggle for life is the order of the world, at which it is vain to repine. I can imagine the burden changed in the way it is to be borne, but I cannot imagine that it ever will be lifted from men's backs. I can imagine a future in which science shall have passed from the combative to the dogmatic stage, and shall have gained such catholic acceptance that it shall take control of life, and condemn at once with instant execution what now is left for nature to destroy. But we are far from such a future, and we cannot stop to amuse or to terrify ourselves with dreams. Now, at least, and perhaps as long as man dwells upon the globe, his destiny is battle, and he has to take the chances of war. If it is our business to fight, the book for the army is a war-song, not a hospital-sketch. It is not well for soldiers to think much about wounds. Sooner or later we shall fall; but meantime it is for us to fix our eyes upon the point to be stormed, and to get there if we can.

Behind every scheme to make the world over, lies the question, What kind of world do you want? The ideals of the past for men have been drawn from war, as those for women have been drawn from motherhood. For all our prophecies, I doubt if we are ready to give up our inheritance. Who is there who would not like to be thought a gentleman? Yet what has that name been built on but the soldier's choice of honor rather than life? To be a soldier or descended from soldiers, in time of peace to be ready to give one's life rather than suffer disgrace, that is what the word has meant; and if we try to claim it at less cost than a splendid carelessness for life, we are trying to steal the good will without the responsibilities of the place. We will not dispute about tastes. The man of the future may want something different. But who of us could endure a world, although cut up into five-acre lots, and having no man upon it who was not well fed and well housed, without the divine folly of honor, without the senseless passion for knowledge outreaching the flaming bounds of the possible, without ideals the essence of which is that they can never be achieved? I do not know what is true. I do not know the meaning of the universe. But in the midst of doubt, in the collapse of creeds, there is one thing I do not doubt, that no man who lives in the same world with most of us can doubt, and that is that the faith is true and adorable which leads a soldier to throw away his life in obedience to a blindly accepted duty, in a cause which he little understands, in a plan of campaign of which he has little notion, under tactics of which he does not see the use.

Most men who know battle know the cynic force with which the thoughts of common sense will assail them in times of stress; but they know that in their greatest moments faith has trampled those thoughts under foot. If you wait in line, suppose on Tremont Street Mall, ordered simply to wait and do nothing, and have watched the enemy bring their guns to bear upon you down a gentle slope like that of Beacon Street, have seen the puff of the firing, have felt the burst of the spherical case-shot as it came toward you, have heard and seen the shrieking fragments go tearing through your company, and have known that the next or the next shot carries your fate; if you have advanced in line and have seen ahead of you the spot you must pass where the rifle bullets are striking; if you have ridden at night at a walk toward the blue line of fire at the dead angle of Spottsylvania, where for twenty-four hours the soldiers were fighting on the two sides of an earthwork, and in the morning the dead and dying lay piled in a row six deep, and as you rode you heard the bullets splashing in the mud and earth about you; if you have been in the picket-line at night in a black and unknown wood, have heard the splat of the bullets upon the trees, and as you moved have felt your foot slip upon a dead man's body; if you have had a blind fierce gallop against the enemy, with your blood up and a pace that left no time for fear—if, in short, as some, I hope many, who hear me, have known, you have known the vicissitudes of terror and triumph in war; you know that there is such a thing as the faith I spoke of. You know your own weakness and are modest; but you know that man has in him that unspeakable somewhat which makes him capable of miracle, able to lift himself by the might of his own soul, unaided, able to face annihilation for a blind belief.

From the beginning, to us, children of the North, life has seemed a place hung about by dark mists, out of which comes the pale shine of dragon's scales and the cry of fighting men, and the sound of swords. Beowolf, Milton, Durer, Rembrandt, Schopenhauer, Turner, Tennyson, from the first war song of the race to the stall-fed poetry of modern English drawing rooms, all have had the same vision, and all have had a glimpse of a light to be followed. 'The end of wordly life awaits us all. Let him who may, gain honor ere death. That is best for a warrior when he is dead.' So spoke Beowolf a thousand years ago . . .

When I went to the war I thought that soldiers were old men. I remembered a picture of the revolutionary soldier which some of you may have seen, representing a white-haired man with his flint-lock slung across his back. I remembered one or two examples of revolutionary soldiers whom I have met, and I took no account of the lapse of time. It was not long after, in winter quarters, as I was listening to some of the sentimental songs in vogue . . . that it came over me that the army was made up of what I should now call very young men. I dare say that my illusion has been shared by some of those now present, as they have looked at us upon whose heads the white shadows have begun to fall. But the truth is that war is the business of youth and early middle age . . .

War, when you are at it, is horrible and dull. It is only when time has passed that you see that its message was divine. I hope it may be long before we are called again to sit at that master's feet. But some teacher of the kind we all need. In this snug, over-safe corner of the world we need it, that we may realize that our comfortable routine is no eternal necessity of things, but merely a little space of calm in the midst of the tempestuous untamed streaming of the world, and in order that we may be ready for danger. We need it in this time of individualist negations, with its literature of French and American humor, revolting at discipline, loving flesh-pots, and denying that anything is worthy of reverence—in order that we may remember all that buffoons forget. We need it everywhere and at all times. For high and dangerous action teaches us to believe as right beyond dispute things for which our doubting minds are slow to find words of proof. Out of heroism grows faith in the worth of heroism. The proof comes later, and even may never come. Therefore I rejoice at every dangerous sport which I see pursued. The students at Heidelberg, with their sword-slashed faces, inspire me with sincere respect. I gaze with delight upon our polo players. If once in a while in our rough riding a neck is broken, I regard it, not as a waste, but as a price well paid for the breeding of a race fit for headship and command.

We do not save our traditions, in our country. The regiments whose battle-flags were not large enough to hold the names of the battles they had fought vanished with the surrender of Lee, although their memories inherited would have made heroes for a century. It is the more necessary to learn the lesson afresh from perils newly sought, and perhaps it is not vain for us to tell the new generation what we learned in our day, and what we still believe. That the joy of life is living, is to put out all one's powers as far as they will go; that the measure of power is obstacles overcome; to ride boldly at what is in front of you, be it fence or enemy; to pray, not for comfort, but for combat; to keep the soldier's faith against the doubts of civil life, more besetting and harder to overcome than all the misgivings of the battlefield, and to remember that duty is not to be proved in the evil day, but then to be obeyed unquestioning; to love glory more than the temptations of wallowing ease, but to know that one's final judge and only rival is oneself: with all our failures in act and thought, these things we learned from noble enemies in Virginia or Georgia or on the Mississippi, thirty years ago; these things we believe to be true.

SOURCE

Holmes, "Memorial Day Address, May 30 1895," Posner, *The Essential Holmes*, 87–95.

"The Path of the Law" (1897)

"The Path of the Law" was an address that Holmes was invited to deliver at Boston University, and essentially summed up his jurisprudential philosophy. It was in some respects a development of many of the themes that he had touched on in his address a decade earlier at Harvard when he had discussed his own early training in the law. Holmes tried to show that within the quotidian grind of legal practice something truly noble could be gleaned. At the same time he emphasized that the law was no mystery, nor was it in any sense morally driven or derived, but was simply a profession with principles similar to those of science. The law was, as he argued, essentially about prediction, hence his emphasis on how the "bad man" might approach the matter: simply with a view to predicting what the courts would most likely do in any given situation (*legal realism*). In many respects this speech represented Holmes' attempt to modernize the law by freeing it from centuries of historical tradition and outdated legal language (see, for example, the more modern language of Holmes' dissent in *Northern Securities* (1904) below) that served, in his view, to confuse rather than to clarify what the law was intended to, and could, achieve.

If you want to know the law and nothing else, you must look at it as a bad man, who cares only for the material consequences which such knowledge enables him to predict, not as a good one, who finds his reasons for conduct, whether inside the law or outside of it, in the vaguer sanctions of conscience. The theoretical importance of the distinction is no less, if you would reason on your subject aright. The law is full of phraseology drawn from morals, and by the mere force of language continually invites us to pass from one domain to the other without perceiving it, as we are sure to do unless we have the boundary constantly before our minds. The law talks about rights, and duties, and malice, and intent, and negligence, and so forth, and nothing is easier, or, I may say, more common in legal reasoning, than to take these words in their moral sense, at some state of the argument, and so to drop into fallacy. For instance, when we speak of the rights of man in a moral sense, we mean to mark the limits of interference with individual freedom which we think are prescribed by conscience, or by our ideal, however reached. Yet it is certain that many laws have been enforced in the past, and it is likely that some are enforced now, which are condemned by the most enlightened opinion of the time, or which at all events pass the limit of interference, as many consciences would draw it. Manifestly, therefore, nothing but confusion of thought can result from assuming that the rights of man in a moral sense are equally rights in the sense of the Constitution and the law. No doubt simple and extreme cases can be put of imaginable laws which the statute-making power would not dare to enact, even in the absence of written constitutional prohibitions, because the community would rise in rebellion and fight; and this gives some plausibility to the proposition that the law, if not a part of morality, is limited by it. But this limit of power is not coextensive with any system of morals. For the most part it falls far within the lines of any such system, and in some cases may extend beyond them, for reasons drawn from the habits of a particular people at a particular time. I once heard the late Professor Agassiz say that a German population would rise if you added two cents to the price of a glass of beer. A statute in such a case would be empty words, not because it was wrong, but because it could not be enforced. No one will deny that wrong statutes can be and are enforced, and we would not all agree as to which were the wrong ones.

The confusion with which I am dealing besets confessedly legal conceptions. Take the fundamental question, What constitutes the law? You will find some text writers telling you that it is something different from what is decided by the courts of Massachusetts or England, that it is a system of reason, that it is a deduction from principles of ethics or admitted axioms or what not, which may or may not coincide with the decisions. But if we take the view of our friend the bad man we shall find that he does not care two straws for the axioms or deductions, but that he does want to know what the Massachusetts or English courts are likely to do in fact. I am much of this mind. The prophecies of what the courts will do in fact, and nothing more pretentious, are what I mean by the law.

Take again a notion which as popularly understood is the widest conception which the law contains—the notion of legal duty, to which already I have referred. We fill the word with all the content which we draw from morals. But what does it mean to a bad man? Mainly, and in the first place, a prophecy that if he does certain things he will be subjected to disagreeable consequences by way of imprisonment or compulsory payment of money. But from his point of view, what is the difference between being fined and taxed a certain sum for doing a certain thing? That his point of view is the test of legal principles is proven by the many discussions which have arisen in the courts on the very question whether a given statutory liability is a penalty or a tax. On the answer to this question depends the decision whether conduct is legally wrong or right, and also whether a man is under compulsion or free. Leaving the criminal law on one side, what is the difference between the liability under the mill acts or statutes authorizing a taking by eminent domain and the liability for what we call a wrongful conversion of property where restoration is out of the question. In both cases the party taking another man's property has to pay its fair value as assessed by a jury, and no more. What significance is there in calling one taking right and another wrong from the point of view of the law? It does not matter, so far as the given consequence, the compulsory payment, is concerned, whether the act to which it is attached is described in terms of praise or in terms of blame, or whether the law purports to prohibit it or to allow it. If it matters at all, still speaking from the bad man's point of view, it must be because in one case and not in the other some further disadvantages, or at least some further consequences, are attached to the act by law. The only other disadvantages thus attached to it which I ever have been able to think of are to be found in two somewhat insignificant legal doctrines, both of which might be abolished without much disturbance. One is, that a contract to do a prohibited act is unlawful, and the other, that, if one of two or more joint wrongdoers has to pay all the damages, he cannot recover contribution from his fellows. And that I believe is all. You see how the vague circumference of the notion of duty shrinks and at the same time grows more precise when we wash it with cynical acid and expel everything except the object of our study, the operations of the law.

SOURCE

Oliver Wendell Holmes, Jr., "The Path of the Law," *Harvard Law Review*, 10:8 (March 25, 1897) 457–478, in Posner, *The Essential Holmes*, 160–177.

Northern Securities Company v. U.S., 193 U.S. 401 (1904): Oliver Wendell Holmes, Jr. Dissent

The Northern Securities Company was a holding company, established by the banker J.P. Morgan in 1893 to control railroad stock, but it was regarded by some, and especially by President Theodore Roosevelt, as an anti-competitive monopoly, or trust, that effectively restricted free commerce. Having appointed Holmes to the Supreme Court in 1902, Roosevelt had assumed that Holmes would support his attempt to break up the Northern Securities Company using the Sherman Antitrust Act of 1890. As Holmes' dissent made clear, however, he felt unable to support the President's "trust-busting" agenda in this case, and stated it as his view that the Sherman Act did not prevent the formation of corporations such as Northern Securities. Holmes believed that the act, invoked as it was in this case, was being used to alter, rather than safeguard, commercial practice, and that this was going beyond what the Constitution permitted (*judicial restraint*). This was Holmes' first but certainly not his last dissent, and one that soured the good relationship that Holmes had, up to that point, enjoyed with Roosevelt.

I am unable to agree with the judgment of the majority of the court, and although I think it useless and undesirable, as a rule, to express dissent, I feel bound to do so in this case, and to give my reasons for it.

Great cases, like hard cases, make bad law. For great cases are called great not by reason of their real importance in shaping the law of the future, but because of some accident of immediate overwhelming interest which appeals to the feelings and distorts the judgment. These immediate interests exercise a kind of hydraulic pressure which makes what previously was clear seem doubtful, and before which even well settled principles of law will bend. What we have to do in this case is to find the meaning of some not very difficult words. We must try, I have tried, to do it with the same freedom of natural and spontaneous interpretation that one would be sure of if the same question arose upon an indictment for a similar act which excited no public attention, and was of importance only to a prisoner before the court. Furthermore, while at times judges need for their work the training of economists or statesmen, and must act in view of their foresight of consequences, yet when their task is to interpret and apply the words of a statute, their function is merely academic to begin with – to read English intelligently – and a consideration of consequences comes into play, if at all, only when the meaning of the words used is open to reasonable doubt.

The question to be decided is whether, under the act of July 2, 1890, c. 647, 26 Stat. 209, it is unlawful, at any stage of the process, if several men unite to form a corporation for the purpose of buying more than half the stock of each of two competing interstate railroad companies, if they form the corporation, and the corporation buys the stock. I will suppose further that every step is taken, from the beginning, with the single intent of ending competition between the companies. I make this addition not because it may not be and is not disputed, but because, as I shall try to show, it is totally unimportant under any part of the statute with which we have to deal.

The statute of which we have to find the meaning is a criminal statute. The two sections on which the Government relies both make certain acts crimes. That is their immediate purpose, and that is what they say. It is vain to insist that this is not a criminal proceeding. The words cannot be read one way in a suit which is to end in fine and imprisonment and another way in one which seeks an injunction. The construction which is adopted in this case must be adopted in one of the other sort. I am no friend of artificial interpretations because a statute is of one kind, rather than another, but all agree that, before a statute is to be taken to punish that which always has been lawful, it must express its intent in clear words. So I say we must read the words before us as if the question were whether two small exporting grocers should go to jail . . . the act of Congress will not be construed to mean the universal disintegration of society into single men, each at war with all the rest, or even the prevention of all further combinations for a common end.

There is a natural feeling that somehow or other the statute meant to strike at combinations great enough to cause just anxiety on the part of those who love their country more than money, while it viewed such little ones as I have supposed with just indifference. This notion, it may be said, somehow breathes from the pores of the act, although it seems to be contradicted in every way by the words in detail. And it has occurred to me that it might be that, when a combination reached a certain size it might have attributed to it more of the character of a monopoly merely by virtue of its size than would be attributed to a smaller one. I am quite clear that it is only in connection with monopolies that size could play any part . . . even a small railroad will have the same tendency to exclude others from its narrow area that great ones have to exclude others from a greater one, and the statute attacks the small monopolies as well as the great. The very words of the act make such a distinction impossible in this case, and it has not been attempted in express terms . . .

In view of my interpretation of the statute, I do not go further into the question of the power of Congress. That has been dealt with by my brother White, and I concur in the main with his views. I am happy to know that only a minority of my brethren adopt an interpretation of the law which in my opinion would make eternal the *bellum omnium contra omnes* and disintegrate society so far as it could into individual atoms. If that were its intent, I should regard calling such a law a regulation of commerce as a mere pretense. It would be an attempt to reconstruct society. I am not concerned with the wisdom of such an attempt, but I believe that Congress was not entrusted by the Constitution with the power to make it, and I am deeply persuaded that it has not tried.

LOCHNER v. NEW YORK, 198 U.S. 45 (1905): OLIVER WENDELL HOLMES, JR. DISSENT

What became known as the "Lochner era" in the history of the Supreme Court (1890–1937) was a period of perceived *judicial activism*. It was terminated by Franklin D. Roosevelt when he was seeking to enact New Deal legislation. During the Lochner era, the Court often used the Due Process clause of the Fourteenth Amendment to effect a *laissez-faire* economic policy at a time when the states were seeking to protect workers' rights by, for example, restricting working hours, as it did in *Lochner v. New York* (1905). In this case, the Court struck down a state statute that prevented a baker, Joseph Lochner, from contracting working hours in excess of ten a day or sixty a week. It argued that his "general right to make a contract in relation to his business is part of the liberty protected by the Fourteenth Amendment," and that the New York labor statute was "an unreasonable, unnecessary and arbitrary interference with the right and liberty of the individual to contract in relation to labor." Holmes' dissent, by proposing that the New York state statute could be viewed as "a proper measure on the score of health," was interpreted as an example of *liberal jurisprudence*, as support for the working man in the face of corporate greed, although the reasoning that informed his dissent was rather more complicated than that.

———

This case is decided upon an economic theory which a large part of the country does not entertain. If it were a question whether I agreed with that theory, I should desire to study it further and long before making up my mind. But I do not conceive that to be my duty, because I strongly believe that my agreement or disagreement has nothing to do with the right of a majority to embody their opinions in law. It is settled by various decisions of this court that state constitutions and state laws may regulate life in many ways which we, as legislators, might think as injudicious, or, if you like, as tyrannical, as this, and which, equally with this, interfere with the liberty to contract. Sunday laws and usury laws are ancient examples. A more modern one is the prohibition of lotteries. The liberty of the citizen to do as he likes so long as he does not interfere with the liberty of others to do the same, which has been a shibboleth for some well known writers, is interfered with by school laws, by the Post Office, by every state or municipal institution which takes his money for purposes thought desirable, whether he likes it or not. The Fourteenth Amendment does not enact Mr. Herbert Spencer's Social Statics . . . a constitution is not intended to embody a particular economic theory, whether of paternalism and the organic relation of the citizen to the State or of *laissez-faire*. It is made for people of fundamentally differing views, and the accident of our finding certain opinions natural and familiar or novel and even shocking ought not to conclude our judgment upon the question whether statutes embodying them conflict with the Constitution of the United States.

General propositions do not decide concrete cases. The decision will depend on a judgment or intuition more subtle than any articulate major premise. But I think that the proposition just stated, if it is accepted, will carry us far toward the end. Every opinion tends to become a law. I think that the word liberty in the Fourteenth Amendment is perverted when it is held to prevent the natural outcome of a dominant opinion, unless it can be said that a rational and fair man necessarily would admit that the statute proposed would infringe fundamental principles as they have been understood by the traditions of our people and our law. It does not need research to show that no such sweeping condemnation can be passed upon the statute before us. A reasonable man might think it a proper measure on the score of health. Men whom I certainly could not pronounce unreasonable would uphold it as a first installment of a general regulation of the hours of work. Whether in the latter aspect it would be open to the charge of inequality I think it unnecessary to discuss.

SOURCE

Lochner v. New York, 198 U.S. 75 (1905).

ABRAMS V. UNITED STATES, 250 U.S. 616 (1919): OLIVER WENDELL HOLMES, JR. DISSENT

Abrams v. United States (1919) was a case that revolved around the First Amendment right to free speech in a conflict situation. In *Schenck v. United States* (1919) Holmes had upheld the prosecution of Charles Schenck for distributing anti-war leaflets, on the grounds that the First Amendment protection of free speech did not hold in times of "clear and present danger." In *Abrams*—on the surface a similar case—he and his colleague Louis D. Brandeis dissented, arguing that, in this case, there was no immediate danger and that the prosecution was no more than an attempt to curb free speech and prosecute for belief rather than action. Long regarded as a powerful defense of First Amendment rights, or what Holmes termed "free trade in ideas," the grounds for the dissent have largely been rejected by the Supreme Court in the twenty-first century in the context of the "war on terror."

─────────

Persecution for the expression of opinions seems to me perfectly logical. If you have no doubt of your premises or your power and want a certain result with all your heart you naturally express your wishes in law and sweep away all opposition. To allow opposition by speech seems to indicate that you think the speech impotent, as when a man says that he has squared the circle, or that you do not care whole heartedly for the result, or that you doubt either your power or your premises. But when men have realized that time has upset many fighting faiths, they may come to believe even more than they believe the very foundations of their own conduct that the ultimate good desired is better reached by free trade in ideas—that the best test of truth is the power of the thought to get itself accepted in the competition of the market, and that truth is the only ground upon which their wishes safely can be carried out. That at any rate is the theory of our Constitution. It is an experiment, as all life is an experiment. Every year if not every day we have to wager our salvation upon some prophecy based upon imperfect knowledge. While that experiment is part of our system I think that we should be eternally vigilant against attempts to check the expression of opinions that we loathe and believe to be fraught with death, unless they so imminently threaten immediate interference with the lawful and pressing purposes of the law that an immediate check is required to save the country. I wholly disagree with the argument of the Government that the First Amendment left the common law as to seditious libel in force. History seems to me against the notion. I had conceived that the United States through many years had shown its repentance for the Sedition Act of 1798 . . . by repaying fines that it imposed. Only the emergency that makes it immediately dangerous to leave the correction of evil counsels to time warrants . . . making any exception to the sweeping command, "Congress shall make no law abridging the freedom of speech." Of course I am speaking only of expressions of opinion and exhortations, which were all that were uttered here, but I regret that I cannot put into more impressive words my belief that in their conviction upon this indictment the defendants were deprived of their rights under the Constitution of the United States.

FURTHER READING

PRIMARY SOURCES

Most of Holmes' papers and the material relating to Mark DeWolfe Howe's biography have helpfully been furnished in digital, searchable format by Harvard Law School: http://library.law.harvard.edu/suites/owh/.

PUBLISHED SOURCES

Adams, Henry, *The Education of Henry Adams*, ed. Ernest Samuels (Boston: Houghton Mifflin Company, 1973)

Berenson, Barbara F., *Boston and the Civil War: Hub of the Second Revolution* (Charleston, SC: The History Press, 2014)

Bryce, James, *The American Commonwealth*, New Edition, 2 Vols. (New York: The Macmillan Company, 1922)

Burton, David H. (ed.), *Holmes-Sheehan Correspondence: Letters of Justice Oliver Wendell Holmes, Jr. and Canon Patrick Augustus Sheehan* (New York: Fordham University Press, 1993)

Cohen, Felix S. (ed.), "Holmes-Cohen Correspondence," *Journal of the History of Ideas*, 9:1 (January 1948) 3–52

Duncan, Russell (ed.), *Blue-Eyed Child of Fortune: The Civil War Letters of Colonel Robert Gould Shaw* (Athens and London: University of Georgia Press, 1999)

Hallowell, Norwood P., *Reminiscences Written for My Children* (Boston: Little, Brown and Company, 1896)

Holmes, Oliver Wendell, *Collected Legal Papers* (New York: Harcourt, Brace and Howe, 1920)

Holmes, Oliver Wendell, Jr., *The Common Law* (1881. Reprint. London: Macmillan and Company, 1882)

Holmes, Oliver Wendell, Jr., "The Path of the Law," *Harvard Law Review*, 10:8 (March 25, 1897)

Howe, Mark DeWolfe (ed.), *Touched with Fire: Civil War Letters and Diary of Oliver Wendell Holmes, Jr., 1861–1864* (Cambridge, MA: Harvard University Press, 1946)

Howe, Mark DeWolfe (ed.), *Holmes-Laski Letters: The Correspondence of Mr. Justice Holmes and Harold J. Laski, 1916–1935*, 2 Vols. (Cambridge, MA: Harvard University Press, 1953)

Howe, Mark DeWolfe (ed.), *Holmes-Pollock Letters: The Correspondence of Mr. Justice Holmes and Sir Frederick Pollock, 1874–1932*, Second Edition: Two Volumes in One (Cambridge, MA: The Belknap Press of Harvard University Press, 1961)

Howe, Mark DeWolfe, (ed.), *Oliver Wendell Holmes: Occasional Speeches* (Cambridge, MA: The Belknap Press of Harvard University Press, 1962)

Hughes, Sarah Forbes (ed.), *Letters and Recollections of John Murray Forbes*, 2 Vols. (Boston: Houghton, Mifflin and Company, 1899)

James, William, *The Will to Believe and Other Essays in Popular Philosophy* (1896. Reprint. New York and London: Longmans Green and Company, 1897)

Lerner, Max (ed.), *The Mind and Faith of Justice Holmes: His Speeches, Essays, Letters, and Judicial Opinions* (1943. Reprint. New Brunswick, NJ: Transaction Publishers, 2010)

Mennel, Robert M. and Christine L. Compston, *Holmes and Frankfurter: Their Correspondence, 1912–1934* (Hanover: University of New Hampshire, 1996)

Morse, John T., *Life and Letters of Oliver Wendell Holmes*, 2 Vols. (London: Sampson Low, Marston and Company, 1896)

Palfrey, Francis William, *Memoir of William Francis Bartlett* (Boston: Houghton, Mifflin and Company, 1881)

Perry, Ralph Barton, *The Thought and Character of William James*, 2 Vols. (London: Oxford University Press, 1935)

Posner, Richard A. (ed.), *The Essential Holmes: Selections from the Letters, Speeches, Judicial Opinions, and Other Writings of Oliver Wendell Holmes, Jr.* (1992. Reprint. Chicago and London: The University of Chicago Press, 1996)

Scott, Robert Garth (ed.), *Fallen Leaves: The Civil War Letters of Major Henry Livermore Abbott* (Kent, OH: The Kent State University Press, 1991)

SECONDARY WORKS

Ackerman, Bruce, *We, The People, Vol. 1, Foundations* (1991. Reprint. Cambridge, MA: Harvard University Press, 1993)

Adams, Michael C.C., *Living Hell: The Dark Side of the Civil War* (Baltimore, MD: Johns Hopkins University Press, 2014)

Aichele, Gary J., *Oliver Wendell Holmes, Jr.: Soldier, Scholar, Judge* (Boston: Twayne, 1989)

Alschuler, Albert W., *Law without Values: The Life, Work, and Legacy of Justice Holmes* (Chicago and London: University of Chicago Press, 2000)

Arnold, Andrew B., *Fueling the Gilded Age: Railroads, Miners and Disorder in Pennsylvania Coal Country* (New York: New York University Press, 2014)

Baker, Carlos, *Emerson among the Eccentrics: A Group Portrait* (New York: Penguin Books, 1997)

Baker, Liva, *The Justice from Beacon Hill: The Life and Times of Oliver Wendell Holmes* (New York: Harper Collins, 1991)

Beckert, Sven, *The Monied Metropolis: New York City and the Consolidation of the American Bourgeoisie, 1850–1896* (Cambridge: Cambridge University Press, 2001)

Berenson, Edward, *Heroes of Empire: Five Charismatic Men and the Conquest of Africa* (Berkeley and Los Angeles: University of California Press, 2011)

Bowen, Catherine Drinker, *Yankee from Olympus: Justice Holmes and His Family* (Boston: Little, Brown and Company, 1944)

Curry, Leonard P., *Blueprint for Modern America: Nonmilitary Legislation of the First Civil War Congress* (Nashville, TN: Vanderbilt University Press, 1968)

Dalzell, Robert F., *Enterprising Elite: The Boston Associates and the World They Made* (1987. Reprint. New York and London: W.W. Norton, 1993)

Driver, Felix, *Geography Militant: Cultures of Exploration and Empire* (New York and Oxford: Oxford University Press, 2001)

Edel, Leon, *Henry James: The Untried Years, 1843–1870* (Philadelphia, PA: Lippincott, 1953)

Farrell, Betty G., *Elite Families: Class and Power in Nineteenth-Century Boston* (New York: State University of New York Press, 1993)

Fehrenbacher, Don E., *The Dred Scott Case: Its Significance in American Law and Politics* (New York and Oxford: Oxford University Press, 1978)

Finkelman, Paul (ed.), *His Soul Goes Marching on: Responses to John Brown and the Harpers Ferry Raid* (Charlottesville: University of Virginia Press, 1994)

Fredrickson, George M., *The Inner Civil War: Northern Intellectuals and the Crisis of the Union* (New York: Harper and Row, 1965)

Gibian, Peter, *Oliver Wendell Holmes and the Culture of Conversation* (New York and Cambridge: Cambridge University Press, 2004)

Gillman, Howard, *The Constitution Besieged: The Rise and Demise of Lochner Era Police Powers* (1993. Reprint. Durham, NC: Duke University Press, 2004)

Gilmore, Grant, *The Ages of American Law* (New Haven, CT: Yale University Press, 1977)

Gould, Stephen Jay, *The Flamingo's Smile: Reflections in Natural History* (London: Penguin Books, 1985)

Hall, Kermit L., James W. Ely, and Joel B. Grossman (eds.), *The Oxford Companion to the Supreme Court of the United States*, Second Edition (New York and Oxford: Oxford University Press, 2005)

Heale, Michael J., *American Anticommunism* (Baltimore, MD: Johns Hopkins University Press, 1990)

Higham, John, *Strangers in the Land: Patterns of American Nativism 1860–1925* (New York: Atheneum, 1963)

Howe, Mark DeWolfe, *Justice Oliver Wendell Holmes*, 2 Vols. (Cambridge, MA: Belknap Press of Harvard University Press, 1957–1963)

Jones, Max, *The Last Great Quest: Captain Scott's Antarctic Sacrifice* (New York and Oxford: Oxford University Press, 2003)

Knights, Peter R., *The Plain People of Boston: A Study in City Growth, 1830–1860* (New York: Oxford University Press, 1971)

Lears, Jackson, *No Place of Grace: Antimodernism and the Transformation of American Culture, 1880–1920* (New York: Pantheon Books, 1981)

Lerner, Max, *Ideas Are Weapons: The History and Uses of Ideas* (1939. Reprint. New Brunswick, NJ: Transaction Publishers, 1991)

McPherson, James M., *Battle Cry of Freedom: The Civil War Era* (New York and Oxford: Oxford University Press, 1988)

Menand, Louis, *The Metaphysical Club* (2001. Reprint. London: Harper Collins, 2002)

Miller, Richard F., *Harvard's Civil War: A History of the Twentieth Massachusetts Volunteer Infantry* (Hanover and London: University Press of New England, 2005)

Novick, Sheldon M., *Honorable Justice: The Life of Oliver Wendell Holmes* (New York: Dell Publishing, 1989)

Novick, Sheldon M., *Henry James: The Young Master* (1996. Reprint. New York: Random House, 2007)

O'Brien, Gerald V., *Framing the Moron: The Social Construction of Feeble-Mindedness in the American Eugenic Era* (Manchester and New York: Manchester University Press, 2013)

O'Connor, Thomas H., *Civil War Boston: Home Front and Battlefield* (Boston: Northeastern University Press, 1997)

Painter, Nell Irvin, *Standing at Armageddon: The United States, 1877–1919* (1987. Reprint. New York and London: W. W. Norton and Company, 1989)

Pohlman, H.L., *Justice Oliver Wendell Holmes: Utilitarian Jurisprudence* (Cambridge, MA: Harvard University Press, 1984)

Rabban, David M., *Free Speech in Its Forgotten Years* (New York and Cambridge: Cambridge University Press, 1997)

Richardson, Heather Cox, *The Greatest Nation of the Earth: Republican Economic Policies during the Civil War* (Cambridge, MA: Harvard University Press, 1997)

Riffenburgh, Beau, *The Myth of the Explorer: The Press, Sensationalism, and Geographical Discovery* (New York and Oxford: Oxford University Press, 1994)

Sergeant, Elizabeth Shepley, *Fire under the Andes: A Group of Literary Portraits* (1927. Reprint. New York: Kennikat Press, 1966)

Sklansky, Jeffrey, *The Soul's Economy: Market Society and Selfhood in American Thought* (Chapel Hill: The University of North Carolina Press, 2002)

Somkin, Fred, *Unquiet Eagle: Memory and Desire in the Idea of American Freedom, 1815–1860* (Ithaca, NY: Cornell University Press, 1967)

Stewart, James Brewer, *Holy Warriors: American Abolitionists and American Slavery* (New York: Hill and Wang, 1997)

Story, Ronald, *The Forging of an Aristocracy: Harvard and the Boston Upper Class, 1800–1870* (Middletown, CT: Wesleyan University Press, 1980)

Stouffer, Samuel A., *Communism, Conformity and Civil Liberties* (Garden City, NY: Doubleday, 1955)

Weinberg, Steven, *Taking on the Trusts: The Epic Battle of Ida Tarbell and John D. Rockefeller* (New York: W.W. Norton and Company, 2008)

Weinstein, Michael, *The Imaginative Prose of Oliver Wendell Holmes* (Columbia; Missouri University Press, 2006)

White, G. Edward, *Justice Oliver Wendell Holmes: Law and the Inner Self* (New York and Oxford: Oxford University Press, 1993)

Wiebe, Robert H., *The Search for Order, 1877–1920* (New York: Hill and Wang, 1967)

Wilson, Edmund, *Patriotic Gore: Studies in the Literature of the American Civil War* (1962. Reprint. London: The Hogarth Press, 1987)

INDEX

early years 11–37
egotism 85, 101
Einstein, Lewis 132
Eliot, Charles William 99–100
Elsie Venner (1861) 17, 62, 90, 159
Emancipation Proclamation 25, 62–3, 65
Emerson, Ralph Waldo 16, 19–21, 29–31, 34, 41, 74, 81, 88, 118
Employers Liability Act (1887) 110
equality 3–4, 147
Erdman Act (1898) 140
Espionage Act (1917) 151, 153
Eugenical Sterilization Act (1924) 158–9
Evening Post (New York) 108, 129–30
Expediting Act (1903) 132

faith 99–128
Farthest North (1897) 117–18
FDR *see* Roosevelt, Franklin Delano
Fehrenbacher, Don 27
Fiechter, Frederick 31
Fifth Amendment 27, 140
Finkelman, Paul 21, 147
First Amendment 151, 153–4, 202–3
First Church in Cambridge address, February 12, 1886 184–5
First Confiscation Act (1861) 63
First World War 3–4, 11, 78, 151, 155–6, 166
Forbes, John Murray 16, 19, 65
Foster, Frank 112
Fourteenth Amendment 77, 111, 137, 140, 145, 158, 200–201
Frankfurter, Felix 2, 101, 104, 136–7, 149–51
Fredericksburg 11, 64
free speech 151, 153, 202–3
free trade in ideas 202
Frémont, John C. 63
French Revolution 94
Frohwerk v. United States (1919) 151–2
"Frontier Thesis" 186
Fugitive Slave Act (1850) 19–20, 25, 27
Fuller, Melville 133, 148

GAR *see* Grand Army of the Republic
Garden of Eden 11, 19
Garfield, James A. 166
Garrison, William Lloyd 20
Gay, George H. 60
General Motors 145
George, Henry 111
Gettysburg 24, 64, 115
ghettoization 110

Gilded Age 5, 93, 102, 131
Giles, Jackson W. 145
Giles v. Harris (1903) 145, 147–8, 157, 168
Gilmore, Grant 2
Gitlow, Benjamin 155
Gitlow v. New York (1925) 155
Gladstone, Thomas H. 21
Grand Army of the Republic 4, 105, 181
Grant, Ulysses S. 51, 65, 94
Gray, Horace 121–2
Gray, John 82, 89
Great Depression 3
Great Dissenter 143–4
"Great Migration" 12
Great Northern Railroad 134
Greenleaf, Simon 76

habeas corpus 147
Hallowell, Norwood Penrose 25, 33, 41–3, 48–9, 56, 59, 62–4, 72, 107, 156–7
Hamilton, Walton H. 1
Hammond, William A. 16
Hand, Learned 153
Harlan, John Marshall 112, 133, 148
Harpers Ferry raid 21, 28
Harper's Weekly 50–52, 60, 72–3
Harrison, William Henry 3
Harrison's Landing 59–60
Harte, Bret 16
Harvard Class Album 22, 73, 173–5
Harvard Commemoration Day 108
Harvard Law Review 120, 153
Harvard Law School 1, 20–21, 25, 27–9, 31, 33–4, 43–6, 74–7, 80
Harvard Magazine 29, 174
Harvard Medical School 21, 72, 173
Harvard Regiment *see* Twentieth Massachusetts
Hasty Pudding club 29, 174
Hayes, Rutherford B. 89
Hegel, Friedrich 113
Hemenway, Alfred 121
hero-worship 150
Higginson, Thomas Wentworth 15, 20–21, 25, 28–9, 33, 46
Hill, James J. 131, 134, 139, 166–7
historical assessment of Holmes 164–9
History of the Standard Oil Company 131
Hobbes, Thomas 113
Holmes, Amelia Jackson 24–5, 173
Holmes, Oliver Wendell, Snr. 1, 11–18, 21–2, 25–8, 30, 41–5, 48–9, 60–65, 72–4, 81–2
Holy War 65